CRITICAL INSIGHTS

George Orwell

CRITICAL
INSIGHTS

George Orwell

Editor
John Rodden
Tunghai University, Taiwan

SALEM PRESS
A Division of EBSCO Publishing
Ipswich, Massachusetts

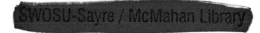

Library of Congress Cataloging-in-Publication Data
George Orwell / editor, John Rodden.
    p. cm. -- (Critical insights)
  Includes bibliographical references and index.
  ISBN 978-1-4298-3728-6 (hardcover)
  1. Orwell, George, 1903-1950--Criticism and interpretation. I. Rodden, John.
  PR6029.R8Z6393 2012
  828'.91209--dc23
                                    2012007780

Contents _____

Resources

About This Volume_____

John Rodden

Critical Insights: George Orwell contains a broad collection of analytical essays dealing with perhaps the best-known English author of the twentieth century. Although famous for his brilliant satire of the failures of the Russian Revolution, *Animal Farm* (1945), and his powerful dystopian novel, *Nineteen Eighty-Four* (1949), Orwell was also a talented journalist and a master of the essay form.

The nineteen essays in this volume reveal Orwell as a complex, multitalented author. By focusing on the themes "Critical Contexts" and "Critical Readings," the authors seek to provide both an overview of Orwell's writings and an analysis of why his influence has remained strong over a half century since his death.

The first four essays in the volume provide a broad overview of Orwell's life as well as examining some of the significant influences on his career. Two essays, my own and one by La Salle University history professor John Rossi, provide the reader with some context for understanding Orwell's work. In another essay, I discuss how Orwell became "a Famous Author," showing how his reputation went through a series of stages in literary and intellectual circles. Finally, in a brief third essay, I describe Orwell as my own "big brother," discussing the influence Orwell had not only on me personally, but also on those generations who fell under his spell.

After this introduction, four essays seek to further understand the critical context of Orwell's work. In the first, James Seaton, professor of English at Michigan State University, sets out to provide some historical context for Orwell's writings, discussing the evolution of Orwell's distinctive point of view on the political issues of his time. He also focuses on the reaction of Orwell's critics and commentators to his political perspective.

Seaton's historical perspective sets the stage for the first of two essays by William Cain, professor of English at Wellesley College. Cain provides an examination of how Orwell and Ernest Hemingway dealt with the crucial conflict that foreshadowed World War II, the Spanish Civil War. Orwell's account of that conflict, *Homage to Catalonia* (1938), based on his firsthand experiences, saw Orwell's final commitment to his own brand of socialism. Cain contrasts Orwell's memoir with *For Whom the Bell Tolls* (1940), Hemingway's fictional account of the war's impact on the life of Robert Jordan, a dedicated foe of fascism. Both books see the republican cause as just but in different ways show the ambiguities involved. Orwell saw the cause of socialism betrayed by communists interested in power, launching him on the path that led him to his last two iconic books, *Animal Farm* and *Nineteen Eighty-Four*. Hemingway, Cain shows, recognized that the republican cause was doomed to defeat but showed the nobility it called forth in the character of the ill-fated Jordan.

Cain's second essay uses an approach derived from the work of literary theorist Stanley Fish to examine Orwell's writings from the perspective of reader-response criticism. Cain argues that this approach demonstrates Orwell's ability to engage in complex intellectual argument with the reader, a quality that contributed to his popularity as a writer.

The last essay in this section is by Loraine Saunders, author of an influential study of the four novels Orwell wrote in the 1930s. Saunders examines Orwell's critical reception and influence by concentrating on a handful of his books. In particular, she dissects the reasons why his early novels, especially *A Clergyman's Daughter* (1935) and *Keep the Aspidistra Flying* (1936), were dismissed by critics as lifeless and amateurish. Her essay also focuses on Orwell's reception history, dividing it into five stages beginning with the reputation as a talented author he established in the 1930s and culminating with *Nineteen Eighty-Four* reaching the top of international best-seller lists thirty-five years after his death.

The third section of the volume presents a series of critical readings of Orwell's writings, including reflections on his essays, his reportage, and his last two crucial works, *Animal Farm* and *Nineteen Eighty-Four*.

First, Loraine Saunders analyzes the significance of Orwell's reportage during the 1930s, especially the two books that honed his documentary prose style: *The Road to Wigan Pier* (1937) and *Homage to Catalonia*. She stresses how these two works completed Orwell's journey to his own brand of idiosyncratic socialism. In the process, Saunders traces Orwell's development as a writer of powerful and controversial prose. James Seaton's second essay in this collection examines Orwell the essayist and journalist. Seaton argues that Orwell's short prose nonfiction is indispensable for appreciating the totality of Orwell's achievement as a writer, pointing out that Orwell grew into the premier essayist of his generation and pioneered a form of personal journalism much imitated by succeeding generations.

The next seven essays in the collection are built around the significance and impact of *Animal Farm* and *Nineteen Eighty-Four*. Leading off, John Rossi provides a close reading of *Animal Farm* as an allegory of the Russian Revolution and events in the Soviet Union between 1917 and 1944. Rossi shows how Orwell cleverly used the beast fable format to elucidate the key events of this period—the overthrow of the tsar, the Russian Civil War, Joseph Stalin's five-year economic plans, his party purges, and World War II. This approach makes the historical context of the fable clearer to the reader.

Next comes the first of two essays I contribute to this section, demonstrating both the diversity of Orwell's writings as well as his continuing relevance today. It discusses the remarkable decision by Chinese Communist political authorities to allow a dramatic performance of *Animal Farm* in 2002. The production, which was seen by thousands of patrons, caused confusion among both the Chinese public and the political leadership. I use this event to analyze how difficult it can be in the twenty-first century to understand the background of *Animal Farm*, especially for those who lack the proper historical context.

In an essay dealing with both *Animal Farm* and *Nineteen Eighty-Four*, Eugene Goodheart, Edythe Macy Professor of English at Brandeis University, argues that the latter is the more significant novel, as well as the more devastating exposé of the Stalinist tyranny. He also explores the themes of the manipulation of language and the mutability of the past, examining the historical dimension of both works for readers unfamiliar with the record of the Soviet Union under Stalin. Finally, Goodheart discusses the question of the continuing relevance of both works, arguing that Orwell's greatest achievement lies in his alertness to the power of propaganda.

Peter Davison, editor of the twenty-volume *The Complete Works of George Orwell*, in a highly original essay examines Orwell's interest in science. In particular, he argues that Orwell was concerned with how science was abused in the Soviet Union, and that this concern influenced his writing of *Nineteen Eighty-Four*. Davison notes how Orwell sensed what the atmosphere or tone of life was like in the Soviet Union, although he never visited the country. Davison also notes how the ideas of the Russian biologist Trofim Lysenko influenced Orwell's treatment of the perversion of science in *Nineteen Eighty-Four*.

Gorman Beauchamp, professor emeritus of humanities at the University of Michigan, takes a different approach from both Goodheart and Davison in his understanding of *Nineteen Eighty-Four*. He asserts that the dystopian format of the novel clashed with the traditions of literary modernism to which Orwell adhered, including psychological complexity, ambiguity, and indeterminacy in narration and characterization. According to Beauchamp, this caused problems for Orwell in the development of the character of Winston Smith, whom Beauchamp sees as too psychologically compromised to convey *Nineteen Eighty-Four*'s ideological message.

Henk Vynckier, professor of foreign languages and literature at Tunghai University in Taiwan, reads *Nineteen Eighty-Four* in yet another way: in psychological terms. Scrutinizing the author-character identification between Orwell and Winston Smith, Vynckier traces the similarities between the two, such as their love of seemingly useless objects and their interest in the past for its own sake, all of which deepens our comprehension of Orwell.

Also writing on *Nineteen Eighty-Four* is Peter Stansky, professor emeritus of history at Stanford University. Stansky was one of the first American scholars to seriously study Orwell's life and times before it was a fashionable topic. His essay discusses to what degree the themes Orwell developed in his dystopian novel—loss of privacy, abuse of language, corruption of technology by totalitarian governments, leader worship, and so on—still have relevance today. He also considers how these questions were rooted in Orwell's own experiences.

The remaining essays in the collection move away from *Animal Farm* and *Nineteen Eighty-Four* to demonstrate the breadth of scholarly interest in Orwell's life and writings.

My final essay in the collection examines different elements of Orwell's career, contrasting his impact and influence with that of another influential twentieth-century literary figure, French author Albert Camus (1913–1960). Both men, I argue, exemplified the rare gift of speaking truth to power, in contrast to the cowardice of governmental authorities and the political and literary intelligentsia. Following a short history of these two extraordinary figures, I show how their careers were parallel in their opposition to the great issues of their time: Communism, fascism, and the corruption of power.

The last and in some ways a truly remarkable essay is by Dione Venables, concerning Orwell's formative years growing up in Henley-on-Thames, England. Her essay casts light in particular on Orwell's relationship with Jacintha Buddicom, his first romantic relationship and one that was revived shortly before his death. Venables's essay is an original contribution to our understanding of a long-neglected aspect of Orwell's life.

The nineteen essays in this collection seek to shed new light in an original way on this fascinating and often controversial literary figure of the first half of the twentieth century. Although he has been dead for over sixty years, these essays are a testament to the hold that George Orwell continues to have on the imagination of each new generation of readers.

Acknowledgments

Having written so much about George Orwell, I find it both a joy and an inspiration to work with colleagues who share my devotion to his work. It has been both stimulating and refreshing to engage in a dialogue about Orwell and his legacy with the outstanding international scholars—a distinguished group hailing variously from North America, Europe, and Asia—whose contributions grace this volume.

Most gratifying in my journey of editing this book about Orwell has been the discovery of still further insights about his writings and life. Time and again, I had suspected there might be little or nothing more to say about Orwell, particularly about his three great classics: *Homage to Catalonia*, *Animal Farm*, and *Nineteen Eighty-Four*. Therefore, it was with surprise and wonder that I repeatedly found myself learning anew from the contributors with whom I discussed these and other works of Orwell, for their contributions to this collection prove to be not only highly accessible to new Orwell readers, but also challenging and original even to well-informed students of Orwell.

Above all, I want to thank John Rossi, my erstwhile undergraduate teacher and ongoing friend and colleague, for both his wise counsel and his superb essays in this collection. I also extend my deepest gratitude to the other authors in the volume for both their forbearance with the editorial process and the excellent contributions that ultimately emerged. These contributors include Dione Venables, Eugene Goodheart, Henk Vynckier, Gorman Beauchamp, Peter Stansky, and Peter Davison, the latter pair of whom are world-renowned for their pioneering Orwell scholarship. Finally, I am especially indebted to William

E. Cain, James Seaton, and Loraine Saunders, all of whom wrote two pieces each for the book. Both novice and long-standing students of Orwell will find the following essays enlightening and edifying. The critics who have written about Orwell for this collection have done him proud.

Last but not least: As a token of my esteem for his own indispensable and pathbreaking contribution to Orwell studies as the coeditor (with Orwell's wife Sonia) of the invaluable four-volume *Collected Essays, Journalism and Letters* (1968)—and most especially for the kindness and generosity that he and his wife showed to a junior scholar visiting from America—I dedicate this book to Ian and Ann Angus, with gratitude and admiration.

CAREER, LIFE, AND INFLUENCE

On George Orwell

John Rodden

Although he has been dead for more than six decades, George Orwell (1903–1950) continues to generate keen interest and intense debate both within the literary academy and in the public at large. It even could be argued that he is the best-known literary figure of the twentieth century. Since 2000, three new biographies have appeared (by Jeffrey Meyers, Gordon Bowker, and D. J. Taylor), along with the final volumes of *The Complete Works of George Orwell*, an exhaustive collection of his writings edited by Peter Davison. Special studies and monographs also appear annually.

Orwell remains widely quoted and internationally recognized for his last two books—both of them unique masterpieces. His powerful exposé of the betrayal of the idea of revolution, *Animal Farm* (1945), modeled on the Russian Revolution and cast in the form of a fable, established his literary reputation first in Great Britain and then around the world. His dystopian portrait of a world gone mad, *Nineteen Eighty-Four* (1948), has haunted generations of readers with its grim portrayal of a society controlled by a brutal, all-powerful dictatorship. Both books reveal Orwell's gift for memorable coinages. Phrases and words such as *Big Brother*, *newspeak*, *doublethink*, and "All animals are equal, but some animals are more equal than others" have entered the cultural lexicon. The combined sales of Orwell's last two works total more than 50 million copies. They have become standard texts in secondary school and university curricula, making them two of the most popular books of the twentieth century. In a 1997 survey of the reading public carried out by Waterstone's, an English book chain, *Animal Farm* and *Nineteen Eighty-Four* ranked second and third (behind J. R. R. Tolkien's *Lord of the Rings* trilogy) as the greatest English-language books of the last century.

Orwell was born Eric Arthur Blair in June 1903 in India, where his father served as an official in the Opium Department of the Indian

Civil Service. Young Eric was brought back to England as a baby and raised there, along with his two sisters. His youth, especially his love of nature and his checkered experience at his preparatory school, St. Cyprian's, shaped his life. Always something of a loner, his aloofness and wariness were significantly conditioned by the events of his childhood, especially his prep school experience.

After St. Cyprian's, about which he wrote scornfully in one of his most powerful autobiographical essays, "Such, Such Were the Joys" (written in 1947 and first published, posthumously, in 1952), Blair matriculated to secondary school at Eton College, England's most elite boarding school. Although he enjoyed his time there, he did not work up to his abilities, partly because he was exhausted by the demands at St. Cyprian's of pursuing a scholarship to attend Eton. Neither did Blair make many lasting friends at Eton—the writer Cyril Connolly representing an important exception. Blair's misery at his prep school turned the writer Orwell into a harsh critic of the British tradition of elite "public school" (as private schools in England are called) education. He accused such schools of inculcating a class prejudice that he believed was England's special curse. Nonetheless, shortly after his son Richard was born in 1945, Orwell put his name down for Eton. This was typical of the numerous paradoxes that characterized Orwell's life.

Blair's disillusion with his English boarding school years launched him on a trajectory that would differ markedly from that of his peers— and doubtless helped form his distinctive voice and vision as a writer. Instead of going on to university at Oxford or Cambridge as did most of his classmates, Blair followed his father's path by joining the Indian Civil Service as a policeman in Burma—an unlikely, if not unprecedented, career choice for an Etonian.

Five years in Burma (also known today as Myanmar) convinced Blair he could be no servant of the British Empire. He came to hate imperialism and all it represented. But Burma provided him with experiences upon which he would draw in his future writings, including the novel *Burmese Days* (1934), as well as such powerful essays as "A Hanging" and "Shooting an Elephant." Almost everything Orwell wrote until *Animal Farm* was drawn from his personal experiences. In this respect, despite his last two remarkable works of fiction, Orwell was not an especially gifted creative writer. He admired authors such as James Joyce and D. H. Lawrence precisely because they could go far beyond themselves and their own experiences in their writings.

Blair returned to England in 1927, determined not only to resign his position as a policeman but also to embark on a new life as a writer. At the age of twenty-three, he opted for a career for which he had as yet shown no talent. But at last he had decisively embarked on his impassioned boyhood wish, his great dream to be (as he once wrote it to his friend Jacintha Buddicom) "a FAMOUS AUTHOR."

It took five more years for this daring decision to emerge as the right choice. From 1927 through 1932 Blair struggled to learn his craft, first in England and then in Paris. He was fascinated by existence on the lower levels of society. Inspired by the writings of authors such as Jack London, and partly also to purge himself of feelings of guilt for a privileged youth, Orwell adopted the lifestyle of a tramp. He lived and worked among transients and the downtrodden, trying to understand their lives, all the while gaining understanding about how the poor live and die.

Like many other English intellectuals of his day, he also spent time in Paris, living a subsistence life for two years as a struggling author. His experiences there and his excursions among the poor in London led to his first major publication, a work that is part autobiography, part imaginative fiction, *Down and Out in Paris and London* (1933), for which he adopted the nom de plume "George Orwell." The book was a success and showed that Orwell had talent for writing vividly descriptive scenes and creating lifelike characters. *Down and Out* was also the first of his writings in which Orwell was both a participant and an observer, dual roles that he would adopt in many of his later writings.

The sordid nature of *Down and Out* induced Orwell to use a pen name so as not to embarrass his respectable middle-class family. Although for a few more years he still occasionally published book reviews under his birth name, "Orwell" gradually replaced "Blair."

Down and Out in Paris and London launched Orwell's literary career. He believed that being an author meant publishing not just nonfiction but also serious fiction, or in his case "enormous naturalistic novels with unhappy endings," as he put it in his 1946 essay "Why I Write." In the next several years Orwell would publish four novels of uneven quality that fit this description. What these novels ultimately demonstrated was that Orwell's greatest literary talents lay in other areas.

Orwell later belittled some of the fiction he wrote in the 1930s, and in his literary will he expressly asked that two of the novels, *A Clergyman's Daughter* (1935) and *Keep the Aspidistra Flying* (1936), not be republished. He had some affection for *Burmese Days* because it captured what he remembered from his five years in Burma. He regarded *Coming Up For Air* (1939) as his best realistic novel, but it was a victim of timing, appearing just as war broke out in September 1939.

During the 1930s, Orwell also reviewed books for a number of English magazines and newspapers. He read widely in both fiction and nonfiction, thereby effectively acquiring the university education he had formally rejected. More important to him than his reviewing, however, were his essays. Long an influential genre in British intellectual life, the essay format received in Orwell's hands new energy and innovative direction. He wrote serious essays on what might be considered ephemeral and even trivial topics, such as working in a bookstore, witnessing a hanging, shooting an elephant, and reading American and English mystery novels and comic postcards. Orwell's essays foreshadowed the emergence of the new academic field of popular cultural studies. They also first showcased his mature prose style, a mode of writing purged of excess words and one in which the author spoke directly to the reader. By 1940, Orwell had found his voice, his dramatic gift for "speaking on paper" and thereby connecting with the reader.

Orwell's simple, unadorned prose style particularly lent itself to the documentary format. In the 1930s he published two such works that meant a great deal to him. *The Road to Wigan Pier* (1937), a powerful examination of economic conditions among the unemployed in the north of England, was a major success and established his reputation in English intellectual circles. *Homage to Catalonia* (1938), which related his experiences as a militiaman in the Spanish Civil War, was a publishing failure, selling less than a thousand copies, and yet a book Orwell cherished. Indeed, both books were important to Orwell personally because they completed his conversion to socialism. Having been something close to a Tory anarchist in his youth, Orwell had become a democratic socialist, albeit an idiosyncratic one, after witnessing poverty in the north of England and fascism in Spain.

Homage to Catalonia also is important for Orwell's political development. As Orwell watched how reportage on the events in Spain was distorted for ideological reasons, he began to fear that the very concept of historical truth was in jeopardy. This theme would surface repeatedly in Orwell's subsequent writings, reaching its fullest treatment in *Animal Farm* and *Nineteen Eighty-Four*. Orwell's criticisms of traditional socialism (first spelled out in the second part of *The Road to Wigan Pier*), along with his denunciations of Communism and Communist fellow-travelers, made him persona non grata among Marxist radicals. He gradually adopted the role of critic of the British Left from within. Many of his sharpest observations were directed at his fellow socialists.

World War II was a turning point in Orwell's life. He had flirted with pacifism after his return from Spain, even briefly joining the antiwar Independent Labour Party. He argued that the outbreak of war would lead to a triumph of fascism. But when World War II arrived, he experienced a conversion and tried to enlist. Because of health problems—he suffered from chronic bouts of bronchitis that eventually led to the tuberculosis that killed him—the military rejected him. He eventually joined the Home Guard, the British civil defense force. Because of his experience as an imperial policeman in Burma and his military service in Spain, he was given the rank of sergeant.

During the first year of war, Orwell published a collection of essays in 1940, *Inside the Whale*, that marked him as a shrewd observer of literary trends, particularly in his defense of the controversial American novelist Henry Miller. The collection showed Orwell the critic at his best. The title essay was an influential analysis of the developments in English literature in the years between the wars. His next collection, *The Lion and the Unicorn: Socialism and the English Genius* (1941), gave critical support to the war effort while calling for an economic and social revolution.

In August 1941 Orwell joined the BBC as broadcaster to India. He spent two largely wasted years organizing programs for an audience that barely existed. At this time, Orwell's literary work was limited mostly to essays and book reviews. He did reach an American audience during the war with a column ("London Letter") for the American left-wing journal *Partisan Review*. But he soon grew bored with his job at the BBC, resigning in November 1943 to work as literary editor of *Tribune*, a small but influential socialist weekly. During this period Orwell was writing *Animal Farm*, which he completed in early 1944. Because of Britain's wartime alliance with the Soviet Union, Orwell encountered great difficulties getting a book critical of the Soviet government published.

The rejection of *Animal Farm* on political grounds by several British publishers deepened Orwell's antagonism toward his fellow leftists and their tendency to parrot a strict party line. In August 1945, after the war ended, *Animal Farm* was finally released by a small radical publisher, Secker and Warburg. The book was a runaway success, first in England and then in 1946 in the United States, where it was made a Book-of-the-Month-Club choice.

Animal Farm made Orwell rich and famous. The book was not only a clever parody of the events of the Russian Revolution, but also brilliantly executed as a simple fable. The fact that children appreciated *Animal Farm* as a fairy tale pleased him. Its success, along with the difficulties he had endured finding a publisher, only furthered Orwell's alienation from those radicals who had accused him of slandering an ally in the war.

Animal Farm's success came at an important juncture in Orwell's life. He and his wife, Eileen, had adopted a child early in 1945, only to have Eileen die during a routine operation later that spring. Shortly thereafter, Orwell's latent tuberculosis flared up. He decided to move from smoky, smog-ridden London to the island of Jura in the Scottish Hebrides. He had long dreamed of an island retreat where he would be close to nature and could write without the distractions of London literary life. Unlike many English writers, Orwell felt no strong attachment to London and its lively literary scene.

From the fall of 1946 until his death in January 1950, Orwell spent his days in the Hebrides or, when his tuberculosis recurred, in various sanatoria. Despite his health problems, he was happy on Jura and began there to compose his greatest work, *Nineteen Eighty-Four*. Written between 1946 and late 1948—he changed the original working title, *The Last Man in Europe*, to a title based on a transposition of the last two digits of the year in which he finished the book—*Nineteen Eighty-Four* ultimately made Orwell a household name.

Orwell's posthumous reputation has been astounding and without parallel. *Animal Farm* and *Nineteen Eighty-Four*, along with his most famous essays (collected in diverse volumes since 1940) have never been out of print. Some of his essays, particularly "Such, Such Were the Joys" and "Shooting an Elephant," have found their way into anthologies used in secondary schools and universities around the world. "Politics and the English Language," with its famous six rules for clear prose, has influenced generations of writers.

As the Cold War (a term many believe he coined) intensified in the years following his death, Orwell's work came to be co-opted by Cold Warriors in Great Britain and the United States. His last two books became ideological weapons in the conflict between the West and the Soviet world, as his strictures against totalitarian Communism were convenient truncheons with which to bludgeon the Left as Soviet sympathizers. In some ways this was predictable. Ever since his experience in the Spanish Civil War, Orwell had profoundly distrusted Communism, and so, despite his generally left-wing inclinations, he became prized on the Right for his anti-Communism.

Some of Orwell's early admirers turned against him. For instance, Raymond Williams, one of the dominant British cultural figures of the 1950s and 1960s, attacked *Nineteen Eighty-Four* for its "totalitarian tactics of arguing against totalitarianism." Nonetheless, Orwell's status as a literary figure and cultural hero continued to ascend. Indeed, every few years a successor would be heralded as the "new Orwell" or the "next Orwell"—only to be soon found wanting.

Events such as the so-called Orwell Year of 1984, or Orwell anniversaries such as the centenary of his birth (2003), have seen revived interest in his writings. Today young scholars discover him and his works and are attracted to this adamantly atheistic ascetic, a strange blend of saint and sinner. His reputation as a public intellectual and canonical author towers above those of his contemporaries; he is among the best-known English-language writers and most frequently cited political journalists of the twentieth century. Predictions are dangerous, but it is probably safe to say that at least until we reach the target date given in *Nineteen Eighty-Four* for the "perfection" of Newspeak—the year 2050—his international status as "a Famous Author" is assured.

How Orwell Became "a Famous Author" _____

John Rodden

The Dynamics of Reputation-Building

George Orwell was an outsider within the intelligentsia during the 1930s and 1940s, yet also with a claim to knowledge of the inside, and so he was perfectly positioned to become, as his fellow British writer V. S. Pritchett eulogized him, "the wintry conscience of his generation." Orwell was the conscience of the Left, and he gradually converted much of his own and the succeeding generations to his point of view about the intelligentsia in general and the Left in particular.

He was hated and relentlessly castigated by the Stalinists of his day, who dominated the London intellectual world. But Orwell viewed such Stalinist attacks on his work as unworthy of a reply and of only passing interest. That is to say, Orwell occupied a position of "optimal marginality" throughout his lifetime. Unlike T. S. Eliot, who acquired a position of "optimal centrality" as London's leading modernist poet and its reigning gatekeeper (as editor of the journal *The Criterion* and editorial advisor at the publishing house Faber and Faber), Orwell remained essentially an outsider for almost his entire career. At least until the publication of *Animal Farm* (1945) and *Nineteen Eighty-Four* (1949)—that is, until the last three or four years of his life—he was little known outside London and New York intellectual circles. Almost immediately upon his death in January 1950, however, his reputation skyrocketed. He became the famous "Saint George" Orwell. The posthumous figure "Orwell" assumed a place of "optimal centrality" as a world-historical author before the next decade was out.[1]

Orwell's early death turned him in the 1950s into an intellectual James Dean, as it were, a romantic icon within the intelligentsia. Like Dean, Orwell had died early and "too young." If he had even lived until 1955, he could not have possibly have maintained his stature on all fronts across the political spectrum. Inevitably, he would have had to take positions—whether on the Cold War or the Vietnam War or some other contentious issue—that would have compromised him among some of his later followers, as occurred with many of his contemporaries who survived in some cases decades beyond him. That is the temporal factor associated with his moment of exit.

The "Right Stuff": The Roles of Timing and Placement

Yet early death is by no means a boon to reputation. In fact, just the reverse: more often than not, longevity, and the attendant capacity to acquire followers or disciples who promote your work, is far more valuable. Yet reputation is contingent on many factors, and there is no way for the cultural historian or sociologist of art to isolate—and thereby analyze discretely and accurately—any particular factor, or even groups of factors, that may increase reputation. The zeitgeist is far too subtle for that. The innumerable complexities involved in being situated in the right place (both geographically and socially) and at the right time (with historical conditions emerging just at the moment when your achievement is ready to be exploited), defy all strategizing and tactics. The artist may employ various image-makers and reputation theorists to promote his or her work, but there is no guarantee their embroidery will result in fame.

Orwell is a very unusual case of someone dying at precisely the right historical location and moment. That is to say, his moment of exit from literary life—or his moment of entrance into his posthumous reputation—was perfectly (if inadvertently) timed to catapult his reputation into the stratosphere. Like Vladimir Lenin, he benefited from an early death, whereby he could never be discredited—and neither could he discredit statements made on his behalf. Thus, an Orwell cult soon arose. He was elevated to something like secular sainthood, at a time when it was common for intellectuals to claim a figure such as Orwell or Lenin as part of their moral and ideological pedigree.

But not merely at the moments of his entrance and exit from this life was Orwell in the right place at the right time. His posthumous reputation was further secured at three crucial moments in his afterlife: the dawn of network television in the mid-1950s, when televised versions of *Nineteen Eighty-Four* first skyrocketed him to stardom; the "countdown to 1984," when his reputation was revived to the unprecedented extent that his last book reached the *New York Times* best-seller list thirty-five years after its original publication date; and the centennial of his birth in 2003, when he once again gained international stature as the intellectual icon claimed by both proponents and opponents of "the War on Terror" and the invasions of Afghanistan and Iraq.

Models of Stardom

Today the "Orwell phenomenon" is without comparison among modern writers and unprecedented in its scope and scale: he is unique in possessing not only high standing among fellow writers, but also with the wider public. That is to say, both his critical standing and his popular reputation are remarkably high. Indeed, Orwell's reputation raises the fascinating question: What does it mean to be a literary "phenomenon"? Is it a matter of name recognition, best-seller lists, and sales totals? Or is it about informed readers, literary esteem from critics, and canonical standing? Size or stature? Breadth or depth? Sales volume or artistic renown? Mass appeal or cult appeal?

To put it in somewhat different terms, Orwell is the last of what could be called "the big-tent authors," a notion deriving from the sales model of stardom, which measures success and fame by the absolute number of book buyers and readers. The big-tent author offers something for everybody, and this Orwell does: he magnificently exemplifies the man of letters of the mid-twentieth century, having excelled at producing opinion columns, prose essays, documentary reportage, literary reviewing, and (of course) political fantasia (the beast fable, the anti-utopia).

Yet the size of Orwell's audience accounts only for his fame, that is, the breadth of his reputation (associated with data such as name recognition or citation counts). By contrast, the intensity with which his readers have identified with him explains the honor, sometimes bordering on reverence, that countless admirers have accorded him. Orwell's audiences *care* about him, both as a writer and as a man. His literary personality and personal life have exerted a spell on generations of readers, so much so that many writers not only prize Orwell as a prose stylist, but also want to *become like Orwell.* Given these facts, Orwell is also an outstanding example of the "niche author." This model scales success and fame according to the passion of a writer's following. Whereas the big-tent author is the old-school exemplum of a public figure whom we all admire, the niche author represents a form of stardom based on the sense of personal investment of his or her admirers. The niche author is precisely *not* for everyone; the cognoscenti pride themselves on being different. They relish the fact that their allegiance to their author-hero is a special, highly cultivated taste, a refined aesthetic judgment.

Is one kind of reputation better than another? Is it ultimately more advantageous to an author's reputation to have a smaller group of fans who care intensely about what he or she writes? Or a bigger number who just care enough to purchase (if not always read) the author's books? Admittedly, more people buy Danielle Steele and Stephen King than Jonathan Franzen and John Updike. However, that doesn't necessarily make Steele and King better authors, let alone literary phenomenons. Orwell possesses a reputation without equal, for he has been both renowned and revered from the entire post–World War II era to the present—a period of astonishing social and technological change.

Surfing the Tides of Time

All this is to say that there is indeed "a tide in the affairs of men," as Shakespeare's Brutus puts it. The conditions must be propitious for a reputation to emerge and flourish.[2] A forgotten story by Stephen Vincent Benét eloquently makes the point. In "The Curfew Tolls," Benét portrays a retired French army officer in the late eighteenth century. The aging officer, a rather cantankerous and curmudgeonly figure, is portrayed as something of a crank—even his own family treats him as such. He is constantly talking about battle plans, political designs, and military campaigns he would like to conduct, but he is usually treated rather patronizingly or even dismissively by the people around him.

We discover at the end of the story—when the officer dies, in May of 1789—that this "little man" with the grandiose fantasies is none other than Napoleon Bonaparte, and that Benét has spun a tale about what Napoleon's life might have been like had he been born about three decades earlier. His fantasies about what he would do if he were in power remain just that, for his life ends immediately prior to the era of revolutionary upheaval. The Napoleon of Benét's story was born too early: His moment of entrance was premature. The moral of the story is that if the conditions are unripe, even a Napoleonic force cannot shift the tides of history. Under such conditions, one is unlikely to go down in history rather than simply down the memory hole.

So reputation is indeed partly a matter of being in the right place at the right time. The conditions must be propitious for one to surf the tide of history; that is to say, a revolutionary moment of upheaval such as the French Revolution was crucial even for a "great man" such as Napoleon Bonaparte to emerge as a French general and ultimately the emperor of France and ruler of most of Europe.

Let us reconsider in Orwell's case the idea of the "moment of entrance" to which we alluded earlier. If Orwell had passed away even three years before his death at the early age of 46, he would have faded into obscurity, largely unread and unknown except perhaps among scholars of British literature specializing in the 1930s and early 1940s. Why? Because he would not have written *Animal Farm* and *Nineteen Eighty-Four.*

Contexts, Contingencies, and Reputations

As we have argued, if the case of Orwell exemplifies what could be referred to as "optimal marginality" during his lifetime, it exemplifies "optimal centrality" posthumously. That is to say, he began as a marginal political writer, but ended his days as the leading Cold War-rior of his generation, soon to become the iconic figure at "the bloody crossroads where literature and politics meet," in the famous phrase of Lionel Trilling (11). In the 1950s, as Raymond Williams acknowl-edged, "Down every road that you traveled, Orwell seemed to be wait-ing" (310).

An unfamiliar comparison is illuminating here. We may note a strong resemblance between how much the reputations of George Or-well and Harriet Beecher Stowe, author of *Uncle Tom's Cabin*, owe to the prevailing conditions of their eras: Stowe to the era of slavery in the United States and Orwell to the Cold War. The point of the comparison is that the rise to literary fame is less a matter of "great works" than of the kind of opportunities available and the fit of various candidates for greatness with the spirit of the times. The "contingencies of repute" are a web of advantages and inheritances that anyone will encounter in forging a life and legacy.

Reputation is based not only—and sometimes not even chiefly—on merit (i.e., aesthetic value). Nor is it a matter of individual achieve-ment alone, but rather a collective matter. It is often difficult to see how the individual is connected to the collective, but it is always crucial to look at the individual's context—that is, to see what is all around the individual yet often lurking in the shadows. These contexts will be historical, generational, cultural, class-oriented, gendered, racial, and so on. But these externalized features, which bear so decisively on the formation of reputation, are often lost to history. What survives and ascends to a peak visible from a vast historical distance is textual rather than contextual: the prose style, the narrative skill, the plotting, and the power of characterization. This is all very useful for the literary critics, but it is misleading and even disadvantageous as a focus for the literary and cultural historian.

For reputation is very different from critical interpretation or evalu-ation. The reputation of a work and author are a matter of context, whereas the latter two functions of criticism are a matter of text. The literary historian must primarily look "around" a work, not at it or into it (Rodden, *Politics*, 62–64). He must recover the scene of the work's reception because that scene explains the conditions that gave rise to what seems to be superhuman exploits or feats of genius.

Let me share here a personal anecdote about the contingencies of reputation and the importance of historical context: my encounter in a London pub in 1982 with a good friend of Orwell's, the crime writer and literary critic Julian Symons. The meeting occurred in the course of my research for my first book devoted to Orwell. Most Americans have never heard of Julian Symons, whereas hundreds of millions of people possess at least passing acquaintance with Orwell's name and work. After my interview with Symons about his relationship to Orwell and his impressions of fellow contributors to *Tribune*, Symons remonstrated: "But I must tell you again that George Orwell was no celebrity when I first got to know him in 1941. He was simply a bloke with whom I would walk down the street and have a drink in a pub like this. If he would have boasted to me that, forty-odd years from now, a young Yank would cross the ocean in order to interview me about him, I would have replied, 'But George, why isn't that chap coming to interview *you* about *me*?!'"

For me, the answer could only be: Because George Orwell became mine and virtually every postwar intellectual's "big brother."

Every Intellectual's "Big Brother"

I am reminded of Leo Tolstoy's remark that all modern Russian writers "came out of Gogol's overcoat." If one considers the roster of prominent Anglo-American intellectuals of the generations since 1950, there is hardly one that you could say didn't come "out of Orwell's overcoat." Indeed, one can speak of an extended family of intellectuals so touched by his work that they feel like they are his progeny. I have referred to them in one of my books, *Every Intellectual's Big Brother* (2006), as Orwell's "literary siblings."

But if Orwell today is indeed "every intellectual's big brother" (my lowercasing is deliberate here), he is also, quite paradoxically, the intellectual who hates intellectuals. He certainly regarded himself as an intellectual, yet he was never particularly proud of that fact. He derided those literary intellectuals who believed that intellectuals must inevitably feud bitterly with their rivals, that they warrant artistic license to indulge their narcissistic excesses, and that they merit public respect for political exhibitionism. He would have concurred with W. H. Auden's ditty: "To the man-in-the-street, who, I'm sorry to say, / Is a keen observer of life, / The word 'Intellectual' suggests straight away / A man who's untrue to his wife." Despite his early castigation of Auden for some of the vices just enumerated, Orwell would have fully agreed with the Auden of this jocular stanza, the mature poet who had befriended Orwell by the later 1930s and 1940s. Both men felt that many intellectuals tried too hard to separate themselves from the masses. Unlike such pretentious intellectuals, snugly ensconced in their literary coteries and writing in abstract jargon exclusively for one another, Orwell has often been considered more of a common man, blessed with a certain common sense precisely because he refused to separate himself in this way.

Nowadays all kinds of consultants, image-makers, and spin doctors have devised tactical and strategic methods for positioning fame seekers to attain renown. Back in Orwell's day—and especially given the kind of person he was—it was inconceivable that he could or would have planned his meteoric rise to international prominence in the last four years of his life. He wrote *Animal Farm* simply out of a sense of righteous indignation and personal passion. He had never written a book like that before. He had written realistic novels in the 1930s; he was eking out an existence as a journalist. Never did he expect that *Animal Farm* would achieve the kind of success it did; it was rejected by two dozen publishers before it was accepted. Of course, its moment of entrance on the literary stage as a published work proved auspicious. Had it reached print soon after its completion in February 1944, it might have disappeared; instead, its appearance was delayed until August 1945, just as World War II was ending and the Anglo-American alliance with the Soviet Union was breaking up.

Orwell could never have planned the circumstances so well! Imagine planning that its publication would be delayed eighteen months because he would send it around to two dozen different publishing houses that would reject it and then suddenly the war would end. Even today it's impossible to imagine such clairvoyance (or promotional ledgermain).

To Be "a Famous Author"

So how do writers become famous? How did George Orwell achieve his boyhood dream of becoming "a Famous Author," as he expressed it to a friend? We have seen that literary reputation is inevitably a matter of historical timing and placement. As Germany's former chancellor Helmut Kohl once expressed it, he and his generation of Germans had received "the blessing of late birth."[3] By that Kohl meant that Germans of his age had been given the accidental fortune of being born too late to have come to maturity during the Third Reich. As a result, they were not responsible for crafting or carrying out Adolph Hitler's policies, unlike their elders. In the case of George Orwell and many other writers, we might think of "the blessing of early death." To reiterate: had Orwell died even as late as 1955, he would have been unlikely to maintain his stature on all political fronts across the ideological spectrum.

How then do writers acquire fame? The short answer would allude to the Greek concept of *kairos*—that is, be in the right place in the right time. A writer must be positioned in relation to the zeitgeist so that he or she will be perceived—once conditions are propitious—as a candidate eligible for elevation. The writer must get out in front of the tides of history to be able to surf the biggest waves when the tsunami hits. Here, in summary, is how Orwell did this: He penned a little fable called *Animal Farm*, which was rejected by publishers because it directly attacked Stalinism, and at the time, the United States and Great

Britain were allies of "Uncle Joe" Stalin. But then the war ended, and political conditions altered; the Cold War began. Stalin became the enemy—and *Animal Farm* and *Nineteen Eighty-Four* were already there as ideological weapons, ready to be used. "Big Brother Is Watching You," Newspeak, doublethink, thoughtcrime, "All animals are equal but some are more equal than others." It was—and has been—an arsenal that could be used against socialism and its history quite effectively by the capitalist democracies.

Then Orwell died, in 1950, just as the Cold War freeze was deepening. His death that January immediately preceded the onset of McCarthyism in the United States a few weeks later—that is, it preceded the rise of a vulgar pro-Americanism or defense of capitalism that might have undermined Orwell's status on some segment of the ideological front. As it was, having died at mid-century, Orwell was spared the difficulty of taking a firm position on a range of issues: McCarthyism and the early Cold War, followed by the counterculture and Vietnam; the communist experiments in Nicaragua; the nuclear freeze in central Europe; and on through September 11, 2001, and beyond. A dead man is a blank slate on which his successors can write as they please. To be in "the right place" means that the structure of conditions will support you; to be there at "the right time" means you'll be sufficiently malleable to be used or abused for whatever purposes the successors deem necessary to achieving their own identity and aspirations.

Reputation and Its Vicissitudes

Orwell's attitude toward the literary establishment of intellectual London, the Marxist Left that ostracized him as an "anti-Socialist," resembled the sentiments expressed by John Keats in a letter shortly before his death about the harsh reviews of his poetry: "This is a mere matter of the moment—I think I shall be among the English Poets after my death" (Keats 177). Posterity has concurred.

But what is literary immortality? According to one of Orwell's favorite boyhood authors, Samuel Butler, immortality is a matter of continued existence in the thoughts and lives of others. Butler conceived of heaven as a gift of posterity whereby we bask in the radiant glow of good wishes from those still alive (Butler 301). If this is so, then it can certainly be said that the literary immortality of George Orwell is affirmed by the esteem felt for him by millions of readers still today, more than six decades after his death. His outsized posthumous reputation discloses the impassioned—if often carefully veiled—vanity of human wishes, given the fact that so many writers of his own and succeeding generations have dreamed of attaining the kind of literary immortality gained by Orwell alone among contemporary writers.

Sherwood Anderson once remarked about literary fame: "Fame is no good, my dear... Take it from me," and "If I could work the rest of my life unknown, unnoticed by those who make current opinion, I would be happier" (qtd. in Carver 201). The posthumous Orwell would probably echo those statements—and let us remember that Orwell achieved real fame only posthumously. He was spared its bittersweet ordeals in this life.

Indeed, a writer identifies with "Orwell" at his own psychological peril. For George Orwell himself could not have imagined "Orwell." In fact, Orwell himself never really sought to be "Orwell"—and how could he have possibly done so? Nothing less than a cascade of unique and fateful events miraculously converged and thereby precipitated the invention of "Orwell." It was a matter of fate or providence, of the hand of *kairos*: the construction of a figure such as "Orwell" was far beyond the design of any image-making machine; even the most skillful, manipulative handlers could not have manufactured an "Orwell"—a project vastly more ambitious and dubious than the successful forgery that Winston Smith at the Ministry of Truth undertakes in fabricating his Comrade Ogilvy in *Nineteen Eighty Four*.

George Woodcock once wrote that Orwell decided not to use his pen name on his tombstone because he understood that, while Eric Blair would return to dust, George Orwell might survive as one of the literary immortals (Woodcock 529). Although Woodcock was a close and insightful friend of Orwell's, he errs in supposing that Orwell the man—his boyhood dream to be "a Famous Author" notwithstanding—possessed even the slightest intuition that he would become arguably the most famous literary figure since Shakespeare, let alone that his neologisms and coinages would become not only part of the contemporary cultural lexicon and political imagination, but also battle-certified ideological weapons in the Cold War.

George Orwell said he would never write his autobiography. One may wonder if he somehow did intuit on his deathbed, as his extraordinary afterlife was dawning, the challenge of such a memoir. If so, he might have voiced his reservations in terms that resemble the celebrated claim of Henri Matisse: "If my story were ever to be written down truthfully from start to finish, it would amaze everyone" (qtd. in Spurling xvii).

Notes

1. See McLaughlin 22.
2. See Rodden, *Unexamined Orwell* 27.
3. The remark is from Kohl's speech delivered on October 10, 1988.

Works Cited

Auden, W. H. "Note on Intellectuals." *The Collected Poems*. New York: Modern Library, 2007. 295.

Butler, Samuel. *The Notebooks of Samuel Butler*. Ed. Sir Geoffrey Keynes and Brian Hill. New York: Cape, 1951.

Carver, Raymond. "Fame Is No Good, Take It from Me." *Call If You Need Me: The Uncollected Fiction and Other Prose*. Ed. William L. Stull. New York: Vintage, 2001.

Keats, John. Letter to George and Georgiana Keats. 13 or 14 Oct. 1818. *Letters of John Keats*. Ed. Frederick Page. London: Oxford UP, 1954. 177.

McLaughlin, Neil. "Optimal Marginality." *The Sociological Quarterly* 42.2 (Spring 2001): 271–288.

Rodden, John. *George Orwell: The Politics of Literary Reputation*. Piscataway, NJ: Transaction, 2002.

_____. *The Unexamined Orwell*. Austin: U of Texas P, 2011.

Spurling, Hilary. Introduction. *Matisse the Master: A Life of Henri Matisse, the Conquest of Colour, 1909–1954.* New York: Knopf, 2007.

Trilling, Lionel. "Reality in America." *The Liberal Imagination.* New York: NYRB Classics, 2008. 3–21.

Williams, Raymond. *Politics and Letters.* London: New Left Review of Books, 1979.

Woodcock, George. "Orwell, Blair and the Critics." *Sewanee Review* 83 (1975): 524–536.

Biography of George Orwell

John P. Rossi

Eric Arthur Blair, better known as George Orwell, was born in Motihari, India on June 25, 1903. He was the second of three children born to Ida Limouzin Blair and Richard Walmsley Blair. His father was an agent in the Indian Civil Service's Opium Department from 1875 until his retirement in 1912. In 1904 Orwell's mother took her three children to England, where they settled in Henley-on-Thames in Oxfordshire.

Orwell had a happy childhood. Evidence for this can be found in a charming memoir by his friend Jacintha Buddicom, *Eric and Us* (1974). A voracious reader, Orwell especially liked the works of Rudyard Kipling, Jack London, George Bernard Shaw, and H. G. Wells (Bowker 15–16). From them he developed affection for the Edwardian world of his youth. In the words of his friend Cyril Connolly, Orwell was "a revolutionary in love with 1910" (qtd. in Bowker 188).

When he was four, Orwell went to a neighborhood school run by French Ursuline nuns in Henley. At age eight he won a partial scholarship to St. Cyprian's, a preparatory school in Sussex with an excellent record of sending its graduates to influential public (meaning private) schools in England such as Eton and Harrow. In his essay "Such, Such Were the Joys" (1952), Orwell painted a damning portrait of the school and its owners. For reasons of libel, the essay wasn't published for years in England. Orwell never deviated from his opinion that preparatory schools did irreparable harm to young boys.

Orwell won a scholarship to two schools, Wellington and Eton. After nine weeks at Wellington, he transferred to Eton, where he was a King's Scholar, one of seventy elite students in a school of a thousand students. Despite his scholarship, Orwell did not apply himself at Eton, instead largely educating himself by reading widely. Although he did not distinguish himself academically, he retained affection for his time at Eton, even putting down the name of his son, Richard, for the school (Bowker 318).

In 1921 after graduation Orwell joined the Indian Civil Service, following in his father's footsteps. He chose Burma as his post, serving as an Imperial Policeman for what he described as "five boring years within the sound of bugles" (Crick, 145). Burma served an important role in his life. From his time there he would produce a novel and two of his greatest essays, "A Hanging" and "Shooting an Elephant." Early in his tenure in Burma, Orwell decided to resign his position. "I felt that I had got to escape," he later wrote, "not merely from imperialism but from every form of man's dominion over man" (*Wigan Pier* 148). This hatred of authority would be the motif of his life for the next decade.

Orwell returned to England in late 1927, shocking his family when they learned that he wanted to become a writer. During the next five years while living with his family and holding down a series of jobs—teacher, bookstore clerk—he wrote short stories, plays, and even attempted a novel. But he was dissatisfied with his efforts and destroyed most of what he wrote.

In 1927, inspired by Jack London's *The People of the Abyss* (1902), a firsthand account of life among the poor of London, Orwell began to investigate the world of the poor, unemployed, and homeless. In the spring of 1928, Orwell moved to Paris, where he lived in the Latin Quarter, joining thousands of other struggling writers of the post–World War I "Lost Generation." His first publication appeared in October 1928, an article on censorship in England for Henri Barbusse's radical weekly, *Monde.* Two months later, the British publication *G. K.'s Weekly* published Orwell's first article in English, an essay about a populist right-wing French journal, *Ami du Peuple* (Bowker 109). Orwell remained in Paris throughout 1929, revising a long manuscript that would eventually become his first book, *Down and Out in London and Paris* (1933). He returned to England in December 1929 when an essay dealing with the life of tramps, "The Spike," was accepted by the literary journal *The Adelphi.* Orwell's literary career was about to be launched.

During the next six years of his life, Orwell struggled to find his voice. Between 1933 and 1938 he produced a book a year: three novels [*Burmese Days* (1934), *A Clergyman's Daughter* (1935), and *Keep the Aspidistra Flying* (1936)] and two prose masterpieces, *The Road to Wigan Pier* (1937) and *Homage to Catalonia* (1938). He also wrote over fifty essays and book reviews. The novels he regarded as failures; although he retained affection for *Burmese Days*, he later recommended the other two not be reprinted.

The Road to Wigan Pier and especially *Homage to Catalonia* demonstrated the unique power of Orwell's reportage and journalism. *The Road to Wigan Pier* was written after Orwell was commissioned in 1936 by the well-known left-wing publisher, Victor Gollancz, to undertake an investigation of economic conditions in the English Midlands. When Orwell completed the manuscript of his research, Gollancz made it an offering of his popular Left Book Club (Crick 309). *The Road to Wigan Pier* not only brought Orwell to the attention of a large audience, selling around 50,000 copies, it also revealed his talent as an investigative journalist. The second half of the book also showed Orwell's gift for controversy, when he wrote that the worst arguments for socialism were the socialists themselves. In spite of this, *The Road to Wigan Pier* marked an important step on Orwell's conversion to socialism.

In 1937, Orwell went to Spain to take part in the civil war there, documenting these experiences in *Homage to Catalonia*. He joined an independent communist party, the POUM (Partido Obrero de Unificación Marxista, or Workers' Party of Marxist Unification), which feuded with the Spanish communists aligned with Joseph Stalin and the Soviet Union. After six months Orwell suffered a serious wound when he was shot in the throat. Spain completed Orwell's conversion to socialism, while also instilling in him an abiding hatred of Communism—especially the Stalinist version that the POUM had opposed.

When Orwell returned to England, he was disgusted to find that events in Spain were being distorted by international communists for ideological reasons, portraying the POUM and their allies as pro-fascist. In his effort to counter this falsehood and tell what he saw in Spain, Orwell ran afoul of the far Left. Gollancz refused to publish *Homage to Catalonia*, or any articles and reviews Orwell wrote that were critical of the Spanish communists. In 1938, Orwell became ill with tuberculosis and spent seven months in Morocco trying to recover his health. While there he wrote the last, and the best, of his traditional novels, *Coming Up For Air* (1939), published on the eve of World War II.

The war completed Orwell's transformation into a major literary figure. Orwell and wife—Eileen O'Shaughnessy, a fellow eccentric whom he had married in 1936—moved to London when the war broke out. While she secured a job with the government's Censorship Department, he tried to join the military, but without success due to his poor health. Orwell published a collection of essays, *Inside the Whale*, in March 1940. The essays, on authors from Charles Dickens to Henry Miller and topics such as weekly publications for boys, were something unique. The essay "Boys' Weeklies" in particular foreshadowed the new academic genre of cultural studies—a serious essay on a seemingly frivolous subject.

The beginning of the German blitzkrieg in April and May of 1940 energized Orwell. His literary output was prolific, including movie and play reviews for the popular journal *Time and Tide*. Later that year he agreed to write a series called "London Letters" for the American left-wing journal *Partisan Review*, which would introduce him to the American intelligentsia (Bowker 272). The crisis of the Battle of Britain in the summer of 1940 convinced Orwell that a genuine revolutionary moment was emerging. In *The Lion and the Unicorn*, a pamphlet published in February 1941, Orwell argued that the patriotism that bound the English middle and lower classes together could be exploited to create what he called a decent form of socialism (Crick 403–409).

That revolutionary moment passed, however, and in June 1941 Orwell began working for the BBC, broadcasting news to India. He held this position for what he described as two and a half wasted years. The position did, however, give Orwell an opportunity to meet with leading members of the English literary and cultural elite, such as Dylan Thomas, T. S. Eliot, and J. P. Priestley, among others. Radio broadcasting proved frustrating, and he found life at the BBC "a mixture of whoreshop and lunatic asylum" (qtd. in Bowker 299). Part of his frustration arose from the fact that, aside from another influential essay of lasting cultural significance, "The Art of Donald McGill," Orwell wrote relatively little during his time at the BBC.

In November 1943, he resigned from the BBC and joined the left-wing weekly magazine *Tribune* as its literary editor, a job that better suited his skills and temperament. While at *Tribune*, Orwell also wrote a column, "As I Please," which tapped his eccentric interests, writing about anything that took his fancy. Indeed, his new job allowed him ample time to write. From November 1943 to January 1945, when he left *Tribune*, Orwell published more than one hundred pieces in the magazine, including essays, book reviews, and his column.

Most importantly, his time at *Tribune* saw Orwell finish his first great masterpiece, *Animal Farm*. Although completed in February 1944, it took Orwell eighteen months to find a publisher for the book. With its clever satire of the failures of the Russian Revolution and the brutalities of Stalin in the form of beast fable, *Animal Farm* was politically unacceptable in the midst of a war in which the Soviet Union and Great Britain were fighting as allies. Rejected by at least a half dozen publishers, including T. S. Eliot at Faber and Faber, *Animal Farm* only appeared in August 1945, just as World War II ended. It was a huge success, first in England and then in the United States, where it was a Book-of-the-Month-Club selection. *Animal Farm* made Orwell famous and financially secure, although the success was offset by the earlier death of his wife Eileen on March 29, 1945. The marriage had been a happy one, especially as Orwell had come to depend a great deal on Eileen's judgment and common sense, and at the time of her death, the couple had recently adopted a son, Richard.

In 1946 the success of *Animal Farm* enabled Orwell to leave London, a city he never really enjoyed, for the island of Jura, a quiet refuge off the coast of Scotland. At this time he began writing his last great work, *Nineteen Eighty-Four*. In December 1947, another bout of tuberculosis forced him to spend seven months in a sanatorium in Scotland where he was not allowed to do any writing. He returned to Jura in July 1948 for five months and there put the finishing touches to *Nineteen Eighty-Four*. In January 1949 Orwell's deteriorating health again required hospitalization. In June 1949, while he was in the hospital, *Nineteen Eighty-Four* was published in Great Britain and the United States. It was an even greater success than *Animal Farm* and again was a Book-of-the-Month-Club selection in the United States. However, Orwell would not have long to enjoy his success.

In September 1949, Orwell was moved to University College Hospital in London. One month later, he married Sonia Brownell, an assistant to Orwell's friend Cyril Connolly at the London literary journal *Horizon*. On January 21, 1950, while preparing to leave for a sanatorium in Switzerland, Orwell died. He was forty-six and at the peak of his fame. Five days later, he was buried at All Saints Cemetery, Sutton Courtenay, Berkshire. His epitaph simply reads: "Here lies Eric Arthur Blair, born June 25th 1903, died January 21st 1950."

Works Cited

Bowker, Gordon. *Inside George Orwell*. New York: Palgrave, 2003.

Buddicom, Jacintha. *Eric and Us*. 1974. Chichester: Finlay, 2006.

Crick, Bernard. *George Orwell: A Life*. Rev. ed. London: Penguin, 1992.

Davison, Peter. *George Orwell: A Literary Life*. New York: St. Martin's, 1996.

Meyers, Jeffery. *Orwell: The Wintry Conscience of a Generation*. New York: Norton, 2000.

Orwell, George. *The Collected Essays, Journalism, and Letters of George Orwell*. Ed. Ian Angus and Sonia Orwell. 4 vols. London: Secker, 1968.

_____. *The Complete Works of George Orwell*. Ed. Peter Davison. 20 vols. London: Secker, 2000.

_____. *The Road to Wigan Pier*. New York: Harcourt, 1958.

Rodden, John. *The Politics of Literary Reputation: The Making and Claiming of "St. George" Orwell.* New York: Oxford UP, 1989.

Shelden, Michael. *Orwell: The Authorized Biography.* New York: Harper, 1991.

Taylor, D. J. *Orwell: The Life.* London: Chatto, 2003.

Homage to My "Intellectual Big Brother"_____

John Rodden

This essay represents a salute of thanks to George Orwell, my "intellectual big brother," for his priceless contribution to my political outlook and literary development. I have no confidence that he would acknowledge me as an intellectual or spiritual sibling. But as the centennial of his birth approached in 2003, I wanted to pay "homage to Orwell" because of my incalculable debt to him. Like so many other writers and critics of my generation—and especially generations previous to mine stretching all the way back to the early post–World War II era—I have felt a compelling affinity to Orwell. In my case, the feeling has run so deep that I have not only devoted a substantial part of my mature energies to studying Orwell's life and work, and in particular to an examination of his multifaceted reputation and unique legacy, but also to meeting and interviewing numerous men and women of earlier generations who have been similarly influenced and felt a comparable kinship.

Yet my debt to Orwell is not only political and intellectual, but also intensely and even intimately personal. For he has introduced me to what Irving Howe, another strong admirer of Orwell, unforgettably termed "the world of my fathers" in a best-selling historical study of that title. Now that I am firmly embedded in middle age, having lived almost a decade longer than Orwell himself, I often ponder: What has prompted me to identify with Orwell so deeply? What is the nature of our own (Anglo-American) "special relationship"? Why has he exerted such a dramatic impact on my life? (Indeed, a student once said to me after a lecture about Orwell's essays: "Was it true that George Orwell was your college roommate? I heard from several friends that he was.")

The answers are difficult to formulate, or at times even to fathom. But let me here discuss two comprehensive ways in which I discovered a second self—the Orwell within myself—through my ever-deepening acquaintance with my intellectual big brother.

II

First, with regard to "the world of my fathers," Orwell was the intellectual Beatrice who accompanied me on the exciting, if uncertain and often baffling, journey to what Henry James famously described as "the visible past." In his 1908 preface to *The Aspern Papers*, James speaks about that vista of history just beyond the horizon of our memories, the past of the immediately preceding generations that is fast receding yet still accessible because its living witnesses are still alive. James writes:

> I delight in a palpable imaginable *visitable* past—in the nearer distances and the clearer mysteries, the marks and signs of a world we may reach over to as by making a long arm we grasp an object at the other end of our own table. The table is the one, the common expanse, and where we lean, so stretching, we find it firm and continuous. That, to my imagination, is the past fragrant of all, or of almost all, the poetry of the thing outlived and lost and gone, and yet in which the precious element of closeness, telling so of connexions but tasting so of differences, remains appreciable. With more moves back the element of the appreciable shrinks—just as the charm of looking over a garden-wall into another garden breaks down when successions of walls appear. (xxiv)

James, like Orwell, possessed a distinctly tactile sense of the past. He acknowledged that his imagination embraced most readily the recent past, the world of his fathers and mothers, a past that was almost a felt experience and could be "grasped" like "an object," a stretch of history still imbued with the multifaceted wealth of associations of his life and times. James adds that the artist must catch hold of the past at just the right moment in order to extract its nectar of nuances, flavored by a fast-receding intensity:

We are divided of course between liking to feel the past strange and liking to feel it familiar; the difficulty is, for intensity, to catch it at the moment when the scales of the balance hang with the right evenness. . . . It would take me too far, however, to tell why the particular afternoon light that I thus call intense rests clearer to my sense on the Byronic age, as I conveniently name it, than on periods more protected by the "dignity" of history. With the times beyond, intrinsically more "strange," the tender grace, for the backward vision, has faded, the afternoon darkened; for any time nearer to us the special effect hasn't begun. (xxiv)

James's conception of the "visitable past" pertains to what one scholar describes as a past that is "before our time and yet so tantalizingly close to it that we feel we must be able to recover it, through contact with those few from that era who still survive" (Rochelson 39).

Like the nameless narrator of *The Aspern Papers*, my relationship with Orwell has inspired me to visit and revisit—with ever greater understanding, insight, and pleasure—the decades immediately before my own. Orwell has thereby introduced me not only to British and American intellectuals of his day and shortly thereafter—men and women ranging from Julian Symons, John Atkins, Mary Fyvel, Diana Trilling, Mary McCarthy, Alfred Kazin, William Phillips, Ian Angus, and other writers and scholars too numerous to mention—but he has also thereby enlivened this increasingly unrecoverable past (no longer readily "visitable" because almost all of the aforementioned guides have departed this life).

In this way, Orwell has silently instructed me about the preciousness and fragility of this past—how suddenly it disappears and how unvisitable it soon becomes, after which one must rely exclusively on hearsay and written records (such as diaries and letters) often even more vexing than the admitted shortcomings of memory and oral history.

James describes in detail the "thrill" of touching the immediate past and discovering that it "overlaps" with one's own lifetime of available experience.[1] I have experienced the same thrill countless times, even long before beginning my scholarly studies of Orwell's afterlife. An intellectual frisson in early boyhood occurred on a visit to my father's sister in Dublin (my parents had immigrated to the United States at mid-century), where I met an elderly neighbor of hers. This acquaintance had lived through the 1916 Easter Rising and the Irish Civil War. With good humor and infinite patience, she tolerated the insatiable curiosity of "the wee Yank." My merciless inquisition of this working-class lady owed to the simple fact that I felt myself to be a time traveler launched back to the Old World. For me, it was as if I had stumbled upon a survivor of the U.S. Civil War, since I had little real sense of the differences in time scale between it and its Irish counterpart. Both were "great historical events." I was to have similar thrills in later years on numerous occasions—in the United States, the United Kingdom, and above all Germany—whenever I met such historical witnesses. These men and women turned me into a kind of participant-historian, a "witness to witnesses," a visitor who gathered up the most perishable stories and gave voice to my storytellers. Ultimately, I wrote full-length books featuring my witnesses, and even books and articles about how to conduct interviews.[2]

Yet I must add an important caveat that applies to all these sallies into the past, including with intellectual acquaintances whom I have called "George Orwell's literary siblings," per the subtitle of my book *Every Intellectual's Big Brother*. Although my quest for entry to the visitable past is ceaseless and unrelenting, only occasionally do I reach it. We can only hope to experience it partially and temporarily. Still, the fact that our connection with it is fragmentary and imperfect should not invalidate the pursuit and the rewards that one may reap from it. Henry James is not the first to remind us of all this, as long ago on 46 B.C.E., Cicero declared in *Brutus the Orator*: "To be ignorant of what happened before you were born is to be ever a child. For what is man's lifetime unless the memory of past events is woven with those of earlier times?"

IIII

Nonetheless, my debt to Orwell is much broader and comprehensive than the priceless bequest of receiving a front-row visiting card to not just his own life and times, but also those of his contemporaries and successors. My second great promissory note to Orwell has to do with my own journey within. Because of the richness and amplitude of Orwell's remarkable oeuvre and ambiguous legacy, I have been led on and on through my human comedy to topics and issues and people that one might never associate with Orwell at all. Nonetheless, as several of my books about his cultural heritage suggest, Orwell has been the hub from which my forays into other languages and societies and histories have been directed. Because of my passion to learn about Orwell's aspirations and achievement, I have investigated numerous themes and motifs associated with his life and literature. I can even conceptualize my life history in terms of my debt to him. Because of a shifting combination of extensions and opportunities associated with Orwell's entry into my life, I have ventured in unexpected ways to visitable pasts (and presents) that I otherwise never would have encountered. For instance, the obvious extensions have to do with meeting fellow admirers of Orwell of my day and earlier—intellectuals such as Christopher Hitchens, Irving Howe, Norman Podhoretz, and others. Those extensions have led me to little magazines such as *Partisan Review* and left-wing papers such as *Tribune*, and, of course, to cultural capitals such as New York and London.

But as I explored Orwell's legacy more and more deeply, I began to extend my extensions, as it were, embracing less and less obvious extensions because of wonderful and often fortuitous opportunities that have arisen. Because of these opportunities, my intellectual and indeed existential priorities have often shifted. A dramatic example has been that Orwell's views of socialism and his engagement with World War II interacted with some other interests to make me fascinated with the condition of postwar Germany—and especially state socialism in East Germany, the so-called German Democratic Republic (GDR), whose forty-year lifespan (1949–1989) almost precisely coincided with the opening decades of Orwell's posthumous fame.

And so I was led to visit and revisit East Germany before and after the fall of the Berlin Wall. I glimpsed the visitable past of its Stalinist dictatorship before German reunification in October 1990. As it turned out, Orwell's neologisms in *Animal Farm* and *Nineteen Eighty-Four* were well known to literate East Germans—and indeed in the German language: "Big Brother Is Watching You"; Newspeak; thoughtcrime; "All animals are equal, but some are more equal than others"; even Orwell's name in adjective form—*Orwellisch* ("Orwellian"). All these have ensconced themselves in the German cultural lexicon. I was astounded to discover all this during my conversations and lectures in the immediate aftermath of the wall's toppling amid my visits to the GDR's Leipzig University (then still called Karl Marx University).

Moreover, because divided Germany represented in microcosm the global Cold War—with East and West Germany mirroring the rivalries and hostilities of their two "Big Brother" superstates, the capitalist United States and the communist Soviet Union—Germany turned out to be the nation outside the English-speaking world where Orwell was best known and most popular. By the year 1984, Orwell's books had sold more than two million copies in West Germany, a remarkable phenomenon. Unlike almost every other English-language author with the exception of Shakespeare, every single one of Orwell's books was in print in German translation—and they remain so today.

A more recent and equally surprising opportunity presented by my intellectual big brother has been an expedition to Asia as the keynote speaker for the "Orwell in Asia" symposium in Taiwan in 2011, which in turn led to a lecture tour devoted to Orwell and related topics in Hong Kong, Singapore, and elsewhere on that continent. Never would I have planned even visiting Asia for an extended period, let alone becoming deeply immersed in its cultural life. The invitations have arisen thanks to my intellectual big brother.

So both "extension" and "opportunity" have altered my priorities as my beneficent (anti-Orwellian!) big brother has guided me on my journey. The opportunity to meet "relatives," as it were, of Orwell—my intellectual siblings and spiritual cousins—has been irresistible and wonderfully enriching. It has stoked my impassioned love of biography and cultural history, so that I have also become a scholar of the American group to which Orwell also belonged, the *Partisan Review* circle, which included intellectuals such as Lionel Trilling, Howe, Podhoretz, Dwight Macdonald, and others. I have published many books and articles about these intellectuals, too, who are in some ways closer to me than Orwell in terms of cultural and historical affinities, since they are fellow American intellectuals.[3] With few exceptions, such as Macdonald, they are almost all Jews, so I have also been stretched anew in yet another direction.

My interest in Orwell has thereby introduced me to more than people or places or even my inner landscape, but also even to new scholarly specialties, such as German intellectual history, American cultural history, the geopolitics of human rights, and so on. I can honestly say that Orwell has been not just the guiding spirit of my intellectual development, but also the inner compass that has helped that development cohere and remain directed.[4] "I form human beings in my own image," says Goethe's Prometheus in that great eponymous lyric. I acknowledge the same about George Orwell. Because of the indelible imprint of my intellectual big brother upon my life journey, I have not merely accumulated interests and acquaintances: A mere accumulation is not truly a "formed" development; yet a group of interests and people mindfully and painstakingly brought together is an invaluable collection, a curriculum vitae. A mere accumulation does not cohere, but an organized and defined collection does indeed.

IV

So Orwell has been the hub of my own "collection development," and as a private collector who has insistently adopted him as my intellectual big brother, I thank him for the genius of his fraternal counsel.[5] Moreover, like any collector, I value the integrity of my collection, and I do believe that it possesses a deep rationale and coherence, even if that fact is not immediately obvious to those acquainted only with my work on Orwell, or on the New York intellectuals, German history, GDR communism, human rights abuses, psychology and the novel, the art of the interview—or on sundry other seemingly unrelated topics to which I have devoted books and articles. These topics are not really "sundry," for they all relate back to the great hub of my intellectual and even personal development, George Orwell, my ever-renewing sun to whom I feel forever grateful.

Regarding my vocational path, I would further acknowledge that Orwell has inspired me to become a "scholar-gypsy," in the phrase of Matthew Arnold. I gave up my academic position to become a freelance journalist, like Orwell. A freelance writer and full-time independent scholar was not so uncommon in his day, but I have never met anyone else who has left a secure position in leading research universities in the United States to follow such a life. It has been a penurious existence materially, but the spiritual and psychological remuneration has been munificent. If it were not for the example of George Orwell, I might never have been emboldened to undertake this passionate pilgrimage.

What a wondrous gift that goes on giving!

Notes

1. See James xxiv. On learning that a contemporary had obtained letters from an elderly lady named Jane Clairmont, the half-sister of Mary Shelley, author of *Frankenstein* (1818), James acknowledged his "thrill of learning that she [Clairmont] had 'overlapped.'"

2. See, for instance, my *Dialectics, Dogmas, and Dissent* and *Performing the Literary Interview*.

3. See, for instance, my *Lionel Trilling and the Critics, The Worlds of Irving Howe,* and *Irving Howe and the Critics.*

4. On this point, see my forthcoming *The Intellectual Species: Post-Gutenberg Prospects.*

5. I also thank William P. Barlow, Jr., for his stimulating lecture about a very different yet not unrelated subject, namely, the motivation for book collecting. I have adapted a few of his ideas about his history as a collector for this essay. See Barlow's *Book Collecting: Personal Rewards and Public Benefits* (Washington, DC: Library of Congress, 1984).

Works Cited

Cicero. *Brutus; Orator.* Cambridge: Harvard UP, 1976.

James, Henry. *The Turn of the Screw and The Aspern Papers.* Ware, England: Wordsworth, 2000.

Rochelson, Meri-Jane. "Revisiting the 'Visitable Past': Reflections on Wayne Booth's Teaching after 29 Years." *Pedagogy* 7.1 (2007): 37–48.

Rodden, John. *Dialectics, Dogmas, and Dissent: Stories from East German Victims of Human Rights Abuse.* University Park: Pennsylvania State UP, 2010.

_____. *Every Intellectual's Big Brother: George Orwell's Literary Siblings.* Austin: U of Texas P, 2006.

_____. *The Intellectual Species: Post-Gutenberg Prospects.* Leicester, England: Troubador, forthcoming.

_____. *Irving Howe and the Critics.* Lincoln: U of Nebraska P, 2005.

_____. *Lionel Trilling and the Critics.* Lincoln: U of Nebraska P, 1999.

_____. *Performing the Literary Interview: How Writers Craft Their Public Selves.* Lincoln: U of Nebraska P, 2001.

_____. *The Worlds of Irving Howe.* Boulder, CO: Paradigm, 2004.

CRITICAL
CONTEXTS

The Historical Background of Orwell's Work_____

James Seaton

George Orwell wrote in response to the events of the day and the comments on those events by politicians and intellectuals. Understanding his journalism and essays and even his novels requires at least a basic knowledge of the historical and intellectual context in which they were written. For example, Orwell's ideas about imperialism, as expressed both in his novel *Burmese Days* (1934) and in his essays and journalism, should be seen against the backdrop both of the British Empire in the first half of the twentieth century, and of the ideas and attitudes about imperialism that dominated public debate in England during that time. Likewise, Orwell's investigations of life among the poor and unemployed in books like *Down and Out in Paris and London* (1933) and *The Road to Wigan Pier* (1937) were written at a time when the Great Depression of the 1930s had raised questions about the future of capitalism that remained in large part unanswered even after the Depression gave way to World War II. Orwell wrote *Homage to Catalonia* (1938) while the Spanish Civil War was still being fought and its outcome still in doubt.

Orwell's two major works were written during a period dominated by the rise and fall of Nazism in Germany, Fascism in Italy, and militant imperialism in Japan. Orwell's statement in 1946 that "every line of serious work that I have written since 1936 has been written, directly or indirectly, *against* totalitarianism and *for* democratic socialism, as I understand it" (*Complete Works* 18: 319) should be seen in the context both of the rise of totalitarian societies in Germany and Russia and of the "united front" campaign carried out by the Communist International and its allies, insisting that the political and social structure of Nazi Germany and the Soviet Union had nothing in common and indeed were polar opposites. Both *Animal Farm* (1945) and *Nineteen Eighty-Four* (1949) were written when Joseph Stalin's power seemed impregnable, and the former was written while the Soviet Union was a vital

British ally in a world war. T. S. Eliot, a director at the publisher Faber and Faber, wrote to Orwell on July 13, 1944, that his firm declined to publish *Animal Farm*, although it was "a distinguished piece of writing," in large part because of the doubt "that this is the right point of view from which to criticize the political situation at the present time" (qtd. in Orwell, *Complete Works* 16: 282). At Orwell's death on January 21, 1950, Stalin had been in power in the Soviet Union for over thirty years, throughout Orwell's writing career. Meanwhile, the victory of Great Britain and the United States in World War II, achieved without political or social revolution, suggested that the possibility of achieving something close to Orwell's conception of democratic socialism in England (or elsewhere) seemed little better in 1950 than in the 1930s, although the English Labour Party had been in power since 1945.

When *Burmese Days* was published in 1934, Great Britain ruled over more than one-fourth of the world's territory and a similar proportion of its population. The nineteenth century, marked by events like Queen Victoria's assumption of the title of Empress of India in 1877, saw a vast expansion of the British Empire, and it grew even larger after England's hard-won victory in World War I. In the interwar period, the empire, celebrated in films such as *Lives of a Bengal Lancer* (1935) and *Clive of India* (1935), remained popular with the British public. In his 2002 history *Empire*, British historian Niall Ferguson observes that "as a source of entertainment—of sheer psychological gratification—the Empire's importance can never be exaggerated" (251).

Imperialism, however, could not be defended after World War I with the same confidence and moral certainty that a Briton could feel in the nineteenth century. The sense that a wholehearted defense of imperialism was impossible for anybody claiming to be enlightened was powerfully conveyed by David Low's cartoon character Colonel Blimp, an unabashed imperialist who, according to Low himself, was "no enthusiast for democracy" whose "remedy to social unrest was less education, so that people could not read about slumps" (qtd. in Ferguson

318). Orwell often refers to "the Blimps" in his journalism, usually with the implication that the ideas held by such people do not deserve to be taken seriously. In proposing "willingness to criticize Russia and Stalin" as the true "test of intellectual honesty" in an August 5, 1944, letter to fellow British writer John Middleton Murry, Orwell makes his case by noting that expressing other seemingly controversial opinions is not nearly so dangerous, because "to do so only gets one into trouble with the Blimps and who cares what they say?" (*Complete Works* 16: 320).

Both defenders of the empire and anti-imperialists agreed that England's control of roughly a quarter of the land surface of the globe contributed significantly to the wealth and prosperity of England itself; they differed in that the defenders thought this was a good thing, whereas anti-imperialists condemned what they saw as immoral exploitation of others, especially non-whites. V. I. Lenin had explained in *Imperialism: The Highest Stage of Capitalism* the failure of the proletariat to become revolutionary by reference to the "enormous *super-profits*" resulting from imperialism that made it "quite possible to *bribe* the labour leaders and the upper stratum of the labour aristocracy (13–14; italics in original). John Strachey in *The Coming Struggle for Power* (1932), probably the most influential work of Marxist analysis in England, repeatedly asserted the same thesis. Unlike Lenin, Strachey felt no need to provide evidence to back up his claim, but instead presented it as a given that would be accepted by all parties—as indeed it was. Strachey went even further, claiming that "the very basis of modern capitalism, without which great empires, such as the British, could not exist for a single day, is super-profits derived from the exploitation of colonial and subject peoples" (385).

Although George Orwell was not a Marxist and certainly not a Leninist, he assumed that Lenin and Strachey were essentially right in claiming that English imperialism provided economic benefits for at least a portion of the English working class, benefits that would be lost if the empire were lost. Believing nevertheless that imperialism was morally wrong, Orwell insisted that those who opposed imperialism should acknowledge that giving up the empire would mean a lower standard of living for English workers, at least for a time. In his fall 1945 "London Letter," a column he wrote for the American journal *Partisan Review*, Orwell stated the problem:

> The British people have never been warned, i.e. by the Left, that the intro-duction of Socialism may mean a serious drop in the standard of living. Nearly all left wingers, from Laborites to Trotskyists, would regard it as political suicide to say any such thing. Yet in my opinion it is probably true, at least in the case of a country like Britain, which lives partly by ex-ploiting the colored peoples. To continue exploiting them is incompatible with the spirit of Socialism, while to stop doing so would entail a difficult reconstruction period during which our own standard of living might fall catastrophically. In one form and another this problem comes up again and again, and, except for the minority who have traveled outside Europe, I have never met an English Socialist who would face it. (*Complete Works* 17: 247)

At other times Orwell was even more emphatic. In a 1942 article on British author Rudyard Kipling, he declared: "We all live by robbing Asiatic coolies. . . . Our standard of living, and hence our 'enlighten-ment,' demands that the robbery shall continue" (*Complete Works* 13: 153). For Orwell, the willingness to acknowledge that imperialism was both immoral and a source of material benefits for English workers was, like the willingness of leftists to criticize the Soviet Union, one of the best ways to demonstrate moral and intellectual honesty.

In retrospect, however, it appears that the consensus shared by Marxists, Colonel Blimp, and Orwell about the economic benefits of empire may have been wrong. Niall Ferguson, looking at the history of the British Empire from the vantage point of 2002, finds it doubtful that imperialism either benefited English workers or made colonial subjects poorer than they would otherwise have been. After a careful survey of relevant issues, Ferguson concludes that "the notion that British imperialism tended to impoverish colonized countries seems inherently problematic" (360). Ferguson argues that it is similarly doubtful that "the Empire [was] really economically beneficial to the mass of British voters." Some companies and individuals undoubtedly profited, but the "benefits of overseas investment were not enjoyed by the majority of people," while "the costs of imperial defence . . . were borne primarily by British taxpayers" (251). When England finally gave up imperial control, it was not only because of moral sentiment but because "Britain was simply no longer able to bear the costs of Empire" (352).

It should be emphasized that Orwell's views on the British Empire were not based on economic data, however interpreted, but on his own lived experience, captured eloquently in this passage from his 1936 essay "Shooting an Elephant":

> And it was at this moment, as I stood there with the rifle in my hands, that I first grasped the hollowness, the futility of the white man's dominion in the East. Here was I, the white man with his gun, standing in front of the unarmed native crowd—seemingly the leading actor of the piece, but in reality I was only an absurd puppet pushed to and fro by the will of those yellow faces behind. I perceived in this moment that when the white man turns tyrant it is his own freedom that he destroys. (*Complete Works* 10: 504)

In his 1939 essay "Marrakech," about the city in Morocco, Orwell observes that imperialism requires a disbelief in the humanity of the colonized, an observation made all the more powerful because Orwell admits that there are times when he cannot help sharing this disbelief:

> When you walk through a town like this—two hundred thousand inhabitants, of whom at least twenty thousand own literally nothing except the rags they stand up in—when you see how the people live, and still more how easily they die, it is always difficult to believe that you are walking

among human beings. All colonial empires are in reality founded upon that fact. The people have brown faces—besides, there are so many of them? Are they really the same flesh as yourself? Do they even have names? Or are they merely a kind of undifferentiated brown stuff, about as individual as bees or coral insects? (*Complete Works* 11: 417)

Whatever research may in the future reveal about the economy of imperialism, it is difficult to believe that Orwell's reflections on its human cost will ever be outdated.

Lenin believed that imperialism was the final stage of capitalism, and English Marxists like John Strachey were confident that the free market was an anachronism that was bound to disappear before long. The Great Depression seemed to many people, not just Marxists, to signal the failure of capitalism, while to observers holding a wide range of political views, various kinds of planned economies in the Soviet Union, Germany, Italy, and Japan seemed successful. John Strachey felt he was on firm ground when he argued in 1932 for the superiority of planning: "The actual comparison which a planned economy must bear is with capitalism as it exists today. And, on that standard of comparison, who in their senses can doubt the immense superiority of a planned system?" (138). For John Strachey, the development of the Soviet Union under Lenin and then Stalin demonstrated that a planned system was not only theoretically desirable but practically achievable: "One hundred and sixty millions of men and women have already taken the road to communism. They have leapt out of the kingdom of necessity towards the kingdom of freedom" (259). The success of the Soviet experiment was already evident to Strachey: "Even today in the Soviet Union, during the very brunt of the initial struggles of a working-class dictatorship, before a classless society has fully emerged, there is perceptible an exhilaration of living which finds no parallel in the world. To travel from the capitalist world into Soviet territory is to pass from death to birth" (359).

George Orwell's writings are free of the tendency to idealize any country or society, except possibly Barcelona for a few months in 1936 and 1937. To his great credit, he did not allow his support for socialism to prevent him from thinking and writing with complete moral and intellectual honesty about the one country where, it was claimed, socialism was being put into practice. Like John Strachey and the Marxists, however, Orwell was virtually certain that capitalism would soon give way to some sort of planned economy. In works like *The Road to Wigan Pier*, he expresses his indignation at the suffering seemingly caused or at least allowed by a capitalist economy. Yet Orwell was by no means sure that a planned economy would be humanly better than one based on the market, despite all the latter's flaws. But if he was doubtful about some aspects of a planned economy, he was determined to face a change he believed was certain to come. Orwell felt in 1941 that H. G. Wells was wrong about many things, most notably how dangerous Hitler and Nazism really were, but he felt that Wells was "probably right in assuming that a 'reasonable,' planned form of society, with scientists rather than witch-doctors in control, will prevail sooner or later" (*Complete Works* 12: 539).

In a 1941 BBC broadcast, later published as "Literature and Totalitarianism," Orwell voiced his certainty both that "liberal capitalism is obviously coming to an end" and that "a collectivized economy is bound to come." He also wanted to believe, however, that "freedom of thought can survive the disappearance of economic individualism." For Orwell, this was "the only hope to which anyone who cares for literature can cling" (*Complete Works* 12: 505). Orwell was a democratic socialist who nevertheless feared that the kind of individuality expressed in the literature he loved was somehow connected with the "economic individualism" he thought responsible for poverty and inequality.

In April 1944, reviewing F. A. Hayek's *The Road to Serfdom*—a defense of the free market against the dangers of government interference—Orwell agreed emphatically with Hayek's thesis that socialism could all too easily lead to a kind of serfdom: "It cannot be said too often—at any rate, it is not being said nearly often enough—that collectivism is not inherently democratic, but, on the contrary, gives to a tyrannical minority such powers as the Spanish Inquisitors never dreamed of." A planned economy was nevertheless inevitable, in Orwell's view, "since the vast majority of people would far rather have State regimentation than slumps and unemployment" (*Complete Works* 16: 149). The only hope, however faint, was that "a planned economy can be somehow combined with the freedom of the intellect, which can only happen if the concept of right and wrong is restored to politics" (16: 150). Hayek's argument that socialism was not only likely to lead to a loss of freedom but was inherently incapable of delivering economic prosperity apparently made no impression on Orwell. Like so many others, Orwell assumed that central planning, whatever political dangers it might involve, was necessarily more efficient and more capable of delivering the economic goods than what he called "free capitalism" (16: 149).

George Orwell's willingness to recognize the dangers of a collectivized economy even while remaining a committed socialist provides another illustration of his refusal to allow his thoughts to be censored by any political considerations, even those he himself valued most highly. In the twenty-first century, meanwhile, it is by no means as evident as it was to John Strachey or George Orwell that a planned economy is inherently superior to capitalism. If the laissez-faire capitalism of nineteenth-century England is a thing of the past, so too is the Soviet Union. Capitalism has spread to India, South Korea, Singapore, and Taiwan, to the formerly planned economies of Eastern Europe, and even into the People's Republic of China. The heritage of the old Soviet Union survives intact only in North Korea and Cuba. New totalitarianisms have arisen, but their claims to superiority have little to do with economics or secular history.

In the 1930s, however, the futures of democracy and liberal capitalism seemed extremely doubtful. Benito Mussolini, a former socialist, had taken power in Italy in 1922 as the leader of the new Fascist

Party. Originally prime minister, Mussolini soon became the dictator of a state that, according to Fascist philosophy, had no limits on its power. In contrast to the liberal notion that individual rights set limits on the authority of the state, Mussolini proclaimed, "Everything within the State, nothing outside the State, nothing against the State" (qtd. in Krieger 275). Adolf Hitler took power in Germany in 1933 as the leader of the National Socialist German Worker's (Nazi) Party, creating a dictatorship even more ruthless and powerful than that of Mussolini. Today, Mussolini and Hitler are almost universally condemned, but it is important to remember that in the 1920s and 1930s they were charismatic figures who seemed to many to represent the wave of the future. The 1917 Russian Revolution first ended the rule of the tsars and then brought Lenin and the Communist Party to power. First Lenin and then Joseph Stalin ruled with the same kind of absolute authority and the same disregard for human rights and human life exhibit by the Fascist and Nazi dictators. Ignoring the similarities between their rule and that of Stalin, Fascists and Nazis condemned Communism, arguing that only Fascism or Nazism could save Europe from Communist revolution. Meanwhile, Communists presented themselves as the fiercest opponents of both Fascism and Nazism.

To his great credit, George Orwell was among those on the Left who from the beginning applied the same moral and political criteria in judging the Soviet Union as in condemning Fascism and Nazism. All three regimes were examples of the totalitarianism that Orwell dedicated his life to opposing. If today the parallels between the dictatorships of Stalin and Hitler seem straightforward, in the 1930s they were not obvious at all to many on the Left, who at the time were only too eager to lump together all opponents of Communism. John Strachey, for one, warned against "what we have called the advocates of action—the Mussolinis, the Churchills and the Hitlers" (376), but could not help admiring what he called the "dazzling audacity" of Lenin and the "colossal tenacity" of Stalin (354).

From 1935 until the nonaggression treaty between Germany and the Soviet Union was signed in August 1939, Communist parties throughout the world espoused the strategy of the "popular front," theoretically comprised of all true opponents of Fascism and Nazism, including liberal and other nonrevolutionary parties. The popular front strategy was first officially proclaimed in August 1935 by Georgi Dimitroff, general secretary of the Communist International, the organization that in theory represented Communist parties from all countries. In Dimitroff's speech announcing the popular front policy, he insisted that Communist parties throughout the world would "defend and shall continue to defend every inch of bourgeois-democratic liberties, which are being attacked by fascism and bourgeois reaction, because the interests of the class struggle of the proletariat so dictate" (34). Dimitroff specified that in England, a popular front would mean cooperation between the Communists and the Labor Party, explaining that "the British comrades are prepared at the forthcoming parliamentary elections to cooperate with branches of the Labor Party" (44).

In Spain, the policy of the popular front meant that the Communist International would aid and if possible control the Spanish Republic in its civil war with the forces of General Francisco Franco. For Dimitroff and for Communist parties generally, the Spanish Civil War, won by Franco's Nationalist forces in April 1939, was not a struggle between factions in Spain but between world Fascism on the one hand and the workers, or "the people," on the other. In a 1937 speech, Dimitroff asserted:

Actually, this bloody plot against the Spanish people was hatched and organized in Berlin and Rome. The fascist war-mongers made use of the counter-revolutionary generals so as to lay their hands on Spain, on its wealth, on its raw materials for the war industry, and so as to establish themselves in the Mediterranean Sea for the new imperialist war they are preparing. (254)

George Orwell volunteered to fight for the Spanish Republic because he too believed that the Spanish Civil War was essentially a war against Fascism. He writes in *Homage to Catalonia* that he originally accepted an interpretation of the war as "the defence of civilization against a maniacal outbreak by an army of Colonel Blimps in the pay of Hitler" (47). He could have added that this was also the Communist version as promulgated by the head of the Communist International. When Orwell arrived in Spain, he was more than ready to accept the leadership of the Communists. As he explains, "The Communists had gained power and a vast increase of membership partly by appealing to the middle classes against the revolutionaries, but partly also because they were the only people who looked capable of winning the war. . . . After all, the one thing that mattered was to win the war" (63). Orwell broke with the Communists only after a pitched and bloody battle between Communists and other leftist factions in Barcelona in May 1937 left him disillusioned about Communist goals.

To the general secretary of the Communist International, the events in Barcelona were a "putsch" that provided "a particularly clear demonstration" of how independent leftist groups could "stab the People's Front in the back" (Dimitroff 265). To Orwell, in contrast, the Barcelona fighting was a particularly clear demonstration that the Communists were more concerned about increasing their own power than in aiding the working class. Before the Barcelona conflict, Orwell had been ready to accept the leadership of the Communists. Afterwards, he "could not join any Communist-controlled unit. Sooner or later it might mean being used against the Spanish working class" (*Homage to Catalonia* 145).

Orwell was certainly right when he argued in *Homage to Catalonia* that, contrary to the party line expressed by Georgi Dimitroff, Franco's rebellion was specifically Spanish in important respects and could not be simply equated with the spread of Mussolini's Fascism or Hitler's Nazism. As Orwell put it, "[Franco's] rising was a military mutiny backed up by the aristocracy and the Church, and in the main, especially at the beginning, it was an attempt not so much to impose Fascism as to restore feudalism" (*Homage to Catalonia* 48). Spain's refusal to become an ally of Germany and Italy in World War II, despite intense pressure from Hitler, made it clear that, whatever crimes might be ascribed to him, Franco was no puppet of either Hitler or Mussolini. Whether Orwell was also right in believing that Franco might have been defeated if a true working-class revolution had occurred throughout Spain seems doubtful, but of course such questions are unanswerable. Orwell's similar belief that England could not win the war against Nazi Germany without undergoing a revolution turned out to be false, as he himself handsomely admitted.

The shape of the world after World War II was negotiated at a series of conferences attended by Joseph Stalin, Winston Churchill, and Franklin Roosevelt (replaced by Harry Truman at the final conference in 1945). As World War II ended, the Soviet Union moved to consolidate its power in Eastern Europe. Churchill would later call attention to what he called the "iron curtain" that the Soviet Union, Great Britain's former ally, had imposed across Europe. In March 1947, President Truman sent assistance to anti-Communist forces in the Greek Civil War, and in June 1947, the U.S.-led Marshall Plan for the reconstruction of Europe was announced. American aid through the Marshall Plan was rejected by all the countries under Soviet control, but contributed greatly to the rebuilding of Western Europe. For the foreseeable future, it appeared that the two dominant powers in the world would be the Soviet Union and the United States.

In February 1945, Orwell speculated that the American political theorist James Burnham had been right in predicting the dominance of world politics by a small number of superpowers, and added his own suspicion that relations among them would closely resemble what in a few years would be known as the Cold War:

> Already, quite visibly and more or less with the acquiescence of all of us, the world is splitting up into the two or three huge super-states forecast

in James Burnham's *Managerial Revolution*. . . . It is likely that these vast states will be permanently at war with one another, though it will not necessarily be a very intensive or bloody kind of war. (*Complete Works* 17: 39)

Orwell's *Nineteen Eighty-Four* is of course a warning and not a prophesy. Just as it should not be taken as a prediction, it should not be taken as a straightforward indication of Orwell's attitudes about the politics of his own time. In *Nineteen Eighty-Four* the eternally warring empires of Oceania, Eurasia, and Eastasia are morally equivalent. They are equally totalitarian, equally miserable societies. The novel gives the reader no reason to doubt that "the conditions of life in all three superstates are very much the same," their official ideologies "are barely distinguishable," and "the social systems which they support are not distinguishable at all" (162). Though Orwell worried about the possibility that current trends such as the centralizing of economic and political power, the weakening of traditional morality, and the growth of technology might, if not curbed, bring about a world dominated by superstates like those in *Nineteen Eighty-Four*, he did not believe that such trends were inevitable, nor was he unable to make moral and political distinctions among the dominant powers of his own time, specifically between the United States and Soviet Russia.

In 1947, Orwell speculated that "it is even possible that if the world falls apart into three unconquerable super-states, the liberal tradition will be strong enough within the Anglo-American section of the world to make life tolerable and even offer some hope of progress" (*Complete Works* 19: 167). Orwell went beyond speculation in a March 1947 letter to Victor Gollancz, the onetime publisher of the Left Book Club, to declare where he himself stood: "I don't, God knows, want a war to break out, but if one were compelled to choose between Russia and America—and I suppose that is the choice one might have to make—I would always choose America" (16: 90). Orwell was aware that such sentiments were not popular on the Left. He noted that same year, in an unpublished essay with the ironic title "In Defense of Comrade Zilliacus," that

> at any given moment there is always an orthodoxy, a parrot-cry which must be repeated, and in the more active section of the Left the orthodoxy of the moment is anti-Americanism. . . . To speak favorably of America, to recall that the Americans helped us in 1940 when the Russians were supplying the Germans with oil and seeing on their Communist Parties to sabotage the war effort, is to be branded as a "reactionary." (*Complete Works* 19: 181–82)

If forced to choose between Soviet Russia and the United States, he was unwilling to give what he called "the usual quibbling answer, 'I refuse to choose.'" Despite what might be fashionable or taboo in leftist circles, it was unthinkable that England would support Russia against the United States: "And in spite of all the fashionable chatter of the moment, everyone knows in his heart that we should choose America. The great mass of people in this country would, I believe, make this choice almost instinctively" (19: 182). In this unpublished essay, Orwell recorded his personal belief that "the only big political questions in the world today are: for Russia—against Russia, for America—against America, for democracy—against democracy" (19: 179–80).

Orwell, for a number of good reasons, was not optimistic that the moral and cultural traditions that together made "common decency" possible would survive in the postwar world. Planning would inevitably replace the market, he believed, but he was not at all confident that the liberal freedoms capitalism had allowed even while generating economic inequality would survive. The events of his lifetime had not given many reasons to be hopeful. In a 1944 essay on the Hungarian British author Arthur Koestler, Orwell observed, "Since about 1930 the world has given no reason for optimism whatever. Nothing is in sight except a welter of lies, hatred, cruelty and ignorance" (*Complete Works* 16: 399). Koestler draws the conclusion, according to Orwell, that all one can do is "keep out of politics, make a sort of oasis within which you and your friends can remain sane, and hope that somehow things will be better in a hundred years." Orwell shares Koestler's bleak estimate of the present and near future, but he himself refuses to leave politics for a private "oasis." It may indeed be the case that "the choice before Man is always a choice of evils," and it may be true that "all revolutions are failures," but, Orwell declares, "they are not all the same failure." No political-economic structure, including socialism, will ever "make the world perfect," but it is at least possible, he insists, to "make it better" (16: 400).

Though *Nineteen Eighty-Four* has contributed to the impression that George Orwell was a pessimist who saw only disaster in the future, a study of Orwell's writings in their historical context demonstrates that his intellectual honesty was matched by a moral courage that allowed him to face the most dispiriting circumstances without evasion and without surrender. In his 1940 essay "Inside the Whale," Orwell praised T. S. Eliot for publishing poems like *The Love Song of J. Alfred Prufrock* during World War I, saying that "by simply standing aloof and keeping touch with pre-war emotions, Eliot was carrying on the human heritage" (*Complete Works* 12: 110). Orwell's generous praise for the great conservative poet applies, surely, to his own writings—letters, journalism, essays, and novels—but it must be added that George Orwell never stood aloof. He carried on and enriched "the human heritage" even while he argued about what was to be done in the face of worldwide depression, the rise of totalitarianism, and world war.

Works Cited

Dimitroff, Georgi. *The United Front: The Struggle Against Fascism and War*. New York: International, 1938.

Ferguson, Niall. *Empire: The Rise and Demise of the British World Order and the Lessons for Global Power*. New York: Basic, 2003.

Krieger, Joel, ed. *The Oxford Companion to Politics of the World*. 2nd ed. New York: Oxford UP, 2001.

Lenin, V. I. *Imperialism: The Highest State of Capitalism.* 1916. New York: International, 1939.

Orwell, George. *The Complete Works of George Orwell.* Ed. Peter Davison. 20 vols. London: Secker, 1998.

_____. *Homage to Catalonia.* 1938. New York: Harcourt, 1952.

_____. *Nineteen Eighty-Four.* 1949. New York: New American Library, 1983.

Strachey, John. *The Coming Struggle for Power.* New York: Covici Friede, 1933.

Comparison and Contrast: Orwell, Hemingway, and the Spanish Civil War_____

William E. Cain

> The Spanish war and other events in 1936–37 turned the scale and thereafter I knew where I stood.
>
> (George Orwell, "Why I Write")

> I think I can truly say for all those I knew as well as one man can know another, that the period of fighting when we thought that the Republic could win the Spanish civil war was the happiest period of our lives.
>
> (Ernest Hemingway, preface to Gustav Regler's *The Great Crusade*)

The best literary treatments of the Spanish Civil War are George Orwell's *Homage to Catalonia* (1938) and Ernest Hemingway's *For Whom the Bell Tolls* (1940). Orwell's nonfiction book sold poorly at first and had little immediate impact, whereas Hemingway's novel instantly became a best-seller, praised by reviewers and critics as his most ambitious and powerful work to date.

By the mid- to late 1950s, following the success of *Animal Farm* (1945) and *Nineteen Eighty-Four* (1949), and spurred by a reprint edition for which the eminent critic Lionel Trilling wrote the introduction, *Homage to Catalonia* became more widely read and discussed: It was, and it remains, an essential text for all who are interested in the Spanish Civil War, fascism, socialism, Communism, and World War II and the Cold War. Meanwhile, during this period, *For Whom the Bell Tolls* lost some of its luster: Critics were more inclined by the 1950s to say that the best of Hemingway was located in his focused, lean short stories and "lost generation" modernist novels of the 1920s, *The Sun Also Rises* (1926) and *A Farewell to Arms* (1929). Even so, with its epic scale and scope, *For Whom the Bell Tolls* retained its status as a major work in Hemingway's career, testifying both to his love of Spain and to his commitment to the campaign against Franco, Mussolini, and Hitler.

For many readers today, both *Homage to Catalonia* and *For Whom the Bell Tolls* are somewhat difficult to get through. Few of us have mastery of the social, political, and military causes, events, and consequences of the Spanish Civil War. Spanish history in the 1930s is a challenge to understand and describe clearly, as teachers have discovered when they attempt to explain to students who the republicans were, who the nationalists were, which nations supported which side and which did not, and so on. Orwell himself noted at the time that the Spanish Civil War was hard even for an insider, someone who had fought there, to comprehend.

To appreciate and learn from these books by Orwell and Hemingway, we do need to know at least the bare bones of the historical narrative. The Spanish Civil War began in July 1936 with a military rebellion led by General Francisco Franco against the left-leaning Republican Popular Front government. The Republican forces, which included Communists, socialists, and other liberal and leftist groups, as well as thousands of volunteers from abroad, and which received support from the Soviet Union, fought bravely against Franco's army and the Italian and German troops and advisers allied with it. Fearing war with Hitler, the western democracies—notably France, Great Britain, and the United States—declared a policy of nonintervention. Early in 1939, Franco took control of Barcelona and Madrid and declared victory, and he established a dictatorship that lasted until his death in 1975.

In a lecture or seminar, a teacher would need to say much more and do his or her best to characterize, and distinguish among, the groups, organizations, and factions on each of the two main sides.[1] This historical context is not essential to our reading experience, but these books might come all the more alive for us if we know what we should be seeking in (and from) them.

One is tempted even to propose that *Homage to Catalonia* and *For Whom the Bell Tolls* are not books about the Spanish Civil War. Of course, in a sense they are: the war is the context, the background, the setting; the political realities and meanings of the war are present in both books. But the real story told in each one is not a story about this war. In each case it is instead a story, with the war as the immediate and urgent occasion, of choice, commitment, and sacrifice.

What makes *Homage to Catalonia* and *For Whom the Bells Tolls* great books is the existential clarity of the questions they raise for us as readers: What do we know? How should we act, given the limits of what we know? And what, for us, is the meaning of an action that we believed was right when we performed it, but which we later see was wrong? What happens to us when we see that the consequences of our choices and actions were the opposite of those we had intended and hoped for? Orwell and Hemingway engage in moral and ethical exploration, and the conclusions they come to are complicated and painful.

For us to feel the moral force of these books, we need to remind ourselves that both Orwell and Hemingway were looking backward: They were writing retrospectively. This is true of *Homage to Catalonia*, in which Orwell tells of his experiences in Spain from the vantage point of some months' distance after his return to England. It is even truer of *For Whom the Bell Tolls*, which Hemingway completed after the triumph of Franco and the fascists. There is an elegiac tone in the titles and in both books. These are affirmative, brave books—books about affirmation and bravery—that, at the same time, evoke disappointment, defeat, and loss: they tell of experiences that can be recalled but not recaptured, that are beyond returning to.

In his book of reportage and analysis, Orwell describes his experiences in the city and countryside and on the frontlines, as they seemed to him at the time and as he reflected on them later. In his novel, Hemingway describes a military action led by a young American, Robert Jordan, who is fighting on the Republican side. Jordan has come to know horrors of war that taint the purity of the cause he believes in: good and evil are separate and the choice for him is clear—but then again, not really. This is a necessary (and grim) truth that Hemingway conveys to us powerfully; he knows that his readers will be aware of what his protagonist was not—that the Republicans would be defeated.

Jordan dies, and Orwell himself was wounded in the throat, his life spared by a fraction of an inch. In the context of defeat, what is the meaning of Jordan's death, and of Orwell's near death?

Orwell begins *Homage to Catalonia* by detailing his brief encounter with a young Italian militiaman with whom he immediately forms an "utter intimacy" (2). He then states: "That was in late December, 1936, less than seven months ago as I write, and yet it is a period that has already receded into enormous distance" (2). Seven months is not a very long time, but Orwell's point is that in this instance it is; throughout the book, even as he describes events, he emphasizes the difference between how he understood them at the time and how he came to understand them afterward.

At the outset, he tells of the inspiring revolutionary atmosphere he witnessed in Barcelona: "All this was queer and moving. There was much in it that I did not understand, in some ways I did not even like it, but I recognized it immediately as a state of affairs worth fighting for" (3). The next sentences, however, are crucial for Orwell's representation of himself as first-person narrator and for our responses to his story and its meanings for him and us: "Also I believed that things were as they appeared, that this was really a workers' State and that the entire bourgeoisie had either fled, been killed, or voluntarily come over to the workers' side; I did not realize that great numbers of well-to-do bourgeois were simply lying low and disguising themselves as proletarians for the time being" (3).

Some have criticized Orwell for presuming to make generalizations about the Spanish Civil War, the internal conflicts on the Republican side, and so forth, on the basis of only a few months' experience. How much could he really have known? How trustworthy are his impressions of military and political leaders, political alliances and struggles, the workers, the operations of the war? But these are questions that Orwell, from the beginning, raises himself. Repeatedly he describes what he saw and heard and experienced and calls attention to his own misunderstandings and misperceptions.

Barcelona was inspiring and thrilling, and yet, Orwell indicates to us, he was unaware of the true situation—he was responding to the surfaces of things, to appearances. His account takes an ominous turn when he reports on something else that was evident to him even then: "Together with all this there was something of the evil atmosphere of war." (4) The roads and buildings were in bad shape, it was dark on the streets at night, and little food was available in the shops. But Orwell then surprises us:

Yet so far as one could judge the people were contented and hopeful. There was no unemployment, and the price of living was still extremely low; you saw very few conspicuously destitute people, and no beggars except the gipsies. Above all, there was a belief in the revolution and the future, a feeling of having suddenly emerged into an era of equality and freedom. (4)

First, Orwell describes Barcelona in positive terms, but then he qualifies the description—he did not know then what he knows now, and, furthermore, even at the time he was there, he could feel evil, something disturbing and sinister, in the atmosphere. Nevertheless, he continues, all was hopeful.

The perspective that Orwell takes, and invites us to share, keeps changing. We cannot settle into any one view, and Orwell's language repeatedly makes us examine and reassess what we thought we knew and understood.

The main narrative line of *Homage to Catalonia* is consistently vibrant and absorbing. Orwell tells of his arrival in Barcelona; his service in the militia; his time (nearly four months) on the Aragon front, including the dangerous, strange, dirty, and tedious routines of trench warfare; his alignment with the Workers' Party of Marxist Unification (Partido Obrero de Unificación Marxista, or POUM) and its suppression by the Communists; his involvement in the street fighting between rival Republican forces that broke out in Barcelona in early May 1937;

his serious war wound (he was shot in the throat on May 20, 1937); his recovery in the hospital; and his escape to France with his wife Eileen when it became evident to him that his connection to the POUM put him at risk of trial and execution. Orwell almost became a victim of political terror—not at the hands of Franco and the fascists, but those of the Communists and their Soviet allies.

Equally compelling in *Homage to Catalonia*, however, is the central drama of knowledge and perception that Orwell conveys. He moves back and forth from past to present—his interpretations then and now—and he structures his sentences and paragraphs to make certain that the reader always is aware of this interplay and, frequently, conflict. Orwell has a position in this book, which is sympathetic to the POUM and hostile to the Communists, but *Homage to Catalonia* is as much or more a profound study of what a political position *is*—what it means to take a political position and how one understands it at the time and later.

Often we say that Orwell is a rare, brave, bold figure who tells the plain truth, who says honestly what he sees, and who names and states the things that must be said and that others are too frightened or hesitant to utter. This is accurate, but it is incomplete. Orwell believes that we can and must say what we see, what is there plainly and clearly before our eyes; yet he also emphasizes that often it is extremely hard to see what *is* before our eyes. As he learned in Barcelona, appearances can deceive us—what is there is apparent, and yet not apparent.

We know what we know, Orwell suggests, only imperfectly. We are obliged to tell hard truths: we know what these are and cannot take refuge in uncertainty when the moral demand is for truth. We must do this, believing we are in the right, having the courage of our convictions—and yet maintaining in ourselves the understanding that we could later be proven wrong. The future may lead us to revise our sense of who we were and what we did when we did what we believed was right at the time.

For Orwell, memory means discipline. To remember well is to bring alive an experience in its complexity. To remember badly is to see the past from a single point of view. Orwell believes that his task as a writer is to describe how he felt at the time—and also what he was feeling but not quite registering or understanding. The challenge for Orwell is also to articulate how he feels in retrospect—or, rather, how he *is feeling*, for he knows his feelings, thoughts, and perspectives will alter and adjust in the future. The discipline for Orwell is in stating the truth, and, simultaneously, in knowing that truth is always provisional and never complete, its story always to be continued.

When Orwell and his comrades prepared to leave by train for the Aragon front, they marched to the station in the midst of a passionate, stirring scene of revolutionary fervor. Orwell builds to a climax, and then immediately deflates it: "A borrowed band played some revolutionary tune or other. Once again the conquering-hero stuff—shouting and enthusiasm, red flags and black flags everywhere, friendly crowds thronging the pavement to have a look at us, women waving from the windows. How natural it all seemed then; how remote and impossible now!" (12).

In the midst of the experience, Orwell felt one way. At the time he was writing about it, the experience was not only distant but also incredible, as if it did not happen and could not have happened. There is a lengthy, lively description—we share in the excitement of it all, followed by the uplift of "how natural" it was—except that "seemed then" intervene, and "remote and impossible" reinforce the sense of disillusionment.

When we read these words, we are prompted to return to the sentences of description that we may have taken at face value, and see them somewhat differently. There is the deliberate imprecision of "some revolutionary tune or other"; the detached, uncomfortable feeling in the phrase "conquering-hero stuff"; and the artifice in the alliteration of, "women waving from the windows." When we look again at the description, rereading it, we perceive in it what was there all along—what we probably did not see, its meanings beneath the surface.

This drama of perception operates in the movement of Orwell's chapters, in the rhythm of his paragraphs, and in pointed single sentences such as these:

It was an extraordinary life that we were living—an extraordinary way to be at war, if you could call it war. (32)

It is curious that when you are watching artillery-fire from a safe distance you always want the gunner to hit his mark, even though the mark contains your dinner and some of your comrades. (60)

I reflected that as he [the sniper who shot Orwell] was a Fascist I would have killed him if I could, but that if he had been taken prisoner and brought before me at this moment I would merely have congratulated him on his good shooting. (139)

The most forceful examples in *Homage to Catalonia* of this dynamic come in its final stages, where Orwell pays tribute to the theory and practice of socialism as he had experienced it in Spain. The first example is in a long paragraph in which Orwell begins:

I had dropped more or less by chance into the only community of any size in Western Europe where political consciousness and disbelief in capitalism were more normal than their opposites. Up here in Aragon one was among tens of thousands of people, mainly though not entirely of working-class origin, all living at the same level and mingling on terms of equality. (83)

Four more sentences follow in this vein, and then: "Of course such a state of affairs could not last. It was simply a temporary and local phase in an enormous game that is being played over the whole surface of the earth" (83). The paragraph could have ended there, but Orwell counters the current of disappointment:

> However much one cursed at the time, one realized afterwards that one had been in contact with something strange and valuable. One had been in a community where hope was more normal than apathy or cynicism, where the word "comrade" stood for comradeship and not, as in most countries, for humbug. One had breathed the air of equality. (83)

The paragraph continues, and as a whole typifies Orwell's rhetorical approach—the movements and counter-movements, statements and resistances to them, reminders of the relationship (and often the difference) between past and present, then and now.

Orwell fills *Homage to Catalonia* with qualification, paradox, and ambiguity. But in the end, this is not an ambiguous book: it is, ultimately, an "homage," a declaration of public respect, an honoring of the best people who fought in the war and the values that they embraced and for which so many of them died. Orwell sums it all up in these terms:

> This war, in which I played so ineffectual a part, has left me with memories that are mostly evil, and yet I do not wish that I had missed it. When you have had a glimpse of such a disaster as this—and however it ends, the Spanish War will turn out to have been an appalling disaster, quite apart from the slaughter and physical suffering—the result is not necessarily disillusionment and cynicism. Curiously enough, the whole experience has left me with not less but more belief in the decency of human beings. (185–86)

Orwell gives evidence for this belief in his accounts of fellowship and community among the troops. But the point is that there is more evidence—concrete, tangible evidence—arguing against his belief in human decency. Disaster, appalling disaster, slaughter, and physical suffering: these are the brutal facts. Orwell accepts them, and he rejects them: he makes a choice, impelled to a choice that he might not have made. "The result is not necessarily disillusionment and cynicism"— but it could have been the result, and for many it was.

Orwell believes that he made the right choice. Or, rather, the movements of his sentences suggest that he *thinks* he made the right choice: *Believe* and *think* are not the same. Orwell knows and he does not know: Knowing is what we think and believe and hope. That is what we know, or try to know. We do not know what is.

In "Why I Write," published in 1946, Orwell called attention to the significance of the Spanish Civil War in his literary career and political development: "The Spanish war and other events in 1936–37 turned the scale and thereafter I knew where I stood. Every line of serious work that I have written since 1936 has been written, directly or indirectly, *against* totalitarianism and *for* democratic Socialism, as I understand it" (*Essays* 1085).

Orwell could have ended the sentence after the word "Socialism," but it is striking, and illuminating about his point of view, that he does not. The phrase "as I understand it" makes clear that while the cause matters, it matters always in relation to the integrity of each person who is committed to it. Ultimately, Orwell's allegiance is to his conscience, and not to the cause, to his perceptions as honestly as he can come to know them, knowing they are always evolving.

Thus the choice is Orwell's and our own: From what we know and do not know, where will we take our stand? What do we believe? We do not know everything; we might know less than we wish we did; we might know more than we want to. Human decency: There it is in *Homage to Catalonia*, fleshed out and enriched through the account of his experience that Orwell has written. What, then, is our choice? Will we stand and fight for human decency, or not? This is a great moment in the Orwell canon, of high moral pressure, of self-definition.

For Whom the Bell Tolls also contains insight and information about the Spanish Civil War, yet the most striking thing about it is its emphasis on duty, commitment, and, above all, sacrifice and death for a cause—which connects *For Whom the Bell Tolls* to *Homage to Catalonia*. In his novel, Hemingway too is speaking about integrity, discipline, and choice—how human beings act, and must act, on the basis of the pieces and bits that they know. Robert Jordan does what he thinks is right, though he is not sure that it will—that he will—make any difference. From Hemingway's perspective years later, with Franco in power, it seems that what Jordan did made no difference. He did what he had to do, everything and nothing.

In a sense, Hemingway's novel is over at its beginning, when Robert Jordan, the American guerilla fighter, flashes back to his meeting with the Republican General Golz. Pointing to the map, Golz tells Jordan that his mission is to blow up a bridge, an action that must be achieved with perfect timing, in coordination with a planned Republican attack. Jordan says he understands, but then, as Golz continues, he is silent: "Robert Jordan had said nothing" (5). If we know how Hemingway writes, with so much implied and unstated, we will realize that the reason Jordan says nothing is because he knows that this mission, whether it succeeds or fails, will end in his death. He knows from this moment on that the end of the story of this mission will be that he will die.

Knowing as we do how the war ended, we could claim that the right response would have been for Jordan to refuse the mission. The odds against its success are bad, and he knows what it means for him. But his duty is to obey orders; his loyalty is to the Republican cause. He makes a choice, or, rather, he does not make a choice: there is no wavering, no hesitation, and no challenge to Golz's authority. Jordan takes in the fact of his imminent death, and says only that this is not a mission he "likes":

> "I understand it," Robert Jordan had said. "I do not say I like it very much."
>
> "Neither do I like it very much. If you do not want to undertake it, say so now. If you think you cannot do it, say so now."
>
> "I will do it," Robert Jordan had said. "I will do it all right." (6)

Confirmation of Jordan's fate comes soon after, when, as we are returned to the scene of the guerilla action, he speaks with the peasant woman Pilar:

> "Let me see thy hand," the woman said. Robert Jordan put his hand out and the woman opened it, held it in her own big hand, rubbed her thumb over it and looked at it, carefully, then dropped it. She stood up. He got up too and she looked at him without smiling.
> "What did you see in it?" Robert Jordan asked her. "I don't believe in it. You won't scare me."
> "Nothing," she told him. "I saw nothing in it."
> "Yes you did. I am only curious. I do not believe in such things." (33)

Pilar does not need to make explicit to Jordan what she sees. He knows and the reader knows, and the word "nothing" links this passage to the earlier exchange with Golz. She sees what Jordan already has seen for himself when he looked at the map and was told what his mission was. Pilar sees that he will die, and he knows that is what she sees, but it does not disturb him—though later he recalls several times her reading his fate in his hand. Her premonition does not disclose to him something new, something he had not imagined. He knows this mission means his death.

Hemingway may intend for us to admire Jordan's bravery, but the questions he is posing are more demanding than that. Very soon Jordan meets the young woman Maria, and he falls in love with her. Critics have objected to a lushness and extravagance in Hemingway's accounts of their love and lovemaking, and we might find some fault with the descriptions in chapter 13 and elsewhere, when Jordan feels "the earth move out and away from under them" (159). But Jordan and Maria's love matters in relation to his mission, and to his knowledge of his impending death. He knows that his relationship with her will last only days: it has to be intense, even extreme, because very soon he is going to die.

Robert Jordan's story is not tragic because he falls in love with Maria and then dies. It is tragic because he falls in love with her knowing beforehand that he will die, and that he will lose what he so briefly had. His death is not a fate that interrupts his experience of love; his knowledge that death is very soon to strike him precedes his falling in love. The fact of his death, its imminence, is the condition of the love affair with Maria: it determines and propels it.

Hemingway made four trips to Spain, the first of which began in March 1937 and concluded in May, which is the month when Jordan's mission takes place. Hemingway started work on *For Whom the Bell Tolls* in February 1939, and he completed the draft in July 1940. After further revision, it was published in late October. Hemingway thus was working on the novel when it became obvious that the Spanish Republic was doomed. As he wrote and revised it and corrected the page proofs, Franco's forces overcame the Republican opposition and the fascists seized control. As soon as they gained power in late March and April of 1939, they proceeded to imprison, torture, and execute tens of thousands of the Republic's supporters. This terrorism and purge had been going on for more than a year, even as Hitler was marching across Europe, conquering France in June 1940, when *For Whom the Bell Tolls* made its appearance in bookstores.

In view of the Republic's defeat, of these horrors, we might conclude that Jordan should have chosen love over duty. He gives his life for a cause, and he loses his love, and for what? His sacrifice was noble. He dies, but he was not obliged to: he could have cheated death, once he and Maria had fallen in love, by withdrawing from this mission. For was it not pointless, a waste? What good had Jordan accomplished? He loses his life; he loses his love.

We as readers of this story know more than Jordan does as he lives it out—which gives complexity and depth to our experience of Hemingway's book. Soon after his first meeting with Maria—it is love at first sight for him—Jordan reflects on the mission, and on his friend Anselmo: "He resented Golz's orders, and the necessity for them. He resented them for what they could do to him and for what they could do to this old man. They were bad orders all right for those who would have to carry them out" (43).

Jordan performs his mission; he stays committed to it even when he discovers that the fascist enemy already knows about the planned Republican attack. He dies; Anselmo dies. If Jordan had refused the mission at the outset, or if later he had called it off, he would have saved his life, his love, and the lives of his friends. What he did made no difference, seen from the point in time when Hemingway wrote the novel and when, from late 1940 to today, readers have experienced it.

One of the gripping features of *For Whom the Bell Tolls* is Jordan's determination to resist, and not surrender to, the reality of his situation. These are "bad orders":

And that is not the way to think, he told himself, and there is not you, and there are no people that things must not happen to. Neither you nor this old man is anything. You are instruments to do your duty. These are necessary orders that are no fault of yours and there is a bridge and that bridge can be the point on which the future of the human race can turn. As it can turn on everything that happens in this war. You have only one thing to do and you must do it. (43)

Jordan begins to think about Maria and tries to stop: "think about something else," he says to himself. What he knows he must think about is what he does not want to think about—that he must do his duty, with all of the deadly consequences that follow from it.

As readers, we want to believe in Jordan's heroism—that he has done the right thing. But Hemingway both encourages this response in us and undermines it. Again, the question is, "Was it worth it?" By doing his duty, is Jordan performing a right and necessary action? Of course he is. Perhaps, though, he is not. His action is futile, absurd. But he had to do it. It was good that he did, and we would—would we not?—have acted as he did if we were in his place. Is this what we would have done? No, Hemingway is asking more pointedly, what would we really have done? No evasion—not what we like to think we would have done, but what we would have done.

Here we see the emptiness and the grandeur of Jordan's dedication to his duty and the meaning of his death. He acknowledges that he knew what he was doing when he made the choice to fight for the Republican cause, and he knew also the consequences for himself and others of accepting this mission: "So now he was compelled to use these people whom he liked as you should use troops toward whom you have no feeling at all if you were to be successful" (162). Jordan has his orders:

> The orders do not come from you. They come from Golz. And who is Golz? A good general. The best you've ever served under. But should a man carry out impossible orders knowing what they lead to? Even though they come from Golz, who is the party as well as the army? Yes. He should carry them out because it is only in the performing of them that they can prove to be impossible. (162)

In the early stages of his work on *For Whom the Bell Tolls*, Hemingway made Jordan a member of the Communist Party. It is important that in the final version, Jordan is not a Party member and, furthermore, that he sees the manipulative and ruthless tactics that the Party uses, supported by Soviet advisers and officers. For most Party members, the interests of Stalin and the Soviet Union come first, not those of Spain. While Jordan sees this, he accepts the Communists' line on the war—that what is crucial is winning, and winning means obeying orders: "How do you know they are impossible until you have tried them? If everyone said orders were impossible to carry out when they were received where would you be? Where would we all be if you just said, 'Impossible,' when orders came?" (162).

We could reply that in this instance, if Jordan had refused to obey orders, he and Anselmo and the others who died in the mission would be alive. It seems probable that Hemingway, writing the novel when he did, wants us to feel the weakness in Jordan's argument with himself. What Jordan says to himself is convincing only if we take for granted at the outset that there is no alternative—that orders must be obeyed.

There is a similar thinness in Jordan's account of the new society he is fighting for. In fact, he admits that he does now know what such a society will look like or amount to: "And what about a planned society and the rest of it? That was for the others to do. He had something else to do after this war. He fought now in this war because it had started in a country that he loved and he believed in the Republic and that if it were destroyed life would be unbearable for all those people who believed in it" (163). The Republic *was* destroyed and life *did* become unbearable for millions of people in Spain under Franco's dictatorial rule. Jordan, then, made a choice, but again, the question is whether his action—his death—made any difference.

What would have made a difference to Jordan, personally, would have been to live a long life with Maria—something he dreams about even as he concedes it will never happen. This is one of the thoughts that, he says, come to his mind yet that he must push down. It is part of the discipline not to take such thoughts and daydreams seriously. Taking them seriously would mean acting on them, which Jordan rejects. Jordan bases his decision-making and action on this principle: "He was under Communist discipline for the duration of the war. Here in Spain the Communists offered the best discipline and the soundest and sanest for the prosecution of the war. He accepted their discipline for the duration of the war because, in the conduct of the war, they were the only party whose program and whose discipline he could respect" (163).

In his speeches and writings while the war was being waged, Hemingway advocated this position. It was not relevant whether the Communists' vision of society was correct or whether in Spain the Soviet Union was exerting too much influence. The essential point, for Hemingway and for his character Robert Jordan, is that the Communists believed, correctly, that the war must be won. This was not the time to argue and debate and fight about the future, for there would be no future if Franco was victorious. There are doubts: Jordan hears of and witnesses cruelty and murder on the side of the Republic, among both Communists and non-Communists. But the discipline is to adhere to the imperative of winning the war, and this, for Jordan, is the program to which the Communists subscribe.

Sometimes it is said in this context that Hemingway was naïve or worse—that in effect he aligned himself with Stalin, that he failed to perceive the damage the Communists inflicted on a good cause through their assaults on and purges of their enemies on the Left. But the significant point about *For Whom the Bell Tolls* is that Hemingway makes his readers ask whether Jordan is naïve. Hemingway is writing with the advantage of hindsight: he knows the outcome of the war; Jordan did not. So what is our response to Jordan's commitments and actions? We could contend that in personal, political, military, and social terms—in every way—he was wrong. It is this possibility, or even probability, that helps to give the novel its power—that makes it moving and painful.

Jordan, then, might have been wrong. We should go further and state directly that everything that he hoped would happen did not. He accomplished nothing; he gave his life, and gave away his love, for nothing. The sense of waste and futility, of the folly of human ambition and effort that Hemingway evokes is almost overwhelming.

Yet I think that Hemingway believes that Jordan was wrong but right—that he did the right thing and that he would have (and should have) done the same thing even if he knew with complete certainty what the outcome would be. At the fateful moments of our lives we do not know for certain what the right decision is, and what the right action is. Nevertheless, we must choose. Very possibly, history will show us that we were in error—the future might mock the present.

History on a grand scale, however, may not matter much. It might not matter at all. What matters is what Robert Jordan did, what George Orwell did. Jordan paid the ultimate price for being true to himself; he died a good death. Hemingway and we know more than Jordan did, and we know more than Orwell did as well. Others coming after us will know more than we do.

Orwell and Hemingway share a position, and one that is both simple and profound: each person must do the absolute best that he or she can. There are more complicated ways of describing what life requires. But this stark principle, which Orwell and Hemingway affirm, is the hardest thing in the world to put into practice. Nothing that we do will make much or any difference. Yet everything that we do matters: it matters to us. Knowing as best we can what to do and actually doing it, in the face of human and historical limits, reveals to us who we are.

Homage to Catalonia and *For Whom the Bell Tolls* thus are books about the Spanish Civil War that in their impact exceed the meanings and consequences of the war, however terrible and anguishing these were and remain. Orwell and Hemingway engage the historical events in which they participated: this is their subject. But they take us through this history into ourselves. These writers, in these permanently valuable books, make us face and appraise the investments in choices, causes, and other persons that we do or do not make.

Notes

1. The standard work in the field is Hugh Thomas, *The Spanish Civil War*, first published in 1961. See also the detailed studies by Beevor (2006), Payne (1969), and Preston (2007). For a concise account, see Graham (2005). The impact of the war on writers, journalists, reporters, and intellectuals is discussed in Benson (1967) and Preston (2009). The bibliography includes these sources and others consulted for this essay. A list of Spanish Civil War websites can be found at Spartacus Educational: http://www.spartacus.schoolnet.co.uk/REVspainW.htm

Works Cited

Baxell, Richard. *British Volunteers in the Spanish Civil War: The British Battalion in the International Brigades, 1936–1939.* New York: Routledge, 2004.

Beevor, Antony. *The Battle for Spain: The Spanish Civil War, 1936–1939.* 1983. New York: Penguin, 2006.

Benson, Frederick R. *Writers in Arms: The Literary Impact of the Spanish Civil War.* New York: New York UP, 1967.

Bolloten, Burnett. *The Grand Camouflage: The Communist Conspiracy in the Spanish Civil War.* New York: Praeger, 1961.

Borkenau, Franz. *The Spanish Cockpit: An Eye-Witness Account of the Political and Social Conflicts of the Spanish Civil War.* 1937. Ann Arbor: U of Michigan P, 1963.

Bowker, Gordon. *Inside George Orwell: A Biography.* New York: Palgrave, 2003.

Casanova, Julián. *The Spanish Republic and Civil War.* New York: Cambridge UP, 2010.

Crick, Bernard. *George Orwell: A Life.* New York: Penguin, 1982.

Daniel, Anthony. "Orwell's 'Catalonia' Revisited." *New Criterion* 25.6 (2007): 11–19.

Davison, Peter, ed. *Orwell in Spain.* New York: Penguin, 2001.

Graham, Helen. *The Spanish Civil War: A Very Short Introduction.* New York: Oxford UP, 2005.

Hemingway, Ernest. *For Whom the Bell Tolls.* New York: Scribner's, 1940.

Hitchens, Christopher. *Why Orwell Matters.* New York: Basic, 2002.

Hobsbawn, Eric. *The Age of Extremes: A History of the World, 1914–1991.* 1994. New York: Vintage, 1996.

Kazin, Alfred. "Not One of Us." *New York Review of Books* 14 June 1984: 13+.

Meyers, Jeffrey. "*For Whom the Bell Tolls* as Contemporary History." *The Spanish Civil War in Literature.* Ed. Janet Pérez and Wendell Aycock. Lubbock: Texas Tech UP, 1990. 85–107.

_____, ed. *George Orwell: The Critical Heritage.* New York: Routledge, 1997.

_____. *Orwell: Wintry Conscience of a Generation.* New York: Norton, 2000.

Miller, Donald L. "Fighting Spain: A Conversation with Steve Nelson." *Salmagundi* 76–77 (1987–1988): 113–32.

Monteath, Peter. *Writing the Good Fight: Political Commitment in the International Literature of the Spanish Civil War.* Westport: Greenwood, 1994.

Neugass, James. *War Is Beautiful: An American Ambulance Driver in the Spanish Civil War.* Ed. Peter N. Carroll and Peter Glazer. New York: New Press, 2008.

Orwell, George. *Essays.* Ed. John Carey. New York: Knopf, 2002.

_____. *Homage to Catalonia.* 1955. Boston: Beacon, 1967.

_____. *The Lost Writings.* Ed. W. J. West. New York: Arbor House, 1985.

Payne, Stanley G. *The Spanish Revolution.* New York: Norton, 1969.

Preston, Paul. *The Spanish Civil War: Reaction, Revolution, and Revenge.* Rev. ed. New York: Norton, 2007.

_____. *We Saw Spain Die: Foreign Correspondents in the Spanish Civil War.* New York: Skyhorse, 2009.

Pryce-Jones, David. "The Visions of Orwell and Waugh." *New Criterion* 27:1 (2008): 4–8.

Radosh, Ronald, Mary R. Habeck, and Grigory Sevostianov, eds. *Spain Betrayed: The Soviet Union in the Spanish Civil War.* New Haven: Yale UP, 2001.

Rodden, John. *The Politics of Literary Reputation: The Making and Claiming of "St. George" Orwell.* New York: Oxford UP, 1989.

_____, and John Rossi. "The Mysterious (Un)meeting of George Orwell and Ernest Hemingway." *Kenyon Review* 31:4 (2009): 56–84.

Rosenstone, Robert A. *Crusade of the Left: The Lincoln Battalion in the Spanish Civil War*. New York: Pegasus, 1969.

Shelden. Michael. *Orwell: The Authorized Biography*. New York: Harper, 1991.

Smyth, Denis. "'We Are with You': Solidarity and Self-Interest in Soviet Policy towards Republican Spain, 1936–1939." *The Republic Besieged: Civil War in Spain 1936–1939*. Ed. Paul Preston and Ann L. Mackenzie. Edinburgh: Edinburgh UP, 1996. 87–105.

Taylor, D. J. *Orwell: The Life*. New York: Holt, 2003.

Thomas, Hugh. *The Spanish Civil War*. Rev. ed. New York: Modern Library, 2001.

Trilling, Lionel. Introduction. *Homage to Catalonia*. By George Orwell. 1955. Boston: Beacon, 1967.

Trogdon, Robert W., ed. *Ernest Hemingway: A Literary Reference*. New York: Carroll, 1999.

Woodcock, George. *The Crystal Spirit: A Study of George Orwell*. Boston: Little, 1966.

Zwerdling, Alex. *Orwell and the Left*. New Haven, CT: Yale UP, 1974.

Orwell and Reader-Response Theory_____

William E. Cain

Near the conclusion of his review of H. G. Wells's *Mind at the End of Its Tether* (1945), George Orwell presents a paragraph that consists of a single sentence: "It would be simply dishonest to pretend that this is one of Mr. Wells's better books" (*Essays* 922). This states the judgment that Orwell makes on Wells's book but, more importantly, he also intends it to perform an action on his reader. The sentence is somewhat surprising, for through it, the reader is instructed not to hold a view that he or she may not have held in the first place. Has the reader been assuming that *Mind at the End of Its Tether* is one of Wells's better books? Maybe, but probably not, given the criticisms of it that earlier in the review Orwell forcefully expressed.

Orwell thus rebukes the reader for a thought that might not have been in the reader's mind. If it was, then the reader must face the fact that he or she is being dishonest. Sheer pretending: it would not be a view that the reader actually holds but one that is straightforwardly false—a view that amounts to hypocrisy and deceit, so much so that it would not fool anyone anyway.

In a new paragraph Orwell says:

> Indeed, it is hardly a book at all, merely a series of short, disjointed essays which have probably been written with considerable effort between bouts of illness. And yet it has the power that Mr. Wells's writings have always had—the power of arresting the reader's attention and forcing him to think and argue. The thesis that it puts forward may be far-fetched, it may even be slightly absurd, but it has a sort of grandeur. (*Essays* 923)

Orwell now takes away the designation that a moment ago (and throughout the review) he assigned to *Mind at the End of Its Tether*— that it is a book. It turns out that it is not really a book, but is, instead, something that Wells has cobbled together. Here again Orwell makes a judgment on Wells, but no sooner does Orwell offer it to the reader than he qualifies it. He extends to Wells the benefit of the doubt after all. This may not be a good book, or even a book, but human effort has nonetheless gone into it. The elderly Wells (he was nearing eighty) did this work when he was ill. He did not have to, but this is who he was— a writer, a maker of books to the end.

With the double conjunction "And yet" that begins the next sentence, Orwell insists that the reader see the strength that inheres even in this flawed book. It has power, and a power that from the start to the finish of his career, Wells demonstrated. Orwell arrests the reader's attention; he compels the reader to think and argue. Even when the reader finds Wells's thesis to be far-fetched or absurd, he or she must acknowledge that grandeur of a sort is there.

This review is not one of Orwell's best known or widely reprinted pieces, but the ways in which its phrases and sentences and paragraphs work on the reader strike me as characteristic of him. I think, too, that this sketch of Wells is a good portrait of Orwell himself—perhaps more accurate and enlightening about Orwell than about Wells. Orwell is as adept as anyone at arresting the attention of the reader, engaging the reader and making him or her think. His style encourages, obliges, the reader to be active and attentive. He puts our minds through a complex process of change.

Orwell is distinctive as a writer less for what he says than for what he does, and what he does in his writing is to work on the minds of readers. For this reason it is misleading to emphasize, as we often do, the positions that Orwell takes. I am not suggesting that Orwell has no positions, but, rather, that he is exploring positions through the organization of his language. As John Rodden has observed, Orwell "registers perceptions rather than devises programs" ("George Orwell" 142; see also "Fellow Contrarians" 156). He writes in order to make us, his readers, think our way into and under and around the positions that he brings forward for our inspection. He is not telling us what to think but making us think. This is why he has endured and why he is endlessly stimulating, always invigorating—why he arrests our attention.

"The reason why Orwell is such an interesting person to read still," Christopher Hitchens has said, "and such an interesting stylist, is that he is permanently in combat with himself. He was always grappling with contradiction" (qtd. in Enright). This is helpful, taking us beyond the view that the rightness of Orwell's positions is the reason he matters. But at the same time, it is incomplete, even misleading. It is true that Orwell grapples with contradiction, yet it is even more pertinent to say that he makes his readers grapple with contradiction: his writing functions to make us know, think, and feel what it is like to be in the midst of complexity, paradox, and contradiction.

As we move from line to line as readers of Orwell, we find that he surprises us; he does the unexpected; he puts us off balance; he undercuts our expectations and impels us to see the familiar and the commonplace in a new light. It is all too easy, Richard Rees notes, "to underestimate the acuteness and power of his mind. . . . His style can be deceptive. It is so swift and simple and unpretentious that his best arguments appear much easier and more obvious than they really are" (8). Orwell should be read with pleasure—but also with care and close attention. Again, this is not so much because of what Orwell is saying, but because of how he is saying it—that is, how he writes, how he makes us experience his words on the page.

Orwell indeed is a wonderfully entertaining writer—so pleasure-giving in his prose, pointed, ironic, and frequently funny, sharp, and smart. As Jeffrey Meyers has remarked, "Orwell's style is spare but never drab. His vigorous prose, engaging honesty, and sly wit immediately engage his readers. And his literary personality—his integrity, idealism, and commitment—shine through his writing like pebbles in a clear stream" (95). I would want to take Orwell's engagement with the reader further than Meyers does. Orwell is a hard thinker, a brave thinker, and a keen, intense thinker about political and moral problems.

He imposes hard thinking on us: he gives us pleasure and he makes us do intellectual work.

We tend not to stress the action of Orwell's language, its organization, as much as we should. For we are too invested in identifying and praising Orwell for what he got right—which may mean that we admire him for saying things that we agree with. The critic George Scialabba has stated: "Orwell was not a contrarian; he simply tried to say what most needed saying" (46). But Orwell *is* a contrarian—a maker of contraries in which he situates us as we read him. He aims simultaneously to see what is directly before his eyes and to see through it; he asks a two-part question: What exactly am I looking at, and how will it look if I tilt or turn it in another way? This is the experience of questioning and revising impressions that Orwell in his writing displays and that he extends to us as readers.

The critic Richard White says of Orwell that his "insistence on plain speaking and his appeal to common sense are themselves a kind of mystification insofar as they imply that the world is not a complicated place and ideological distortion is never an issue" (91). To me this is mistaken. Orwell is not mystified but, rather, is aware that he and we are prone to mystification: He writes to equip us intellectually to resist the mystifying to which we are inclined.

Orwell's plain speech and common sense are integral to his commitment to the world as a tangled place and to his recognition that ideological distortion is everywhere, including in his own perception of the world. The movements of Orwell's writing are not inadvertent or accidental, or the result of Orwell's own sins of mystification. His writing is strategic and purposeful: he knows what he is doing and enacts it in his writing for us to go through.

"His way of writing," Alfred Kazin says about Orwell, "is always more or less an argument. He writes to change your mind" (18). I would add that Orwell's writing is extraordinary in that it will not allow our minds to rest—the argument never ends. Someone could say—and many have—that reading Orwell has changed his or her mind about an issue. This is a conversion, a transformation of attitude that we welcome. But it must be remembered that Orwell aims to keep the reader's mind perpetually alert. There is something about the notion of being right, of saying the right thing, of taking the correct position, which misses the major measure of Orwell's accomplishment—not why he matters but why he truly matters. For Orwell, taking a stand means both taking a stand and maintaining a self-critical, self-examining relationship to it.

For me, one of the most effective ways to explain and dramatize the claims I am making about Orwell as a writer is through reader-response criticism, as articulated by the literary theorist Stanley Fish. In a series of powerful essays, published in the 1970s and collected in *Is There a Text in This Class?*, Fish argues that critics, teachers, and students should turn from the text to the reader. Breaking with the New Critics' emphasis on the intrinsic meaning of the text—the view that the features and forms of significance are embedded in it—Fish proposes that instead we should examine the responses of the reader. The focus is not on what is in the text but on how the reader responds to the text. The key word, says Fish, is "experience"—the experience of the reader as he or she responds to the text from moment to moment. It is this experience, not something in the text, that constitutes meaning: what a literary work means is what it does to the reader.

Fish defines the reader as "an actively mediating presence." When he interprets a sentence in an essay or a story, he substitutes "for one question—what does this sentence mean?—another, more operational question—what does this sentence do?" (*Is There a Text* 25). As a critic of prose and poetry, Fish is interested in "the *temporal* flow of the reading experience" (27):

Essentially what the method does is *slow down* the reading experience so that "events" one does not notice in normal time, but which do occur, are brought before our analytical attentions. It is as if a slow motion camera with an automatic stop-action effect were recording our linguistic experiences and presenting them to us for viewing. Of course the value of such a procedure is predicated on the idea of *meaning as an event*, something that is happening between the words and in the reader's mind, something not visible to the naked eye but which can be made visible (or at least palpable) by the regular introduction of a "searching" question (what does this do?). (28; italics in original)

This approach strikes me as illuminating for understanding how Orwell operates as a writer. Sometimes he almost seems to anticipate the approach Fish describes, as though Orwell were putting into practice a strategy that Fish much later would make explicit as a theory.[1]

Here, for example, is Orwell's first sentence in chapter one of *Homage to Catalonia* (1938), his book about the Spanish Civil War: "In the Lenin Barracks in Barcelona, the day before I joined the militia, I saw an Italian militiaman standing in front of the officers' table" (1). As in the later Wells review, Orwell uses a single sentence to form a paragraph. It is direct, crisply stated. It also is disorienting: we are given a fact but are not told how to interpret it. We might have some associations with the name Lenin (the effect would be different if Orwell had written "the barracks in Barcelona") and could hazard an assumption based on this name—for instance, that these are Communist, or perhaps Soviet-led, barracks. Then again, the militiaman is Italian, and as readers, we might wonder about this man's presence, since the majority of Italians who served in the military in Spain were on the Fascist side.

The function of this sentence is to make us ask questions—and to expect that Orwell will answer them. A glance down the page seems to support this expectation. It is a much longer paragraph of description that he writes next, and we can see that it shifts into dialogue. When we read these next sentences, however, Orwell both does and does not fulfill our expectations: "He was a tough-looking youth of twenty-five or -six, with reddish-yellow hair and powerful shoulders. His peaked leather cap was pulled fiercely over one eye. He was standing in profile to me, his chin on his breast, gazing with a puzzled frown at a map which one of the officers had open on the table" (1). He is not a militia-man but a youth. On the other hand, he is tough looking and powerful. Yet he gazes at a map with puzzlement on his face. He is formidable, even scary, but how scary could he be, this youth who frowns at his own inability to read a map?

Orwell continues: "Something in his face deeply moved me. It was the face of a man who would commit murder and throw away his life for a friend—the kind of face you would expect in an Anarchist, though as likely as not he was a Communist" (1). What Orwell says may sur-prise us. It is not just that the man's (or should we say, the youth's) face moved Orwell. It "deeply moved" him. We take in what Orwell tells us even as we recoil when he writes that this is the face of a man "who would commit murder." Could Orwell or anyone be deeply moved by a man whom one feels could commit murder? It is not as simple as that, for this same young man would "throw away his life for a friend"—the casual thoughtlessness of the gesture is part of its splendor and grace. This young man is, potentially, both a killer and a Christlike sacrificer of his life for that of another.

Orwell says more about this face:

There were both candour and ferocity in it; also the pathetic reverence that illiterate people have for their supposed superiors. Obviously he could not make head or tail of the map; obviously he regarded map-reading as a stupendous intellectual feat. I hardly know why, but I have seldom seen anyone—any man, I mean—to whom I have taken such an immediate lik-ing. While they were talking round the table some remark brought it out that I was a foreigner. The Italian raised his head and said quickly:
    "Italiano?"
    I answered in my bad Spanish: "No, Inglés. Y tú?'
    "Italiano."

When Orwell says that this is the kind of face we would expect in an anarchist, he is being ironic—the point that he already has established is that the interpretation of faces is difficult to get right. Our preconceptions do not hold up, not when who or what we are looking at combines such opposites and shades of difference and opposition.

"Candor" we take to be good: we admire it. "Ferocity": This is harder to endorse, and it is meant to be in conjunction with candor. Candid and ferocious—are these versions of the same trait or are they different traits? Orwell puts them next to one another to make us think about how such terms, two such attributes in a person, could make sense together. There is more to a person, to this person, than we might have assumed: in Orwell's place, what would we have seen when we saw this militiaman, and what would have been our response?

Orwell pursues this strategy, this engagement with the reader, throughout *Homage to Catalonia* and in his other books and essays. His writing is full of surprises and turns that we must—with delight and effort—negotiate. It is beautifully, brilliantly done. It might seem effortless, which is why Lionel Trilling praised Orwell as someone whom we feel is like us, someone who "is not a genius" and who "communicates to us the sense that what he has done, any one of us could do" (xi). In fact, it requires genius to write like this—Trilling underestimates the writer he esteems. When we focus on what Orwell's organization of language is doing, we appreciate the craft that Orwell has mastered. He does what we could not do: he is a great writer, an artist, and a genius.

Orwell says that the man's face moved him—and notice that the connection to the militia has not been mentioned since the first sentence. Orwell brings himself close to this person; he feels an emotional bond. The bond is fervent enough to absorb the man's illiteracy and overestimation of others ("supposed superiors") who are essentially no better than he is. Not only is he not an intellectual; he cannot read or write at all. Yet Orwell likes him—immediately. Everything that he is telling us, and that we have been following in our reading, happened, Orwell says, instantly.

Orwell acknowledges that his writing is not faithful to the experience he is describing. Hence I now am slowing down something that Orwell already slowed down himself when he stated it in a sequence of words. He is using his writing to tell us about an encounter that literally was too momentous for phrases and sentences to capture it. The point for Orwell was that he connected to this young man right away. The small bit of dialogue that he gives to us is simultaneously a human touch and an irrelevance: it reinforces a connection that Orwell felt immediately. It existed before any words were spoken: words for the feeling come belatedly in its wake.

In a hostile essay on *Homage to Catalonia*, Bill Alexander rebukes Orwell for his "fantasized, romanticized account" of the militiaman (95). This verdict ignores the actual experience of reading the sentences that Orwell has written. Fantasy and romance—Alexander's terms—simplify the effects that Orwell has devised. Or, rather, they constitute part of the effect: Orwell understands them as elements of his response to the young man, but the effect of the passage as a whole is more intricate. Alexander's statement is true only for someone who is judging the writing but not experiencing it.

The critic Robert Stradling also harshly judges *Homage to Catalonia*, objecting among other things to the title. Why, he asks, the word "homage"? In what sense is this book an "homage"? What about "to Catalonia"? Catalonia, says Stradling, "has no observable existence in Orwell's book. . . . It displays awareness of no aspect of the history of the country, nor of its culture and society, either *sui generis* or in the context of Spain as a whole." He concludes: "Anyone who turns to *Homage to Catalonia* in the hope of being informed about its apparent subject is totally wasting his or her time" (105).

This is not the case, yet in a way Stradling is making an astute observation. If the reader turns to *Homage to Catalonia* in order to be informed in the sense of receiving information from Orwell, he or she will be disappointed. Orwell is not in the business of giving information. It is not that the title is wrong, but instead that it gives us as readers something significant to think about—questions to ask and explore. In what sense is this book an "homage"? How much, how little, does it tell us about Catalonia? If it is not a book that satisfies the expectations its title creates, why is that? What is Orwell doing? What does, and how does, he want you and me to think about this book? How do we think about what *Homage to Catalonia* is, what its purposes are, why it matters? What, in sum, is it *about*?

It is about its reader—about Orwell's writing in its relation to his reader. Consider how Orwell concludes his opening account:

> As we went out he stepped across the room and gripped my hand very hard. Queer, the affection you can feel for a stranger! It was as though his spirit and mine had momentarily succeeded in bridging the gulf of language and tradition and meeting in utter intimacy. I hoped he liked me as well as I liked him. But I also knew that to retain my first impression of him I must not see him again; and needless to say I never did see him again. One was always making contacts of that kind in Spain. (1–2)

The gesture is eager, aggressive. If Orwell had not made his account of the militiaman complex, the action here could be unnerving—and maybe it still is. "Very hard": Orwell could have omitted this phrase, but he wanted it there for the reinforcement that it supplies for "gripped." Orwell says no more about the gesture; we might have assumed he would flesh it out—what, in physical terms, happened next. He does not tell us. He pivots on the word "queer"—the strange, odd nature of his response. He uses the pronoun "you," which enlists us in the action. His feeling for this youth was deep, but he concedes that it was fleeting. A stranger for whom we feel deep affection is still a stranger: we do not know who he is.

Orwell invites readers to imagine that we can be intimate—utterly, completely, absolutely—with someone whom we do not know. For a moment we might be. But then Orwell lessens intimacy to liking. He admits that for such a feeling to linger, nothing can be allowed to add to it—and nothing did. Utter intimacy, then liking, and at the end it is simply a contact, and a kind that happened often. It was special, but not really.

Orwell is a writer who surprises and startles us as we read him. Sometimes he shocks us: He can be not only bold, but also outrageous. Here he is in his provocative mode, in a review of *Mein Kampf* (1940):

> Suppose that Hitler's programme could be put into effect. What he envisages, a hundred years hence, is a continuous state of 250 million Germans with plenty of "living room" (i.e. stretching to Afghanistan or thereabouts), a horrible brainless empire in which, essentially, nothing ever happens except the training of young men for war and the endless breeding of fresh cannon-fodder. How was it that he was able to put this monstrous vision across? It is easy to say that at one stage of his career he was financed by the heavy industrialists, who saw in him the man who would smash the Socialists and Communists. They would not have backed him, however, if he had not talked a great movement into existence already. Again, the situation in Germany, with its seven million unemployed, was obviously favourable for demagogues. (*Essays* 250)

With vivid economy, Orwell describes the vision that Hitler has put forward, and he then raises the obvious question: how could Hitler have succeeded in winning support for a future so monstrous? Orwell offers an answer, linked to the backing that Hitler received from industrialists—the easy answer, he says. He touches too on the extensive unemployment that supplied Hitler with a mass audience of the disaffected. This, though, is only Orwell's setup for his jarring next move:

> But Hitler could not have succeeded against his many rivals if it had not been for the attraction of his own personality, which one can feel even in the clumsy writing of *Mein Kampf*, and which is no doubt overwhelming when one hears his speeches. I should like to put it on record that I have never been able to dislike Hitler. Ever since he came to power—till

then, like nearly everyone, I had been deceived into thinking that he did not matter—I have reflected that I would certainly kill him if I could get within reach of him, but that I could feel no personal animosity. The fact is that there is something deeply appealing about him. One feels it again when one sees his photographs—and I recommend especially the photograph at the beginning of Hurst and Blackett's edition, which shows Hitler in his early Brownshirt days. (*Essays* 250–51)

Orwell knows that he is saying something scandalous, and he knows that we will be scandalized: how could anyone find this monster likeable? Orwell reports that he has never been able to dislike Hitler; the implication is that he has tried and tried again, but is unable to bring himself to feel what he should. He should hate the man. He does not. He would kill him if he could, yet all the while he likes him—Hitler is deeply appealing to look at.

There is more:

It is a pathetic, dog-like face, the face of a man suffering under intolerable wrongs. In a rather more manly way it reproduces the expression of innumerable pictures of Christ crucified, and there is little doubt that that is how Hitler sees himself. The initial, personal cause of his grievance against the universe can only be guessed at; but at any rate the grievance is there. He is the martyr, the victim, Prometheus chained to the rock, the self-sacrificing hero who fights single-handed against impossible odds. If he were killing a mouse he would know how to make it seem like a dragon. One feels, as with Napoleon, that he is fighting against destiny, that he can't win, and yet that he somehow deserves to. The attraction of such a pose is of course enormous; half the films that one sees turn upon some such theme. (*Essays* 251)

The portrait is demeaning (pathetic, dog-like) and grand (Christ-like). Hitler is mythic. He takes on the universe, crying out against injustice done to him as if he were a modern-day Prometheus. Yet he is absurd, as Orwell's mouse and dragon metaphor implies. Then again, this illustrates how huge Hitler is, as he combats destiny like another Napoleon.

One of the benefits of reading as much of Orwell as we can is that we see each piece of his writing connecting to, reflecting upon, other pieces. Literary theorists of various kinds—Roland Barthes, Jacques Derrida, Harold Bloom, and Geoffrey Hartman, among others—have said in their different ways that we should speak less of a discrete text than of intertextuality—of the connectedness of all texts as they weave in and out of one another.[2] Each text that Orwell writes is a special piece of work, a performance of a particular task, but we might also refer to "the Orwell text"—to everything he wrote, as if it constituted a network of writing, an active and ongoing commentary on itself that the reader experiences.

Or perhaps we should say that Orwell gives the reader a world of figures and events, a world of experiences. In this instance we encounter Hitler—visionary, monster, Christ, Prometheus, and Napoleon. He is different from the militiaman described in *Homage to Catalonia*. But maybe he is not. After all, Hitler was once no more than a corporal in the German army. We do not know which persons will become the makers of history, these near-invisible, anonymous figures whom we glimpse for a moment—pathetic, moving, candid, ferocious.

Orwell's review of *Mein Kampf* was published in late March 1940. By then, Germany had invaded and conquered Poland. Rationing had begun in Britain, conscription was underway, and the Germans had bombed the British naval base at Scapa Flow in Scotland. Orwell wrote the review knowing the effect that these sentences would produce in readers. Soon thereafter, Germany attacked Denmark, Norway, France, Belgium, Luxembourg, and the Netherlands. Neville Chamberlain resigned as prime minister and was replaced by Winston Churchill. We know the horror that Hitler inflicted on Europe in the months and years that lay ahead. We could say that in his review Orwell is being glib and gullible. But we also could say that he is being honest, and that his strategy in this piece of writing is to state what he feels and thinks in order to oblige us to come up against (that is, to tell the truth about) our response to Hitler. Of course we say that Hitler was vile, loathsome, evil. Is that all? Is this, really, what we feel, or what we would have felt at the time?

We praise Orwell because he tells the truth. Yet his distinction as a writer and teacher is that he knows that even the most profound truths harden into orthodoxy. Truth—the orthodox version of it—then becomes something that everyone takes for granted and deploys to deny or restrict freedom of opinion, the spirit and activity of relentless inquiry. Truth, the real truth, is something that exists and that we must inspect and dare to criticize. It is there and it is not. Truth exists; truth changes. For it exists in history, not outside or beyond it.

Orwell says in his essay "The Freedom of the Press" (1945), responding to critics of *Animal Farm*: "For all I know, by the time this book is published my view of the Soviet régime may be the generally accepted one. But what use would that be in itself? To exchange one orthodoxy for another is not necessarily an advance. The enemy is the gramophone mind, whether or not one agrees with the record that is being played at the moment" (*Essays* 895–96). The gramophone mind, someone who thinks the thoughts of others and sings their tunes, is Orwell's metaphor for the enemy. His ultimate enemy is not so much capitalism, Fascism, or Communism as it is the mind that subscribes, permanently, to any of them—a mind that is complacent, and dangerous and oppressive, threatening to itself and others under its sway.

This is the fearful thing that Orwell fights against, and that in his work he insists the reader grapple with. What are Orwell's words and sentences and paragraphs doing to us as we read them? The answer is that through them Orwell is reminding us that we are not machines but human beings. The point of having a mind is to use it and never to stop using it—a lesson that in his organization of language and his relationship to his readers, Orwell promotes and teaches.

Notes

1. The best introductions to Fish's work in literary theory are his collection *Is There a Text in This Class?* and *The Stanley Fish Reader*, ed. Veeser (1980). For critical commentary, see the study by Olson (2002) and the collection edited by Olson and Worsham (2004); and for surveys of the field of reader-response and reception theory in general, see Freund (1987) and Holub (1984, 1992). Selections by Fish and other theorists who have argued for or against the role of the reader in making meaning are included in Tompkins (1980) and Leitch et al. (2010).

2. This is, I think, richly true of Fish's conception of the poetry and prose of John Milton, whom he has studied in many essays and influential books. See, for example, *Surprised by Sin* and *How Milton Works*.

Works Cited

Alexander, Bill. "George Orwell and Spain." *Inside the Myth: Orwell: Views from the Left*. Ed. Christopher Norris. London: Lawrence, 1984. 85–102.

Enright, Michael. "Why Orwell Matters: Interview with Christopher Hitchens." *Queen's Quarterly* 109.4 (2002): 533–43.

Fish, Stanley. *How Milton Works*. Cambridge: Harvard UP, 2001.

_____. *Is There a Text in This Class? The Authority of Interpretive Communities*. Cambridge: Harvard UP, 1980.

_____. *Surprised by Sin: The Reader in "Paradise Lost."* New York: St. Martin's, 1967.

Freund, Elizabeth. *The Return of the Reader: Reader-Response Criticism*. New York: Methuen, 1987.

Hitchens, Christopher. *Why Orwell Matters*. New York: Basic, 2002.

Holub, Robert C. *Crossing Borders: Reception Theory, Poststructuralism, Deconstruction*. Madison: U of Wisconsin P, 1992.

_____. *Reception Theory: A Critical Introduction*. New York: Methuen, 1984.

Kazin, Alfred. "Not One of Us." *New York Review of Books* 14 June 1984: 13+.

Leitch, Vincent B., et al., eds. *The Norton Anthology of Theory and Criticism*. 2nd ed. New York: Norton, 2010.

Meyers, Jeffrey. "George Orwell and the Art of Writing." *Kenyon Review* 27.4 (2005): 92–114.

Olson, Gary A. *Justifying Belief: Stanley Fish and the Work of Rhetoric*. Albany: State U of New York P, 2002.

_____, and Lynn Worsham, eds. *Postmodern Sophistry: Stanley Fish and the Critical Enterprise*. Albany: State U of New York P, 2004.

Orwell, George. *Essays*. Ed. John Carey. New York: Knopf, 2002.

_____. *Homage to Catalonia*. London: Secker, 1997. Vol. 6 of *The Complete Works of George Orwell*. Peter Davison, gen. ed. 20 vols.

Rees, Richard. *Orwell: Fugitive from the Camp of Victory*. London: Secker, 1961.

Rodden, John. "Fellow Contrarians? Christopher Hitchens and George Orwell." *Kenyon Review* 28.1 (2006): 142–65.

_____. "George Orwell, Pickwickian Radical? An Ambivalent Case." *Kenyon Review* 12.3 (1990): 139–49.

Scialabba, George. "Facing Orwell's Way." *Raritan* 29.1 (2009): 42–52.

Stradling, Robert. "Orwell and the Spanish Civil War: A Historical Critique." *Inside the Myth: Orwell: Views from the Left*. Ed. Christopher Norris. London: Lawrence, 1984. 103–125.

Tompkins, Jane, ed. *Reader-Response Criticism: From Formalism to Post-Structuralism*. Baltimore: Johns Hopkins UP, 1980.

Trilling, Lionel. Introduction. *Homage to Catalonia*. 1955. Boston: Beacon, 1967. v–xxiii.

Veeser, H. Aram, ed. *The Stanley Fish Reader*. London: Blackwell, 1999.

White, Richard. "George Orwell: Socialism and Utopia." *Utopian Studies* 19.1 (2008): 73–95.

George Orwell's Critical Reception⎽⎽⎽⎽⎽⎽⎽⎽⎽⎽⎽

Loraine Saunders

This essay will survey the major pieces of criticism surrounding Orwell's major works and look at the chief concerns that have preoccupied his critics, both during his lifetime and posthumously. We will examine each book separately and proceed with a selection of key essays by the same method. Though we shall be looking at the works in a largely individual and linear fashion, the essay overall will be exploring broader, all-inclusive questions such as why his early novels, such as *A Clergyman's Daughter* (1935) and *Keep the Aspidistra Flying* (1936), were hastily and unfairly dismissed by notable critics both then and now.

From the outset, owing to his literary connections, Orwell was a writer whose work would receive critical attention. However, it was not until the publication of *Animal Farm* in 1945 that Orwell began to enjoy worldwide fame. Both during his lifetime and posthumously, the critical reception of Orwell's novels has tended to fall into two camps: those who value and appreciate his novels as well as his essays, and those who dismiss him as a novelist but rate him highly as a journalist and documentary writer. This dichotomy is a little crude because there is diversity within these positions; however, it does reflect a strong trend. Typifying a popular sentiment among critics in the latter group is this comment by Morris Dickstein: "Orwell is not Shakespeare. Orwell is not John Milton. Orwell is not in the class with the greatest of all writers" (qtd. in Rodden, *Every Intellectual* 141). Timothy Garton Ash's review of Peter Davison's *The Complete Works of George Orwell*, entitled "Orwell in 1998," has exactly the same lament: "Yet Orwell was no Shakespeare. He was not a universal genius. Nor was he a natural master of the English language" (10). Garton Ash even compares Orwell to John Milton, coming to the conclusion that Orwell is inferior. But why compare Orwell to a playwright and composer of sonnets in the first place? Is it really of any critical value, particularly when there is no textual example to support the claims? Garton Ash says *Nineteen Eighty-Four* "is marred by patches of melodrama and weak writing" (10). Again, absolutely no textual example of this melodrama and weak writing is provided, and this is something that needs to be borne in mind when evaluating the worth of critical commentary applied to Orwell.

Since Orwell's death there has been a steady flow of critical attention to his work, with scholars such as Roger Fowler (since the 1970s) and John Rodden (since the 1980s) bringing out several in-depth studies. There have also been studies showing the influence that the nineteenth-century novelist George Gissing had on Orwell, most notably by Mark Connolly, on which my own study of Gissing's influence builds. The year 1984 was a feverish date in the Orwell reception-history calendar, owing to the prophetic title of his last and most famous novel. In 1968, Sonia Brownell (Orwell's second wife) and Ian Angus brought out *The Collected Essays, Journalism, and Letters of George Orwell*, which was the main academic study of reference until the publication of Peter Davison's brilliant *The Complete Works of George Orwell* in 1998. Both publications have done much to keep interest in Orwell alive. The next major event was the centenary of Orwell's birth, June 25, 2003. Two weighty biographies, one by D. J. Taylor and one by Gordon Bowker, marked the occasion, and added to the many existing Orwell biographies. Regarding Orwell's popularity today, there is the Orwell Prize for British political writing, established in 1974, and now Dione Venable has created an Orwell Society. Let us now turn to the works.

Down and Out in London and Paris (1933)

George Orwell's first literary publication, *Down and Out in Paris and London*, was finally published (after several rejections under the title *A Scullion's Diary*) by Victor Gollancz in 1933. Orwell's firsthand account of life among the poor and destitute in the two European metropolises was well received, generally. J. B. Priestley in the *Evening Standard* echoed C. Day Lewis and Compton Mackenzie when he said it was "the best book of its kind that I have read in a long time" (qtd. in Lucas 15). Most agreed that it was a reliable record of life below the poverty line. Some hoteliers were outraged by its suggestion that expensive meals came out of filthy kitchens; however, that was where the outrage stopped. When it was published in the United States, there was more critical scrutiny; some critics doubted the truth of Orwell's claims of really living below the poverty line. "*How* down and out was George Orwell, actually?" became and still is a common refrain. Writing much later in the twentieth century, Lynette Hunter questions in the same manner, writing that Orwell comes off initially in the book as "blinkered, ignorant, prejudiced, sentimental, clichéd, or worse, snide and supercilious" (*George Orwell* 15). Hunter believes Orwell's narrative is patronizing and unsympathetic because of his upper-class background, though it should be said that Hunter goes on to delineate how Orwell "moves on" from this position. Taylor's 2003 biography confidently rejects much of Orwell's documentary: "The first half of *Down and Out* is a conspicuously Gallic affair, full of somewhat stagy 'French' conversation, whose local colour has been laid on with a trowel" (99).

In the *London Review of Books* in 1998, Ian Hamilton, reassessing Orwell's work through Davison's *The Complete Works of George Orwell*, referred back to Orwell's essay "Confessions of a Book Reviewer." Hamilton says that in this essay Orwell was "piling on the agony" regarding the daily trials facing a book reviewer. He talks of the "glum theatricals" of Orwell's testimony, in much the same way Taylor does about the trials documented in *Down and Out*. The title of Hamilton's piece is "Eric the Nerd" (referring to Orwell's real name, Eric Blair). Orwell comes in for a great deal of this kind of derision. His old-time school friend and literary peer, Cyril Connolly, once commented that Orwell "could not blow his nose without moralizing on conditions in the handkerchief industry" (qtd. in Rodden, *Every Intellectual* 4). Undoubtedly, getting fed up with Orwell at times is and always has been a common side effect of reading his work. Again, the question arises: Is this fair criticism?

Burmese Days, a fictionalized critique of the British Empire drawing on Orwell's own time as an imperial police officer in Burma, was also received rather well, though initially rejected for publication in Britain. Writing in the *New Statesman*, Cyril Connolly described it thus: "I liked it and recommend it to anyone who enjoys a spate of efficient indignation, graphic description, excellent narrative, excitement and irony tempered with vitriol" (qtd. in J. Meyers, *Orwell: Wintry Conscience* 117). In sharp contrast, an American reviewer, Margaret Carson Hubbard in the *New York Herald Tribune*, referred to the "ghastly vulgarity" of *Burmese Days*. Stansky and Abrahams say of her review: "Hubbard found that all of Orwell's sympathies were with the natives, which does not suggest a close reading of the text" (43). The distinguished *Boston Evening Transcript* gave it an impressive write-up and questioned why Orwell had not been able to find a British publisher. The review went on to say that Orwell's depictions of Burma under British rule presented "realities faithfully and unflinchingly realized" (qtd. in Stansky and Abrahams 44). Despite this praise, the novel would soon go out of print.

Today most critics view the novel as having as many strengths as weaknesses, although one or two critics are wholly negative. D. J. Taylor is in this latter camp; he dismisses the entire book, as he does Orwell's succeeding 1930s novels, as "a study in failure." He writes that Orwell's British protagonist, John Flory, "is a lonely fantasist, his best years squandered in drink and whoring" (319). However, most critics are more balanced and apply closer reading. David Seed appreciates the novel's political subtlety: "Orwell's protagonist Flory enacts the novelist's dissatisfaction with the Anglo-Indians by renouncing the club" (276). Regarding the novel's political integrity and treatment of character overall, Seed finds it limited by Orwell's inability to distinguish between Flory's thoughts and his own: "The combination of guilt and over-involvement with his protagonist . . . vitiates Orwell's presentation of empire" (278).

The examination of the next two novels will go into a little more textual detail in order to provide an understanding of why their critical reception has been so varied, and why one should not take at face value many of the critical assertions made about them.

A Clergyman's Daughter (1935)

From the outset, Orwell was not happy with *A Clergyman's Daughter*, an experimental novel about a pious young woman, Dorothy, whose life is thrown into chaos when she suffers an attack of amnesia. The book underwent a great deal of in-house censorship, with Orwell forced to change and cut out parts of the story, much to his despair. Yet Orwell's French translator, R. M. Raimbault, read it and liked it, commenting: "It is a book which is often powerful and makes remarkable observations, strange—in particular your Trafalgar Square—full of humour, sometimes fierce, and written boldly and with captivating originality" (qtd. in Orwell, *Lost Orwell* 46). Raimbault was not without sound critical credentials, being a professor of English at Le Mans University.

Raimbault's Trafalgar Square comment refers to the third chapter, presented entirely in the form of dialogue, in imitation of the "Nighttown" chapter in James Joyce's modernist masterpiece *Ulysses* (1922). The various critical reactions to Orwell's inclusion of this chapter show an unwillingness on the critics' part to trust Orwell's literary judgment. Norman Collins went so far as to hint that "the chaotic structure of [*A Clergyman's Daughter*] would suggest some kind of mental instability" (qtd. in J. Meyers, *Orwell: Wintry Conscience* 119). Others were more constructive: Douglas Kerr's assessment, for example, praised the chapter's artistic merits, noting that its characters "have no possessions at all except their voice, and to tell their story Orwell recognizes that he has to allow them to speak for themselves. So the controlling narrative voice falls silent, and a chattering polyphony takes over" (27). In detailing how Orwell reconstructs Joyce's experimental narrative, Kerr challenges those critics who insist that the Trafalgar Square scene is "written unsuccessfully in the manner of James Joyce" (Fyvel 54).

Robert Lee expertly delineates how the varying, disparate narrative elements in *A Clergyman's Daughter* actually harmonize to strike a greater political note. Alluding to the passages where the third-person narrator disappears, Lee writes: "Such passages spoil the conventional unity and justify the designation episodic. But this need not be pejorative. If we think of the novel as picaresque, the seemingly random adventures the protagonist experiences must conventionally be disparate, revealing varied inequities in the society which is explored" (27).

Daphne Patai offers a feminist reading of the story that finds much fault. She writes, "Dorothy does not suffer a breakdown; she suffers from a creator, Orwell, who, having invented a female protagonist, does not know how to get her out of the house and into the street where he wants to place her" (97). Similarly, Jenni Calder insists that "Dorothy . . . is the least successful of Orwell's fictional rebels. He is just not able to get far enough inside an unfamiliar consciousness" (87). Dorothy is often described by feminists as "pathetic." Lynette Hunter points out that much feminist reading of Orwell is ungenerous, and I would second this.

Keep the Aspidistra Flying (1936)

Again, from the outset, Orwell disparaged *Keep the Aspidistra Flying*—his novel about a man, Gordon Comstock, who tries to rise above the materialism of his society and suffers great hardship as a result—to anyone who would listen; and sadly they mostly did and still do. In a letter about it to his agent Leonard Moore, Orwell wrote, "I have made the alterations Gollancz asked for. . . . It seems to me to have utterly ruined the book" (*Collected Works* 10: 434). In the *Telegraph*, Cyril Connolly gave a far different review from the one he gave *Burmese Days*, objecting a great deal to what he reads as the "disagreeable" truths circulating in the book. Here Connolly has fallen into the (still-familiar) trap of confusing opinions expressed in the novel with those of the author. Connolly is clearly reading the complaining protagonist as a stand-in for Orwell, failing to grasp Orwell's experimentation with narrative voice.

John Mander, too, follows Connolly's reading of the character's thoughts as a reflection of the author's:

> Instead of allowing the money theme to develop out of the talk and behaviour of his characters, Orwell tells at the start that his novel is going to be about money. He hammers this into us page after page: "For after all, what is there behind it, except money? Money for the right kind of education. . . . Give me not righteousness, give me money, only money." (74)

But these are Gordon's outpourings and not the author's. Mander goes on to say, "*Keep the Aspidistra Flying* is not, by general consent, a very good novel. But are the others so very different? In *Coming Up for Air* . . . there is a similar intrusion of Orwellian prejudice" (74). Another critic, Samuel Hynes, finds the novel and its author morbid: "The Orwell-character in *Keep the Aspidistra Flying* imagines civilisation dying . . . and Orwell was just as gloomy with his friends" (373). Similarly, Valerie Meyers writes, "Orwell's depiction of Gordon's anger, frustration and difficulties as a writer are completely serious" (79).

Wholeheartedly rejecting the idea that the novel is defeatist is Robert Bierman's 1997 film adaptation of the story. At its close, the film celebrates the happiness between Gordon and Rosemary, the woman he opts to marry, as they look forward to a life together as a family with their baby. There is one niggle, however, and this is the film's depiction of Gordon and Rosemary's smugness at being members of the middle class. I would argue that this does not chime with the novel's sensitivity toward "class feeling."

The Road to Wigan Pier (1937)

The reception of *The Road to Wigan Pier*, which pairs with *Down and Out in Paris and London* as another of Orwell's nonfiction documentaries on the plight of the lower classes, was predictably mixed. There was much praise for the first part, which documented the lives of the poor in Wigan and other towns in the north of England, but the second part angered and provoked left-wing sensibilities with its criticisms of socialists and leftist politics. Walter Greenwood gives a good example of this in his 1937 review of the book for the socialist weekly *Tribune*. Toward the first part he is all adulation, saying that Orwell is "at his best as a keen observer with great skill at character drawing"; however, of the second part he writes, "I cannot remember having been so infuriated for a long time than by some of the things he says here" (qtd. in J. Meyers, *George Orwell* 13). Greenwood does end on a positive note though, saying how readable the book is. The amount of critical commentary on *The Road to Wigan Pier* since its publication certainly shows it has enduring power. I say much more about the controversy surrounding this book in the chapter "Orwell's Documentaries of the 1930s."

Homage to Catalonia (1938)

From the outset, *Homage to Catalonia* was destined to be controversial because of the book's denunciation of the bloody intervention in the Spanish Civil War by Soviet leader Joseph Stalin. Orwell had been fighting in Spain with the POUM (Partido Obrero de Unificación Marxista, or Workers' Party of Marxist Unification), which was eventually outlawed as a splinter group by the increasingly Communist-dominated government of the Spanish Republic. Orwell, by then officially labeled a Trotskyist, became at risk of being charged with high treason and executed. In fact, Andrés Nin, leader of the POUM, was arrested by Stalin's agents and murdered, making it highly likely that the same end would have befallen Orwell had he not evaded capture.

It is not surprising, then, that Victor Gollancz, Orwell's Communist-sympathizing publisher, rejected *Homage to Catalonia*, much to Orwell's disgust. When finally published by Secker and Warburg, it was received rather coolly by the Left (selling just 600 copies). It was not published in the United States until 1952. Jeffrey Meyers, in his *Orwell, Wintry Conscience of a Generation*, gives a good account of the reception of *Homage to Catalonia*. Geoffrey Gorer praised the book, saying it was of "first-class" importance. Philip Mairet agreed, stating, "The book is likely to stand as one of the best contemporary documents of the struggle" (qtd. in Meyers 176). Meyers summarizes Douglas Woodruff in the Catholic *Tablet* as viewing Orwell as "a romantic who did not understand the Fascist point of view" (176). V. S. Pritchett in the *New Statesman* stated, "There are many strong arguments for keeping creative writers out of politics and Mr. George Orwell is one of them" (qtd. in Meyers 176). However, Pritchett was later responsible for the description of Orwell as "the wintry conscience of a generation," giving Meyers the title of his book. Stephen Spender described the book as "one of the most serious indictments of Communism which has been written" (qtd. in Meyers 176).

Coming Up for Air (1939)

On its publication there was much enthusiasm for *Coming Up for Air*, in which the middle-aged protagonist, George Bowling, reflects on his life and the things he has lost due to social "progress"—among them his childhood and his old hometown, which he visits and finds unrecognizable. Again, though, critics voiced lament for how the novel was written. Margery Allingham in *Time and Tide* was full of praise, but said of its being written in the first person: "This device … tends to falsify the character slightly" (qtd. in Shelden 340). In a 1987 study, David Wykes also cited the point of view as a problem: "Like his other novels, this too deals with a solitary character, but Orwell has compounded this fact with the greater failing—as he himself was soon to pronounce it—of making it a first-person narrative" (106). Raymond Williams strikes a familiar chord when he writes that the book exhibits a "characteristic coldness, an inability to realise the full life of another," a problem he sees as typical of Orwell's characterizations: "Relationships are characteristically meagre, ephemeral, reluctant, disillusioning, even betraying" (89). Terry Eagleton is of the same opinion: "Failure was Orwell's forte, a leitmotif of his fiction. For him, it was what was real. . . . All of his fictional protagonists are humbled and defeated; and while this may be arraigned as unduly pessimistic, it was not the view of the world they taught at Eton" ("Reach-Me-Down" 6).

On the other hand, Peter Goodall views *Coming Up for Air* and its narrator in a far more positive light: "The deepest analysis of common decency in the novel . . . is in the life of George Bowling. Bowling is really the prototype of the proles, despite the fact that he is from a different social class from the proles in *Nineteen Eighty-Four*" (80). But despite such constructive readings, most critics see the novel as gloomy. Writing in 1978, Bernard Bergonzi, for example, reads Bowling as a reflection of a depressed novel by a depressed author:

> George Bowling is very much a vehicle for Orwell's vision of English life, and his responses suggest that the troubled ambivalence expressed in Orwell's poem of 1934, "On a Ruined Farm near the His Master's Voice Gramophone Factory" has now been resolved into outright rejection of the new architecture of the factory and the way of life associated with it. (107)

Today it is not a novel that receives a great deal of attention. George Bowling certainly does not exist in the public consciousness, and *Coming Up for Air* has never been adapted for television or film. There is, however, a glimmer of hope: British theater critic Dominic Cavendish adapted the novel for the stage in 2008, and it was well received. So we may well see more of this production.

Animal Farm (1945)

Gordon Bowker's Orwell biography provides an excellent account of the publishing history and reception of *Animal Farm*, Orwell's allegory of totalitarianism set in a farmyard. Bowker details Gollancz's rejection of the novel, despite having particularly asked to be considered as the publisher. Orwell now was aggressively anti-Communist, and the British Left was distancing itself from him, partly for fear of alienating a key ally—the Soviet Union—during World War II. Another publisher, Jonathan Cape, rejected the book after consulting Peter Smollett—an official at the Ministry of Information who was later discovered to be a Soviet spy. Bowker details T. S. Eliot's rejection of the book for Faber and Faber, on the grounds that *Animal Farm* was "Trotskyite"; he quotes Eliot's now-famous conclusion that "what was needed, was not more communism but more public-spirited pigs" (qtd. in Bowker 313). The publication news was equally bleak in France, and again Orwell was astonished. Bowker reveals that Yvonne Davet, a translator, wrote, "I am afraid that no French publisher will agree to compromise himself by publishing a book which speaks ill of the Communists" (qtd. in Bowker 338).

Finally, Secker and Warburg published *Animal Farm* in London in 1945, and Harcourt followed in New York a year later. It became a great success. Peter Davison also provides full details of the publishing history, showing that by the time of Orwell's death in 1950, 617,000 copies had been issued worldwide. Davison cites a number of important reviews from the many written at the time of initial publication. Tosco Fyvel in *Tribune* called it a "gentle satire on a certain State and on the illusions of an age which may already be behind us" (qtd. in Orwell, *Complete Works* 17: 253). Julian Symons called this insufficient: "Should we not expect, in *Tribune* at least, acknowledgement of the fact that it is a satire not at all gentle upon a particular State—Soviet Russia?" (qtd. in Orwell 17: 253). Another reviewer, Simon Watson Taylor, concludes, "I am prepared to claim on behalf of Mr. Orwell that *Animal Farm* is of far greater significance than its unassuming title would suggest" (qtd. in Orwell 17: 253). Today, it is a world classic; although Raymond Williams argues that it lives in the shadow of *Nineteen Eighty-Four*. He says that *Animal Farm* "is seen as a text appropriate for secondary level teaching, while its successor is 'for grown ups'" (101).

Nineteen Eighty-Four (1949)

Upon the publication of *Nineteen Eighty-Four*, Aldous Huxley, creator of another famous dystopia, wrote to Orwell saying, "The nightmare of *Nineteen Eighty-Four* is destined to modulate into the nightmare of a world having more resemblances to that which I imagined in *Brave New World*" (qtd. in Orwell, *Collected Works* 20: 177). Huxley appears to have read the novel as pure prophecy and not as a disguised attack on the nature of global politics being played out in the decade of the 1940s. In both the United States and Great Britain, *Nineteen Eighty-Four* was read widely, and there was a critical frenzy surrounding what it meant. Peter Davison's *The Complete Works of George Orwell* gives full details of the critical storm that followed publication. Some read the book as an attack upon socialism; others read it as being too pessimistic and alarming; and one dismissed Orwell as "not in full command of his material" (qtd. in Orwell, *Collected Works* 20: 128).

Such was the furor and misunderstanding surrounding *Nineteen Eighty-Four* that Orwell issued a statement saying that in no way was his book an attack on the state or socialism per se, and that as a member of the British Labour Party, he supported Labour Prime Minister Clement Attlee and his government (see *Collected Works* 20: 134–36).

A critical body of work largely hostile to Orwell's writing appears in Christopher Norris's *Inside the Myth*, published in 1984. Subtitled *Orwell: Views from the Left*, many (though not all) of its essays were strongly anti-Orwell; and the book's pro- and anti-Orwell tug-of-war is a good example of how Orwell's work tends to polarize critical opinion. Alan Brown cautioned that Orwell's kind of moral writing leads to a false feeling of objectivity. The reader is somehow *bound* or seduced into swallowing the point of view whole and uncritically: "The binding together of morality and objectivity works to erase our sense of point of view in reading Orwell. . . . Statements attributed to the author take on an oracular and incontestable value" (Brown 43). However, Antony Easthope did not share Brown's and the others' views. He noted that Patrick Parrinder was too hasty in his judgment when he wrote, "*Nineteen Eighty-Four*, after two decades in which it was read with the utmost seriousness as a political prophecy, is now taking its place . . . as a science fiction story" (qtd. in Easthope 263). Easthope's reply to the clamor of dismissive comment was: "It is hard to know what one is doing in trying to *refute* or bring evidence against *Nineteen Eighty-Four*" (267). Extending such a view would be Robert Giroux, who wrote, "With two notable exceptions—Anthony Burgess and Mary Lee Settle—no writer seems to have perceived that Orwell's book was dealing not with the future but the present" (qtd. in Orwell, *Collected Works* 20: 19).

Some reactions to Orwell's depiction of the "proles" in this novel are strong indeed. Beatrix Campbell, among others, believes that Orwell has nothing but contempt for "the people." She writes: "Despite his wish to invest his revolutionary optimism in the people, what [Orwell] feels for the common people edges on contempt. Actually, he thinks they're dead common" (127). John Rodden argues that such negative assertions have perhaps had the effect of fomenting critical prejudice against Orwell. He says that reception of Orwell's work is often tinged with preconceptions about his dislikes. In fact, Rodden has identified an ideological bias against Orwell running through much feminist criticism (and his analysis could equally apply to class-sensitive treatment of Orwell's work): "'Gender-tinged' images of the author get disseminated. . . . Gender-sensitive critiques bear on the formation of reputations. . . . Intellectual reference groups and ideological allegiances shape critical response" ("Sexist" 33).

Rodden further provides an excellent breakdown and analysis of what he calls the "incredible and unprecedented" impact *Nineteen Eighty-Four* had on the media when the year 1984 approached. He also points out that it topped the best-seller list, again unprecedented for a book thirty-five years old. In the chapter "Countdown to 1984: The Public Writer" in his 1989 book *The Politics of Literary Reputation*, Rodden details the numerous television broadcasts, particularly in Great Britain and the United States, that celebrated everything from Orwell's life to the relevance and meaning of the novel for the late twentieth century. He refers to the pop-cultural "absurdities and spinoffs" the novel generated. Rodden also makes a strong case for thinking that the title of the book is actually one of the reasons for its enduring legacy: "In seizing a calendar year as his own, Orwell not only etched his own name in history but blackened a segment of time" (*Politics* 284). Daniel Lea's *George Orwell:* Animal Farm/Nineteen Eighty-Four: *A Reader's Guide to Essential Criticism* (2001) is a good guide to the varying critical receptions of the novel.

"A Hanging" (1931) and "Shooting an Elephant" (1936)

These two essays remain classic pieces, much revered for their symbolic depiction of the evils of colonial domination. However, arguably since Bernard Crick's questioning of the truth of both incidents in his 1980 Orwell biography (that is, Orwell may not have actually witnessed a hanging or shot an elephant), reception of Orwell's journalistic accounts has been complicated to an even greater degree than it was in the wake of *Down and Out in Paris and London* and *Homage to Catalonia*. Since Crick's biography, critics seem almost obligated to temper their appreciation with the question, "Did this actually happen?"

Peter Davison urges us to ignore the question altogether: "Orwell's fictionalising . . . is acceptable because the 'truth' being offered is independent of the artistic reorganisation" (43). Peter Marks agrees. He writes, referring to both essays, "Orwell's use of the personal in eyewitness, then, has importance both in terms of the narrative and ideology. . . . It seems clear that it is unnecessary to situate Orwell within either piece to validate interpretation. . . . The invocation of Orwell as narrator is superfluous to an understanding of that tale" (91).

"The Sporting Spirit" (1945)

This essay shows very well how Orwell could ignite debate instantly, and also drive people to disagree with him violently. In "The Sporting Spirit," Orwell makes the claim that "sport is an unfailing cause of ill-will" (*Complete Works* 17: 440). The match he observed was between a Russian soccer team, the Moscow Dynamos, and England's Arsenal. It was part of the Dynamos' 1945 tour of Britain. Orwell records that "a British and a Russian came to blows and the crowd booed the referee" (440–41). He concludes, "If you want to add to the vast fund of ill-will existing in the world at this moment, you could hardly do it better than by a series of football matches between Jews and Arabs, Germans and Czechs, Indians and British, Russians and Poles" (442). The essay was published in *Tribune* and triggered a deluge of letters to the editor. E. S. Fayers wrote, "George Orwell is always interesting. But he does write some bilge"; Fayers believes that Orwell is "falling into the error of intellectual contempt for the 'mob'" (17: 443). He feels Orwell sees ordinary people as "sadistic morons." He ends by saying Orwell has missed a lot of fun in not liking football. The debate highlights the familiar contrasting reactions to Orwell's ideas. Another response runs, "I wish to thank George Orwell for his article . . . the most intelligently written on the subject I have read" (17: 445).

"Politics and the English Language" and "The Prevention of Literature" (both 1946)

These two essays are yet another example of how Orwell polarizes critical opinion. "Politics and the English Language," with its six rules for good writing, remains one of Orwell's most-referenced essays. John Rodden calls it Orwell's "most famous essay." Marshall Berman says of the essay: "I've taught [it] many times to very different groups in different decades, with uniformly great results" (qtd. in Rodden, *Every Intellectual* 152). D. J. Taylor notes that in this essay, Orwell "foreshadows the basis of 'Newspeak,'" the language of political control he created for *Nineteen Eighty-Four* (Taylor 376). However, Geoffrey Pullum considers "Politics and the English Language" to be "pointless and unfollowable." The title of his 2008 essay is a provocatively open insult to Orwell: "A Load of Old Orwellian Cobblers from Fisk," deriding another author's list of clichés to avoid.

"The Prevention of Literature," about freedom of expression on the Left, received a similar response. Randall Swingler wrote a lengthy and spirited reply ("The Right to Free Expression") to Orwell's essay, demanding that Orwell define what he meant by terms such as "totalitarianism." It also, among other things, asked that Orwell support his claims against Communists (of which Swingler was one) with factual evidence. Orwell did indeed reply, to each question. He ends with: "As to the Russian 'myth,' I was referring—as I think Mr. Swingler knows—to those glowing prospectuses presented to us day after day and week after week by Messrs. Pat Sloan, the Dean of Canterbury, Ivor Montagu and all the other paid and unpaid apologists of totalitarianism in this country" (*Complete Works* 18: 442–43). One can feel the sarcasm in Orwell's reply to someone he clearly counts among the apologists for Soviet Communism.

"Inside the Whale" (1940)

Jeffrey Meyers says that, in "Inside the Whale," Orwell "defined his own place in contemporary literature by means of a sympathetic contrast to Henry Miller and to the main literary traditions of the Twenties and Thirties" (*Orwell: Wintry Conscience* 206). Orwell greatly admired Henry Miller's work. In this essay, Orwell is discussing the American novelist's first book, *Tropic of Cancer* (1934). Orwell maintains that Miller's is a "human voice among the bomb-explosions, a friendly American voice, 'innocent of public-spiritedness'" (*Collected Works* 12: 110). In many respects, through praise of Miller, Orwell is hinting at his own preference for writing about ordinary, nonpolitical people. Meyers gives a good account of how "Inside the Whale" was received:

> Critics responded favorably to Orwell's blend of political and literary analysis, and praised its sanity and sharpness. . . . V. S. Pritchett praised the "lucid revelation of a mind that is alive, individual and nonconforming." Queenie Leavis, in *Scrutiny*, was one of the first critics to draw attention to the distinctive qualities of Orwell's criticism, and recognized the value of his personal experience: "He has lived an active life among all classes and in several countries, he isn't the usual parlour-Bolshevik seeing literature through political glasses" (*Orwell: Wintry Conscience* 207).

I say more about "Inside the Whale" in my essay "Orwell's Documentaries of the 1930s."

"The Lion and the Unicorn: Socialism and the English Genius" (1941)

In this essay about the political situation in Great Britain during World War II, Orwell is demonstrating that he is not interested in political theory but in what can be done practically to improve society. Again, Jeffrey Meyers summarizes this essay well, noting that it "offered socialistic solutions to wartime problems: nationalization of major industries, limitation of incomes, reform of education, Dominion status for India," and so on (*Orwell: Wintry Conscience* 207).

D. J. Taylor writes that the essay "is the first considerable statement of Orwell's view of 'Englishness' and national identity" (289). Describing Orwell's assertion that in order to win the war, socialism had to be established, Taylor points to the radicalism of the essay's message: "In the context of 1940 this was incendiary stuff" (290).

"Such, Such Were the Joys" (1952; published posthumously)

Regarding "Such, Such Were the Joys," Orwell's grim account of his English preparatory school experience, Peter Davison draws attention to the unexpected beginning of the essay. He writes that Orwell does not begin with a description of his school, as one might expect, "but with a vivid and painful account of how, soon after his arrival, he reverted to wetting the bed and the physical punishment that induced. Because he writes so personally, this has been assumed by many readers to be factual. However, it is likely that Orwell has imaginatively taken the experience of another boy as his own for dramatic effect" (in Orwell, *Lost Orwell* 202–03).

Jacintha Buddicom, Orwell's childhood friend, reinforces this view and states in her book of reminiscences, *Eric and Us*, "I can guarantee that the 'I' of 'Such, Such Were the Joys' is quite unrecognizable as

Eric as we knew him then" (45). Again, Orwell, while conceivably misrepresenting what actually happened, is not misrepresenting his own emotional experience.

Conclusion

From all that has been said and referred to so far, it is clear that there has and continues to be a mixed reception to Orwell's literary output. Geoffrey Wheatcroft repeats a familiar sentiment when he writes that Orwell's books are no more than "projections of his own self-pity," and that "[his] posthumous reputation is close to being literary fraud" (10–11). Yet what is striking when scrutinizing Orwell criticism is the dearth of reference to his actual words. In his study of Orwell's essay-istic and novelistic style, Håkan Ringbom writes, "Among other words used to describe [Orwell's] style are 'nervous, flexible and lucid'. . . . Only rarely would such statements be supported by explanatory com-ments or even by illustrative quotations from Orwell's works." (9) One needs to bear this in mind when reading conclusions such as the following: "[Orwell's] four prewar efforts constitute a sort of amateur throat clearing" (Hitchens 133).

We can end this essay with John Carey, who noted the dismissive and negative strain running through the reception history of Orwell's work. Of D. J. Taylor's commentary he writes: "[Taylor] leaves out [Orwell's] greatest achievement. The secret of his style is its invisibil-ity. [Orwell] wrote the most vibrant, surprising prose of the twentieth century, but disguised it as ordinary prose" ("Invisible Man" 35).

Works Cited

Alldritt, Keith. *The Making of George Orwell: An Essay in Literary History*. London: Arnold, 1969.

Ash, Timothy Garton. "Orwell in 1998." *New York Review of Books* 22 Oct. 1998: 10+.

Beddoe, Dierdre. "Hindrances and Help-Meets: Women in the Writings of George Orwell." *Inside the Myth: Orwell: Views from the Left*. Ed. Christopher Norris. London: Lawrence, 1984. 139–54.

Bergonzi, Bernard. *Reading the Thirties: Texts and Contexts*. London: Macmillan, 1978.

Bowker, Gordon. *George Orwell*. London: Little, 2003.

Brown, Alan. "Examining Orwell: Political and Literary Values in Education." *Inside the Myth: Orwell: Views from the Left*. Ed. Christopher Norris. London: Lawrence, 1984. 39–61.

Buddicom, Jacintha. *Eric and Us*. London: Frewin. 1974.

Calder, Jenni. *Chronicles of Conscience: A Study of George Orwell and Arthur Koestler*. London: Secker, 1968.

Campbell, Beatrix. "Orwell: Paterfamilias or Big Brother?" *Inside the Myth: Orwell: Views from the Left*. Ed. Christopher Norris. London: Lawrence, 1984. 126–38.

Carey, John. *The Faber Book of Utopias*. London: Faber, 1999.

_____. "The Invisible Man." *Sunday Times* 18 May 2003: 35–36.

Connolly, Mark. *Orwell and Gissing*. New York: Lang, 1997.

Crick, Bernard. *George Orwell: A Life*. London: Secker, 1980.

Davison, Peter. *George Orwell: A Literary Life*. London: Macmillan, 1996.

Eagleton, Terry. *Exiles and Emigrés: Studies in Modern Literature*. London: Chatto, 1970.

_____. "Reach-Me-Down Romantic." *London Review of Books*, 19 June 2003: 6–9.

Easthope, Antony. "Fact and Fantasy in *Nineteen Eighty-Four*." *Inside the Myth: Orwell: Views from the Left*. Ed. Christopher Norris. London: Lawrence, 1984. 263–85.

Fowler, Roger. *The Language of George Orwell*. London: Macmillan, 1995.

_____. *Literature as Social Discourse: Structuralism, Linguistics and the Study of Literature*. Oxford: Oxford UP, 1986.

_____. *Style and Structure in Literature*. Oxford: Basil Blackwell, 1975.

Fyvel, T. R. *George Orwell: A Personal Memoir*. London: Weidenfeld, 1982.

Goodall, Peter. "Common Decency and the Common People in the Writing of George Orwell." *Durham University Journal* 80.1 (1991): 75–83.

Hamilton, Ian. "Eric the Nerd." *London Review of Books* 29 Oct. 1998: 18–20.

Hannington, Wal. *The Problem of the Distressed Areas*. London: Gollancz, 1937.

Hitchens, Christopher. *Orwell's Victory*. London: Lane, 2002.

Hunter, Lynette. *George Orwell: The Search for a Voice*. Milton Keynes: Open UP, 1984.

_____. "Stories and Voices in Orwell's Early Narratives." *Inside the Myth: Orwell: Views from the Left*. Ed. Christopher Norris. London: Lawrence, 1984. 163–82.

Hynes, Samuel. *The Auden Generation: Literature and Politics in England in the 1930s*. 1972. New York: Viking, 1976.

Kerr, Douglas. *George Orwell*. Tavistock, England: Northcote House, 2003.

Lea, Daniel, ed. *George Orwell: Animal Farm/Nineteen Eighty-Four: A Reader's Guide to Essential Criticism*. Basingstoke, England: Palgrave, 2001.

Lee, Robert A. *Orwell's Fiction*. Notre Dame: U of Notre Dame P, 1969.

Mander, John. *The Writer and Commitment*. London: Secker, 1961.

Marks, Peter. "The Ideological Eye-Witness: An Examination of the Eye-Witness in Two Works by George Orwell." *Subjectivity and Literature from the Romantics to the Present Day*. Ed. Philip Shaw and Peter Stockwell. London: Pinter, 1991. 85–92.

Meyers, Jeffrey, ed. *George Orwell: The Critical Heritage*. 1975. New York: Routledge, 1997.

_____. *Orwell: Wintry Conscience of a Generation*. London: Norton, 2000.

_____. *A Reader's Guide to George Orwell*. London: Thames, 1975.

Meyers, Valerie. *George Orwell, 1903–1950*. Basingstoke: Macmillan, 1991.

Orwell, George. *The Collected Essays, Journalism, and Letters of George Orwell*. Ed. Ian Angus and Sonia Orwell. 4 vols. London: Secker, 1968.

_____. *The Complete Works of George Orwell*. Ed. Peter Davison. 20 vols. London: Secker, 2000.

_____. *The Lost Orwell: Being a Supplement to "The Complete Works of George Orwell."* Ed. Peter Davison. London: Timewell, 2006.

Patai, Daphne. *The Orwell Mystique: A Study in Male Ideology*. Amherst: U of Massachusetts P, 1984.

Pullum, Geoffrey. "A Load of Old Orwellian Cobblers from Fisk." *Language Log* 31 Aug. 2008. Web. 13 Oct. 2011.

Ringbom, Håkan. *George Orwell as Essayist: A Stylistic Study*. Abo: Abo Akademi, 1973.

Rodden, John. *Every Intellectual's Big Brother: George Orwell's Literary Siblings*. Austin: U of Texas P, 2006.

_____. *The Politics of Literary Reputation: The Making and Claiming of "St. George" Orwell*. Oxford: Oxford UP, 1989.

_____. "'A Sexist After All?': The Feminists' Orwell." *New Orleans Review* 17.1 (1990): 33–46.

Seed, David. "Disorientation and Commitment in the Fiction of Empire: Kipling and Orwell." *Dutch Quarterly Review of Anglo-American Letters* 14.4 (1984): 269–80.

Shelden, Michael. *Orwell: The Authorised Biography*. London: Heinemann, 1991.

Smyer, Richard I. *Primal Dream and Primal Crime: Orwell's Development as a Psychological Novelist*. Columbia: U of Missouri P, 1979.

Stanksy, Peter, and William Abrahams. *Orwell: The Transformation*. London: Constable, 1979.

Taylor, D. J. *Orwell: The Life*. London: Chatto, 2003.

Ward, Colin. "Orwell and Anarchism." *George Orwell at Home (and Among the Anarchists): Essays and Photographs*. Ed. Vernon Richards. London: Freedom, 1998. 15–48.

Wheatcroft, Geoffrey. "George At 100." *Prospect* June 2003: 10–11.

Williams, Raymond. *Orwell*. 1971. Glasgow: Collins, 1978.

Wykes, David. *A Preface to George Orwell*. London: Longman, 1987.

CRITICAL READINGS

Orwell's Documentaries of the 1930s_____

Orwell first gained national recognition as the author of *The Road to Wigan Pier* in 1937, a gritty documentary of the plight of coal miners in the industrial north of England that included bracing autobiographical testimony about Orwell's own views of socialism. It was a selection of the Left Book Club and sold more than 40,000 copies. Yet the book differed radically from the socialist reportage of the day and offended many left-wing sensibilities. After finishing the book, Orwell traveled to Spain, from which emerged his eulogy to the anti-Franco forces, *Homage to Catalonia*, in 1938. Many would challenge his view of events, and we shall look at the key areas of controversy. These two books were preceded by Orwell's debut as a writer, the brilliant nonfiction work *Down and Out in Paris and London* (1933), his report on poverty and transient life in London and Paris during the Depression (also not without its detractors). This essay will focus on these three major works as it discusses Orwell's development as a controversial and complex prose writer with a simple humanitarian message.

Down and Out in Paris and London (1933)

Arguably, one of the reasons for writing this book was for Orwell to demonstrate his firm belief that "the average millionaire is only the average dishwasher dressed in a new suit" (Orwell 1: 152). Throughout the book, Orwell demonstrates his conviction that "all men are equal" (the revolutionary ideal corrupted into "all animals are equal, but some animals are more equal than others" in *Animal Farm*). Orwell wrote *Down and Out* after he had resigned his post as a colonial policeman in Burma, turning his back on privilege and power. He returned to a Europe in the depths of an economic depression. Clearly Orwell was worried about what kinds of inequalities would be exploited by a desperately poor society.

One must remember that ideas of eugenics (a movement popular in the early twentieth century that sought to strengthen society by discouraging reproduction in whole classes of people deemed undesirable) had been aired for some decades, particularly by intellectuals like Aldous Huxley (author of *Brave New World*). Consider H. G. Wells's famous *Anticipations of the Reaction of Mechanical and Scientific Progress upon Human Life and Thought*, written in 1901:

> It has become apparent that whole masses of human population are, as a whole, inferior in their claim upon the future, to other masses, that they cannot be given opportunities or trusted with the power as the superior peoples are trusted, that their characteristic weaknesses are contagious and detrimental in the civilizing fabric, and that their range of incapacity tempts and demoralizes the strong. To give them equality is to sink to their level, to protect and cherish them is to be swamped in their fecundity. . . .
>
> The ethical system of these men of the new republic, the ethical system which will dominate the world state, will be shaped primarily to favor the procreation of what is fine and efficient and beautiful in humanity. (314, 322)

Orwell's lifelong ambivalence about Wells, his love/hate relationship with the man and his work, had much to do with Wells's scientific extremism. Strong in Orwell's mind, too, was Jonathan Swift's eighteenth-century novel *Gulliver's Travels*, which Orwell had read and enjoyed as a young boy. While greatly appreciating Swift's story, as he did much of Wells's work, Orwell was nevertheless alarmed and appalled by the views it expressed. Referring to Swift's portrayal of human beings as savage "Yahoos"—which Orwell, like many other readers, saw as a direct attack on the masses or working classes—he wrote: "[Swift's] vision of society was so penetrating, and yet . . . it's false. He couldn't see what the simplest person sees, that life is worth living and human beings, even if they're dirty and ridiculous, are mostly decent" (14: 161).

Thus, despite his admiration of Wells and Swift, and in contrast to his contemporaries' dalliances with eugenics, Orwell began his writing career strongly opposed to the idea of innate privilege. However, it must be said that, for the most part, *Down and Out* does not hammer out a political message, but rather details Orwell's experiences, presenting a straightforward exploration of the effects of poverty on individuals:

> It is altogether curious, your first contact with poverty. You have thought so much about poverty—it is the thing you have feared all your life, the thing you knew would happen to you sooner or later; and it is all so utterly and prosaically different. You thought it would be quite simple; it is extraordinarily complicated. You thought it would be terrible; it is merely squalid and boring. (1: 76)

Yet questions about Orwell's reportage—specifically, the question of his reliability as an objective observer when detailing the lives of the poor—have often shadowed this work. A prominent and respected critic who raised such questions is Lynette Hunter. Hunter's analysis of Orwell's depiction of the poor is interesting because she believes, as many critics do, that Orwell is incapable of escaping his upper-class prejudice; however, she argues that Orwell is actually attempting to draw our attention to his own biases. She insists, as many have done in relation to Orwell's authority, that "any observer is governed by the condition of his background" (Hunter 15). Significantly, hard evidence of this so-called bias is missing. There are no clear-cut examples of Orwell's class feeling, and this is precisely what makes her analysis interesting: even someone taking the time to be sympathetic appears to be operating within a bias of her own. She is *convinced* that Orwell cannot escape his background.

Down and Out opens with a description of a landlady, Madame Monce, who is described as yelling in the street. Orwell details how "her bare feet [were] stuck into sabots and her grey hair was streaming down" (1: 1). The street is described as "a ravine of tall leprous houses, lurching towards one another in queer attitudes, as though they had all been frozen in the act of collapse" (1). If anything, particularly when one compares this opening to that of *The Road to Wigan Pier* (as we shall see later), Orwell is steering well clear of condescension in these scenes. The narrative continues: "The Paris slums are a gathering-place for eccentric people—people who have fallen into solitary half-mad grooves of life and given up trying to be normal or decent. Poverty frees them from ordinary standards of behaviour, just as money frees people from work" (7). In these descriptions, Hunter says Orwell was "blinkered" and "prejudiced." Orwell biographer D. J. Taylor dismisses the scenes, particularly the dialogues, as "stagy" (see "George Orwell's Critical Reception" on page 95). In describing his lodging house, Orwell says it is dirty, but "homelike," and the owners are "good sorts." Of the varied population in the quarter, Orwell says of some that they are "fantastically poor." How one can read prejudice into such adjectives is unclear. Orwell finishes the first chapter with this: "I am trying to describe the people in our quarter, not for the mere curiosity, but because they are all part of the story. Poverty is what I am writing about, and I had my first contact with poverty in this slum" (9).

For the first part of the book, Hunter believes that Orwell is attempting to point out his own naïveté. She feels that he at first believed the outlandish and perverse tales of sexual exploits told to him by a local eccentric named Charlie. Hunter argues that Orwell shows himself to have later moved to a place of enlightenment: "Charlie's third story . . . provides the denouement to Part One of the book. He [Orwell] prefaces the story with the remark, 'Very likely Charlie was lying as usual, but it was a good story.' There is no doubt how we are to read it. Unlike the first tale which took the narrator in . . . this tale is retold specifically as a story" (Hunter 18). I would suggest that the phrase "as usual" indicates Orwell had never believed a word that was said by Charlie and therefore was never taken in. Interestingly, Charlie is from a well-off family and lives on an allowance—if anything, one could imagine Orwell having a good deal of inverted snobbery for such a "parasitic" figure. He is the only person described with revulsion: "[Charlie] is, somehow, profoundly disgusting to see." Orwell also writes: "[Charlie] was a curious specimen. . . . I describe him, just to show what diverse characters could be found flourishing in the Coq d'Or quarter" (1: 14).

I detail Hunter's interpretation of Orwell's so-called prejudice because it appears, owing to her inability to provide examples, that this is a widely held assumption that has failed to prove its case. Certainly, it demonstrates well the evils of which critics suspect the "old Etonian." And yet Orwell's narration is not altogether trustworthy as a faithful account of *his* experiences alone; for though an exercise in reportage, *Down and Out* shows signs of literary borrowings—a liberty Orwell would constantly allow himself when writing. In the second part, where Orwell is living the precarious life of a vagrant tramp in southern England, one finds echoes of nineteenth-century novelist George Gissing. Of the animosity Orwell and his fellow tramps sometimes felt toward the people who gave them charitable assistance, he writes: "What could a few women and old men do against a hundred hostile tramps? They were afraid of us, and we were frankly bullying them. It was our revenge upon them for having humiliated us by feeding us" (1: 163). This frank portrayal of ungratefulness and hostility to charity is reminiscent of Gissing's "soup-kitchen revolt" in his 1889 novel *The Nether World*: "Gratitude, quotha?—Nay, do *you* be grateful that these hapless, half-starved women do not turn and rend you. At present they satisfy themselves with insolence. Take it silently, you who at all events hold some count of their dire state; and endeavour to feed them without arousing animosity!" (252).

Orwell's strongest attack in the book, however—or at least the one that caused most offense when the book was published—was not his socialist contention that all men are equal (invariably paid scant attention by critics then and now), but rather, his verdict on the quality and necessity of expensive hotels, taken from his time employed as a dishwasher at a grand hotel (Hotel X, he called it). After describing cockroaches in the bread bin and filthy, grimy preparation surfaces, he writes:

In the kitchen the dirt was worse. It is not a figure of speech, it is a mere statement of fact to say that a French cook will spit in the soup. . . . He is an artist, but his art is not cleanliness. . . . When a steak, for instance, is brought up for the head cook's inspection he does not handle it with a fork. He picks it up in his fingers and slaps it down, runs his thumb round the dish and licks it to taste the gravy. (1: 73)

Orwell concludes that "the more one pays for food, the more sweat and spittle one is obliged to eat with it." This was in the days before government health inspectors and therefore entirely feasible. Moreover, Orwell does go into some detail about how demands on appearance create a skewed focus by waiters and chefs who are driven by efficiency. Certainly such radically challenging ideas were to be Orwell's signature tune, as we will see in our examination of his next two books.

The Road to Wigan Pier (1937)

The Road to Wigan Pier appeared in the same year as Wal Hannington's book of social reportage, *The Problem of the Distressed Areas.* Both were released by left-leaning publisher Victor Gollancz as part of the same general awareness-raising project. The differences in the respective treatments of the distressed areas Orwell and Hannington visited are marked. And here it is worth giving some background to the writers: Hannington was a founding member of the Communist Party of Great Britain, which Orwell despised, seeing its members as no more than Stalinist apologists. Of the CPGB members, Orwell wrote, "After all the years they have had on the job, none of these men can imagine any occupation except boosting Soviet Russia" (15: 107). He also described Hannington as "a poor speaker, using all the padding and clichés of the Socialist orator, and with the wrong kind of cockney accent (once again, though a Communist entirely a bourgeois)" (10: 424). Given this picture of Orwell's views on the far-Left orthodoxy of his day, one can imagine Orwell deliberately going down another path that was not politically correct.

The beginning of *The Road to Wigan Pier* introduces the reader to the filthy lodging house owned by the Brooker family, where Orwell slept in a room that stank like a "ferret's cage," and where he looked on in horror as he was handed bread and butter with the indentation of a dirty black thumbprint; he would eventually flee from the house because of the sight of an over-flowing chamber pot under the table. Almost in its entirety, Orwell's introduction to England's industrial north through the Brooker's lodging house (which also doubled as a tripe shop) is not a flattering portrait: "Mrs. Brooker used to lament by the hour, lying on her sofa, a soft mound of fat and self-pity, saying the same things over and over again" (5: 10).

Douglas Kerr considers the implications of such a beginning in a book where one might expect the voice of a sympathetic socialist correspondent. Kerr writes:

> In its way it is a memorable portrait, but it is not one that you would choose to illustrate a theme of the dignity of working people, nor (since the narrator, a middle-class visitor from the south of England, is the principal victim of the Brookers) their exploitation. It raises the question of what the narrator is doing, and what he is doing there. These are questions that open into the perennial Orwell issues of subjectivity and genre. (40)

Indeed, why *would* Orwell wish to begin a documentary on the working-class poor in such a deliberately incendiary manner? One answer could be that Orwell prefers to upset expectations, desiring instead to lift the subject matter from its somewhat scripted framework in order to give a more realistic and balanced account of working-class life; they are people, after all, and thus subject to the same folly and vice as the rest of the population.

This theory gains ground when one compares Orwell's opening with Wal Hannington's: "During the winter months of 1933–4, the distressed areas of South Wales, Cumberland, Durham, Northumberland, and the West of Scotland were the scenes of turbulent working-class demonstrations and agitations against the Government on the question of unemployment" (Hannington 1). This is clearly far more in keeping with a book of social reportage, and is what a reader would expect from a man who is also the leader of the National Unemployed Workers' Movement (NUWM). Orwell actually wrote a review of Hannington's book praising it (see 11: 98–99). However, Hannington's opening, like much of his book, is a mere tabulation of facts. It is not memorable or literary.

Another answer to why Orwell would seek out the seedier side of working-class life, with the express intent of beginning his commissioned documentary with a focus on all that is squalid, may lie in Orwell's review of Henry Miller's *Tropic of Cancer* (1936). Orwell's praise of Miller's novel says much about his dislike for the idealization of humanity. Despite what Orwell sees as a callous coarseness in the treatment of the sexual encounters of Miller's characters, whom Orwell describes as the "out-at-elbow, good-for-nothing type," Orwell praises the book because he finds it a welcome departure from "the monstrous soppification," or sentimentalization, of sexuality that he believes has been prevalent "in most of the fiction of the past hundred years" (10: 405). Orwell admires Miller for "brutally insisting on the facts," and while Miller may, as far as Orwell is concerned, have swung "the pendulum too far," he adds that nevertheless Miller "does swing it in the right direction" (405).

The pendulum analogy is useful in thinking of Orwell's treatment of his subject in *Wigan Pier*. In his review of *Tropic of Cancer*, Orwell writes that "man is not a Yahoo, but he is rather like a Yahoo and needs to be reminded of it from time to time" (10: 404). Orwell concludes that such honest treatment of human behavior, even if debased and seemingly cruel, is preferable to, for example, "the tee-heeing brightness of *Punch*" and H. G. Wells's "utopiæ infested by nude schoolmarms" (405). Perhaps Orwell felt that the pendulum had swung too far in the direction of an idealized view of the working class. In light of this kind of counteralignment it would seem that Orwell is wishing to smear a little dirt on what he perceives to be an all too squeaky-clean portrayal of the working class and unemployed. This is Orwell, like Miller, "brutally insisting of the facts." The essential point, however, is that Orwell will feel himself to be humanizing rather than insulting and dehumanizing his subject, in the same manner as he perceives Miller to be doing. Orwell insists that *Tropic of Cancer*, while appearing to be "a vilification of human nature" (404), is in fact something approaching its opposite. Orwell wrote his review two years before he went to Wigan, and, of course, after he chronicled his tramping exploits in *Down and Out in Paris and London*, so we must grant that Orwell certainly would have known what his motivations were in focusing on the Brookers and the overall physical and mental squalor of their lodging house.

Interestingly, it was actually the second part of *Wigan Pier* that caused the most outrage, on account of invective such as this: "One sometimes gets the impression that the mere words 'Socialism' and 'Communism' draw towards them with magnetic force every fruit-juice drinker, nudist, sandal-wearer, sex-maniac, Quaker, 'Nature Cure' quack, pacifist and feminist in England" (5: 161). There hardly exists a piece of criticism (either hostile or sympathetic) of *Wigan Pier* that does not cite this quotation. In the main, it has been seen as Orwell losing balance in his treatment of the Left. At a lecture held in England at Wedgwood Memorial College to commemorate the centenary of Orwell's birth (June 25, 2003), Colin Ward, author of the essay "Orwell and Anarchism," was asked to leave out the quotation from his talk because it had been used by every single speaker who had gone before. I believe it was meant to stir debate. Orwell gives many accounts in *Wigan Pier* of the alienating effects of "eccentric" socialists on ordinary people. The insult could also be a lesson in how to make writing memorable; Wal Hannington's book is now utterly forgotten.

In view of the tense and uncertain times in which Orwell was living (fascism was taking hold in Europe, and there was sky-high unemployment, mass poverty, and looming war), Keith Alldritt hints at an excuse for Orwell's rudeness. Referring to Orwell calling Anglo-American writer W. H. Auden "a sort of gutless Kipling," Alldritt writes, "The bad temper which informs these value judgments derives most significantly from Orwell's sense of the triviality of contemporary literary culture" (81). Orwell was out of patience with Auden for writing about "necessary murder" in his poem "Spain," relating to the Spanish Civil War; Orwell saw Auden as someone who could afford to trivialize murder because he had not engaged in war himself. (Auden later omitted the line.) One could extend Alldritt's mitigating view to Orwell's attack on socialists (above), seeing it as Orwell's exasperation with what he saw as the socialists' failure to achieve positive social change in the 1930s; this is essentially what the second half of *Wigan Pier* is arguing. Leading up to the insulting quotation above, Orwell meticulously catalogues the failure of the Left to get the people on their side when Britain is "in a very serious mess" (5: 158). His frustration is everywhere apparent: "Yet the fact that we have got to face is that Socialism is *not* establishing itself" (159; emphasis in original).

What has been discussed so far does not do justice to the positive treatment Orwell also gives to his subject matter, that is, to the ordinary nonpoliticized poor. The following (now an oft-quoted passage) concerns a young woman he witnessed attempting to unblock a drain. One should notice that Orwell here is airing his convictions about human equality in highlighting how clearly the downtrodden woman is aware of her circumstances:

> It struck me then that we are mistaken when we say that "It isn't the same for them as it would be for us," and that people bred in the slums can imagine nothing but the slums. For what I saw in her face was not the ignorant suffering of an animal. She knew well enough what was happening to her—understood as well as I did how dreadful a destiny it was to be kneeling there in the bitter cold, on the slimy stones of a slum backyard, poking a stick up a foul drain-pipe. (5: 52)

Again, this demonstrates Orwell's desire to make everyone understand that all people are equal, and more, that underprivileged groups need a voice and should not be considered beneath notice, or worse, *eliminated*.

One of the most enduring criticisms of the book is that Orwell neglected to include the work of the trade unions and political activists, particularly those who helped him understand the political situation in the north, and for this reason, Orwell was then and often still is suspected of obscuring the reality or the totality of life in the deprived areas. Given Orwell's dislike of union leaders such as Hannington, it is not difficult to understand why he would wish working people to avoid such ideological contamination. In the book, Orwell talks of the "horrible jargon" used by socialists. He hates such phrases as "bourgeois ideology," "proletarian solidarity," "expropriation of the expropriators," and the "burbling about dialectical materialism"; and furthermore, he writes, "Even the single word 'Comrade' has done its dirty little bit towards discrediting the Socialist movement" (5: 210). Orwell would not wish ordinary people to lose their sound common sense and take up such obfuscating language. Another point to consider is that of John Newsinger, who reminds us of Orwell's true subject, the working class itself:

> More important is the way that [Orwell] makes invisible in the book the network of political activists who assisted him in his investigations. The point is, of course, that he was not writing about working-class political activists, but about the working class. This is not to say that he ignores the role of the Left. According to Orwell, "the best work for the unemployed is being done by the NUWM." (Newsinger 37)

What is clear is that Orwell has a keen sense of selection and the determination to pursue his own literary priorities no matter how potentially damaging to the work's reception.

Homage to Catalonia (1938)

Orwell's experience of fighting in the Spanish Civil War on the side of the anti-Franco forces drew him closer to embracing the idea of socialism; it did much to remove the cynicism with which he had viewed it before. This is from the passage in which he details what he called a "foretaste of Socialism":

> Many of the normal motives of civilised life—snobbishness, money-grubbing, fear of the boss, etc.—had simply disappeared. . . . One had been in a community where hope was more normal than apathy or cynicism, where the word "comrade" stood for comradeship and not . . . humbug. One had breathed the air of equality. . . . And it was here that those few months in the militia were valuable to me. (6: 83–84)

While Orwell had not expressed clear doubts about his commitment to socialism before, the following testifies that in fact he had: "The effect was to make my desire to see Socialism established much more actual than it had been before" (84).

Significantly, Orwell knew he had found himself in the most revolutionary part of Spain. Douglas Kerr stresses that "the book is Orwell's homage to Catalonia (not to Spain)" (56). Orwell was fighting alongside anarchists, among other people; it was their views and behavior that had the most influence on him. Franz Borkenau's *The Spanish Cockpit*, the only book Orwell recommends on the Spanish Civil War in *Homage to Catalonia*, explains the uniqueness of the anarchist attitude: "Anarchism does not believe in the creation of a new world through the improvement of the material conditions of the lower classes, but in the creation of a new world out of the moral resurrection of those classes which have not yet been contaminated by the spirit of mammon and greed" (Borkenau 22). This is not to suggest that Orwell was an anarchist. Take Orwell's own explanation for his brand of socialism:

A Socialist is not obliged to believe that human society can actually be made perfect, but almost any Socialist does believe that it could be a great deal better than it is at present, and that most of the evil that men do results from the warping effects of injustice and inequality. The basis of Socialism is humanism. It can coexist with religious belief, but not with the belief that man is a limited creature who will always misbehave himself if he gets half a chance. (18: 63)

Regarding Orwell's record of his experiences during the Spanish Civil War, it is interesting that in his later essay "Looking Back on the Spanish War," there are significant additions. The essay begins, "Early one morning another man and I had gone out to snipe at the Fascists in the trenches outside Huesca" (13: 501). When a fascist finally comes within sight, Orwell aims his rifle and prepares to fire. However, the enemy soldier, Orwell informs us, "was half-dressed and was holding up his trousers with both hands as he ran. I refrained from shooting at him." The reason Orwell gives for staying his shot is this: "I had come here to shoot at 'Fascists'; but a man who is holding up his trousers isn't a 'Fascist,' he is visibly a fellow creature, similar to yourself, and you don't feel like shooting at him" (501). Why was this account not included in *Homage to Catalonia*? Could it be that it did not actually happen as he recorded it? Regarding the episode, Orwell asks, "What does this incident demonstrate? Nothing very much, because it is the kind of thing that happens all the time in all wars" (501). Given Orwell's deeply moral attitude, one would have to infer that the incident (however real or unreal) is there to demonstrate a moral dilemma that should be no dilemma at all; that is, one is *obliged* to behave as a human being with common human feeling and not as an instrument of mechanical slaughter.

Orwell's meeting with an Italian militiaman in the opening of *Homage to Catalonia* would be another depiction of an encounter with others told specifically to serve as a point. Orwell first sees the soldier attempting, without success, to understand a map. Here is the scene:

"He was standing in profile to me, his chin on his breast, gazing with a puzzled frown at a map which one of the officers had open on the table. . . . Obviously he could not make head or tail of the map; obviously he regarded map-reading as a stupendous intellectual feat" (6: 1).

Orwell continues to detail what he read as great strength of character and innate heroic goodness in the soldier, who moments later steps forward to shake hands with Orwell. This is Douglas Kerr's analysis of their meeting: "Whether or not it actually happened, or happened like that, the meeting is highly charged, crackling with ideological and personal significance. The handclasp represents entry into a community (Orwell was there to enlist), masculine like Orwell's other communities. . . . The image might be that of a propaganda poster—Peasants and Intellectuals Unite!" (54).

Unfaithful recording (or suspicion of it), however, is not so easily forgiven when considering representations of truth that must be historically responsible and that must reflect accurately the political twists and turns as they happened during any given event. A case in point is the crucial question of *what* really was the reason for the Communists'—meaning Stalin's—suppression of, among others, the leftist faction with which Orwell fought? Orwell had joined the POUM, or Partido Obrero e Unificación Marxista (Workers' Party of Marxist Unification), an alliance of leftists not directly affiliated with the Spanish Communists sponsored by the Soviet Union. Did Stalin really believe that Orwell and his comrades were Trotskyist sympathizers, in the pay of Franco, and therefore deliberately attempting to sabotage the Republican cause? At the time, Orwell was adamant that it was almost lunacy to believe anything so blatantly false.

Orwell goes into great detail about the POUM's passionate loyalty to the cause of releasing Spain from Franco's forces. He points out repeatedly that if the POUM were indeed treacherous, it would simply have fought openly on Franco's side. In an appendix, Orwell debunks completely the accusation of treachery, showing that the loyal actions of his fellow soldiers invalidate the allegation that they were all "fascist traitors." Of the notion that the POUM's revolutionary fervor was inadvertently aiding Franco by causing dissent among the leftist militias, Orwell says: "It was arguable—though finally I do not agree—that by pressing for a more revolutionary policy the POUM divided the Government forces and thus aided the Fascists; I think any Government of reformist type would be justified in regarding a party like the POUM as a nuisance. But this is a very different matter from direct treachery" (6: 240–41). Finally, of the dark motives of Stalin, i.e., his wish to scupper the Spanish Civil War while pretending to help it, Orwell was clear: "The Russians were in a position to dictate terms. There is very little doubt that these terms were, in substance, 'Prevent revolution or you get no weapons'" (6: 195).

Undoubtedly, Orwell is obliged on this crucial issue to represent events as they actually happened, as far as he can tell; he cannot afford the artistic license of inventing encounters to suit a moral agenda. If we now compare Orwell's representation of events in Spain with Bill Alexander's account, Orwell can be seen as a distinctly disinterested and objective journalist. Alexander—commander of the British Battalion of the XVth International Brigade—accused Orwell of "obscur[ing] and denigrat[ing] the real issues in the struggle against fascism" (90). Alexander sneers at Orwell's contention that the revolution was cynically betrayed by Stalin. However, from as early as 1936—the beginning of the Spanish Civil War—documents now reveal that Stalin had determined to eliminate the POUM and the other revolutionary militias from the moment he decided the Soviet Union would intervene in the war. Moreover, Alexander's publisher, Lawrence and Wishart (publishers of *Inside the Myth*, in which Alexander's account appears), produced the London edition of Georges Soria's *Trotskyism in the Service of Franco: Facts and Documents on the Activities of the P.O.U.M.* Soria's book repeats claims that the POUM were at times collaborating with Fascist troops. Orwell rejects these claims completely, and was right to do so: Historical evidence has since proven that these claims were false. Moreover, Soria's book was actually part of a Communist

misinformation campaign to blacken the name of the POUM and fo-
ment hatred toward those linked with Leon Trotsky (a Russian Communist, but an enemy of Stalin; see 11: 30–37). In light of this information, Bill Alexander's attempt to undermine Orwell's testimony is
suspicious to say the least.

Now, having made the case for Alexander's clarity of vision regarding Stalin's motives in the Spanish Civil War, Orwell later wavered on
his interpretation of events. In his essay "Looking Back on the Spanish
War," he writes:

> As to the Russians, their motives in the Spanish War are completely in-
> scrutable. Did they . . . intervene in Spain in order to defend democracy
> and thwart the Nazis? . . . Or did they, as the Catholics maintained, inter-
> vene in order to foster revolution in Spain? . . . Or did they, as the Trotsky-
> ists suggested, intervene simply in order to *prevent* a Spanish revolution?
> Then why not have backed Franco? (13: 508)

Orwell wrote this essay around 1942, when Stalin was on the Allied
side, fighting with Britain against the Nazis. Perhaps the emotional atmosphere of the new war served to shake Orwell's conviction or cloud
memory.

Regarding Orwell's depiction of the Italian militiaman (quoted
above), to whom Orwell would dedicate his poem "The Crystal Spirit," Orwell also wrote, "But I . . . knew that to retain my first impression of him I must not see him again" (6: 2). Orwell here is hinting
at his tendency to elevate and beatify individuals; however, perhaps
he feels there are times when it is necessary to do so. It is part of his
balancing of attitudes (perhaps his intent with regard to softening his
condemnation of Stalin at a time when the Soviet Union was helping
defeat an immediate enemy). This resembles Orwell's championing of
Henry Miller's focus on the seedier side of life when there is a trend
toward sanitizing human experience. And this seems to be one of the
prevailing aspects of Orwell's reportage; although seemingly on the

verge of extremism himself, as when living among the "fantastically poor" in Paris, or ridiculing the idle rich (Charlie), or dressing as a tramp in England, or through the varied insults in *Wigan Pier*, or in extolling the values of virtual outcasts such as Miller (whose books were banned in many countries for obscenity), or when siding with the anarchists in Spain—Orwell was in fact trying to find the middle ground and to demonstrate his firm belief that, whether rich or poor, intellectual or uneducated, all men are in the end equal and most are born with innate good sense. Critics may well laugh at Orwell for having such a simplistic view. They may write, as Christopher Norris does, that "Orwell's homespun empiricist outlook—his assumption that the truth was just there to be told in a straightforward, common-sense way—now seems not merely naive but culpably self-deluding" (242). However, the lifelong unshakable devotion Orwell showed in delivering his "simple" message would suggest very strong conviction indeed.

Works Cited

Alexander, Bill. "George Orwell in Spain." *Inside the Myth: Orwell: Views from the Left*. Ed. Christopher Norris. London: Lawrence, 1984. 85–102.

Alldritt, Keith. *The Making of George Orwell: An Essay in Literary History*. London: Arnold, 1969.

Borkenau, Franz. *The Spanish Cockpit: An Eye-Witness Account of the Political and Social Conflicts of the Spanish Civil War*. London: Faber, 1937.

Carey, John. "The Invisible Man." *Sunday Times* 18 May 2003: 35–36.

Gissing, George. *The Nether World*. 1889. Oxford: Oxford UP, 1999.

Hannington, Wal. *The Problem of the Distressed Areas*. London: Gollancz, 1937.

Hunter, Lynette. George Orwell: *The Search for a Voice*. Milton Keynes: Open UP, 1984.

Kerr, Douglas. *George Orwell*. Tavistock: Northcote House, 2003.

Newsinger, John. *Orwell's Politics*. Basingstoke: Palgrave, 2001.

Norris, Christopher, ed. *Inside the Myth: Orwell: Views from the Left*. London: Lawrence, 1984.

Orwell, George. *The Complete Works of George Orwell*. Ed. Peter Davison. 20 vols. London: Secker, 2000.

Taylor, D. J. *Orwell: The Life*. London: Chatto, 2003.

Wells, H. G. *Anticipations of the Reaction of Mechanical and Scientific Progress upon Human Life and Thought*. London: Harper, 1901.

Orwell the Essayist and Journalist_____

James Seaton

George Orwell is known primarily as a political writer. He himself stated, in an often-quoted sentence from his 1946 essay "Why I Write": "Every line of serious work that I have written since 1936 has been written, directly or indirectly, *against* totalitarianism and *for* democratic Socialism, as I understand it" (*Complete Works* 18: 319). Some Orwell commentators stress that Orwell was "*against* totalitarianism" and others emphasize that he was "*for* democratic Socialism." Sometimes a scrupulous interpreter attempts to understand the relationship between what Orwell was "for" and what he was "against." What is rarely questioned, however, is the central importance of Orwell's political opinions themselves, whatever interpretation of them is offered by the critic.

Orwell's essays and journalism are permanently important not because of the political opinions they express but because, when taken as a whole, they articulate a distinctive point of view, a way of looking at the world, a perspective on life comparable in scope, depth, and intensity to that of a great novelist (which Orwell was not). More than half a century later, it seems clear that Orwell was often wrong in his political judgments about contemporary events. Furthermore, he never succeeded in working out a clear vision of the socialism in which he believed so strongly. Orwell remains, however, supremely exemplary as a writer on politics because he refused to subordinate his principles and his outlook to his political opinions, important to him as those opinions were. In the paragraph following Orwell's oft-quoted statement asserting the centrality of politics in his writing, he offers a fuller statement of his writing creed that not only emphasizes the nonpolitical aspects of his outlook, but suggests that he would prefer not to write about politics at all:

> But I could not do the work of writing a book, or even a long magazine article, if it were not also an aesthetic experience. Anyone who cares to examine my work will see that even when it is downright propaganda it

contains much that a full-time politician would consider irrelevant. I am not able, and I do not want, completely to abandon the world-view that I acquired in childhood. So long as I remain alive and well I shall continue to feel strongly about prose style, to love the surface of the earth, and to take a pleasure in solid objects and scraps of useless information. It is no use trying to suppress that side of myself. The job is to reconcile my ingrained likes and dislikes with the essentially public, non-individual activities that this age forces on all of us. (18: 319–20)

From the perspective of the twenty-first century, Orwell's opinions about some of the most important events of his time seem radically wrongheaded. That Orwell was often mistaken in his judgments about contemporary politics does not at all detract from the permanent significance of his writings, but it does suggest that attempts to prove that Orwell would have agreed with one's own views about political events in the twenty-first century are even more pointless than they first appear. George Orwell himself never claimed any special ability to predict the future, and when he became aware that he had been mistaken, he had no qualms about straightforwardly admitting his error. In *Homage to Catalonia* (1938) he went out of his way to "warn everyone against my bias, and I warn everyone against my mistakes" (160), and he repeated his warning at the end of the book: "Beware of my partisanship, my mistakes of fact and the distortion inevitably caused by my having seen only one corner of events" (231). Orwell recorded his belief that no matter which side was victorious in Spain, "the tendency of the post-war Government is bound to be Fascistic," but he characteristically added, "Once again I let this opinion stand, and take the chance that time will do to me what it does to most prophets" (182). In his "London Letter" to *Partisan Review* published in the winter 1944–1945 issue, Orwell declares that "up to at any rate the end of 1942 I was grossly wrong in my analysis of the situation." Although he "tried to tell the truth in these letters," he could see that he had made "many mistaken predictions," as well as "many generalizations based on little or no evidence, and also, from time to time, spiteful or misleading remarks about individuals" (16: 411). As these quotations suggest, Orwell distinguished himself from other political commentators not in his acumen about events but in the moral and intellectual honesty he brought to bear on any subject, political, cultural, or personal, that he discussed.

In the months before and after Prime Minister Neville Chamberlain's capitulation to Adolph Hitler at Munich, Orwell was condemning Chamberlain not as an appeaser but as a warmonger. In June 1938 Orwell explained his decision to join the Independent Labour Party by declaring that it was the only party capable of resisting "the temptation to fling every principle overboard in order to prepare for an imperialist war" (11: 168). In July 1938 Orwell complained that "Chamberlain is preparing for war against Germany," adding that "various sinister mumbles about conscription cannot be explained in any other way" (11: 183). In a letter to Herbert Read dated January 4, 1939, Orwell argued that opposing war against Hitler by words alone was not enough, telling Read, "I believe it is vitally necessary for those of us who intend to oppose the coming war to start organising for illegal anti-war activities" (11: 313).

When nine months later Hitler invaded Poland, and Great Britain declared war against Nazi Germany, Orwell made no attempt to engage in "illegal anti-war activities" but instead tried unsuccessfully to take part in the war effort. The brief explanation of his reversal offered in a January 10, 1940, letter to Geoffrey Gorer seems the fullest Orwell ever offered: "I have so far completely failed to serve HM [His Majesty's] government in any capacity, though I want to, because it seems to me that now we are in this bloody war we have got to win it & I would like to lend a hand" (12: 6). Perhaps because he did not go through any reexamination of his ideas, Orwell immediately began arguing for another thesis that was soon to be proved wrong, declaring that unless England underwent a socialist revolution it could not defeat Nazi Germany. In 1940 Orwell was looking forward to a bloody revolution and decrying as "idiots" those who thought that revolutionary violence was neither necessary nor desirable: "We shall see changes that will surprise the idiots who have no foresight. I dare say the London gutters will have to run with blood. All right, let them, if it is necessary" (12: 272). The "changes" Orwell welcomed were, he insisted, entirely compatible with true patriotism, despite appearances to the contrary: "But when the red militias are billeted in the Ritz I shall still feel that the England I was taught to love so long ago and for such different reasons is somehow persisting" (12: 272). In "The Lion and the Unicorn: Socialism and the English Genius," published in February 1941, Orwell tried to reconcile his support for both the war and revolutionary socialism by arguing that "the war and the revolution are inseparable" (12: 418), so much so that "we cannot win the war without introducing Socialism, nor establish Socialism without winning the war" (421). He offered a program that, as he put it, "aims quite frankly at turning this war into a revolutionary war and England into a Socialist democracy" (422). According to Orwell in early 1941 in "The Lion and the Unicorn," "Either we turn this war into a revolutionary war . . . or we lose it" (428).

In arguing that England could only win the war against Hitler by first undergoing a revolution, Orwell was making an argument similar to the thesis he had advanced in *Homage to Catalonia*, that the Spanish Republic could defeat the fascist leader Francisco Franco only if it first went through a revolution that would establish true socialism. In *Homage to Catalonia* Orwell explains that he arrived in Spain ready to accept "the Communist viewpoint, which boiled down to saying: 'We can't talk of revolution till we've won the war'"(67). Shortly, however, he passionately embraced the opposite view. In *Homage*, Orwell argues that genuine socialist revolution would have increased the chances for victory over Franco not only by raising the morale of the Loyalist forces themselves but also by increasing support for the Loyalist cause from "the workers of the world" (69) outside Spain, encouraging the growth in Spain of a "real popular movement in Franco's rear" (69) and inciting revolt in Morocco.

Later, Orwell came to feel that he had been mistaken in believing that Franco could have been defeated if only Loyalist Spain had undergone a socialist revolution. In an essay probably written in 1942, he conceded that "the Trotskyist thesis that the war could have been won if the revolution had not been sabotaged was probably false. To nationalise factories, demolish churches, and issue revolutionary manifestos would not have made the armies more efficient. The Fascists won because they were the stronger; they had modern arms and the others hadn't. No political strategy could offset that" (13: 507). Orwell, however, never did renounce the conception of the socialist ideal that he gained in his experience in Spain and especially in Barcelona, described so eloquently in *Homage to Catalonia*.

However, it is this conception that, perhaps more than any other aspect of Orwell's legacy, raises questions about his standing as a political thinker. In Barcelona he had found himself for the first time "in a town where the working class was in the saddle" (*Homage* 4). Orwell reports, "I recognized it immediately as a state of affairs worth fighting for" (5). There was scarcity, but "so far as one could judge the people were contented and hopeful" and "Above all, there was a belief in the revolution and the future, a feeling of having suddenly emerged into an era of equality and freedom. Human beings were trying to behave as human beings and not as cogs in the capitalist machine" (6). It is surely the Barcelona of those months that Orwell had in mind when he wrote to Humphrey House in April 1940 that "I have never had the slightest fear of a dictatorship of the proletariat, if it could happen, and certain things I saw in the Spanish war confirmed me in this" (12: 141). In "Looking Back on the Spanish War" Orwell holds on to and reaffirms his memories of that experience as a moral touchstone. In *Homage to Catalonia* he had singled out an Italian volunteer who typified for him "the special atmosphere of that time" (4). In 1942 he hangs on to his memory of the man, whom he met only briefly, as a source of moral certainty: "When I remember—oh, how vividly!—his shabby uniform and fierce, pathetic, innocent face, the complex side-issues of the war seem to fade away and I see clearly that there was at any rate no doubt as to who was in the right" (13: 509).

And yet a look at Orwell's own description in *Homage to Catalonia* of the Italian youth and, more importantly, the situation in Barcelona raises many more questions than it answers about what Orwell presents as a vision of a brief but inspiring realization of the socialist ideal. The Italian volunteer is described on the first page of *Homage to Catalonia* as "a tough-looking youth of twenty-five or six" with "the face of a man who would commit murder and throw away his life for a friend" (3). His face has "both candour and ferocity in it" as well as "the pathetic reverence that illiterate people have for their supposed superiors" (3). It is not clear why encountering a man Orwell describes as both a potential murderer and one willing to die for a friend leads him to feel certainty that the cause such a man is fighting for must be morally right. Orwell, after all, in "Inside the Whale" memorably reproved W. H. Auden for writing about murder like a person "to whom murder is at most a *word*" (italics in original), adding: "Personally I would not speak so lightly of murder. It so happens that I have seen the bodies of numbers of murdered men—I don't mean killed in battle, I mean murdered. Therefore I have some conception of what murder means—the terror, the hatred, the howling relatives, the post-mortems, the blood, the smells" (12: 103). Yet in *Homage to Catalonia* the capacity for murder Orwell intuits in the young Italian somehow helps convince him that the cause for which the youth is volunteering must be morally right.

Rereading Orwell's description of Barcelona, "where the working class was in the saddle," raises second thoughts about the moral standing of the socialist ideal that Barcelona apparently embodied for Orwell. Barcelona was a place where "almost every church had been gutted and its images burnt," where Orwell himself saw some churches "being systematically demolished by gangs of workmen" (*Homage* 4). On the streets "revolutionary posters were everywhere" and "the loud-speakers were bellowing revolutionary songs all day and far into the night" (5). Everybody "wore rough working-class clothes, or blue overalls or some variant of the militia uniform" (5). Orwell found all this "queer and moving," "a state of affairs worth fighting for" (5). From the point of view of the twenty-first century, the scene Orwell describes seems closer to something from Mao's Cultural Revolution or perhaps a scene from Cambodia under the Khmer Rouge than a state of affairs worth fighting for.

Perhaps the most serious moral question arises, however, not from the scene Orwell describes but from his own thoughts taking in what he sees: "Also I believed that things were as they appeared, that this was really a workers' State and that the entire bourgeoisie had either fled, been killed, or voluntarily come over to the workers' side. I did not realize that great numbers of well-to-do bourgeois were simply lying low and disguising themselves as proletarians for the time being" (*Homage* 5). Orwell, that is, on his own showing, did not know and did not care if the "state of affairs worth fighting for" had been achieved by killing a whole class of individuals, apparently including men, women, and children ("the entire bourgeoisie") or by some other means. The discovery that many had been "simply lying low" is presented as a disillusioning fact. If only they had really all been killed, Orwell could have continued to believe "that things were as they appeared, that this was really a workers' State" (5).

Orwell's writings reveal a continuing struggle to work out a conception of socialism that was both morally inspiring and able to withstand critical examination. Often he seemed to admit that socialism had no necessary connection with individual freedoms and was perhaps intrinsically opposed to them. Reviewing Franz Borkenau's *The Totalitarian Enemy*, in May 1940, Orwell asserted emphatically it must be admitted that Nazi Germany was indeed an example of socialism: "National Socialism *is* a form of Socialism, *is* emphatically revolutionary, *does* crush the property owner just as surely as it crushes the worker" (12: 159; italics in original). In 1941, Orwell expressed his belief that a "collectivised economy is bound to come," together with his hope for the emergence of "a form of Socialism which is not totalitarian, in which freedom of thought can survive the disappearance of economic individualism" (12: 505).

Here and elsewhere, Orwell seems to believe that a "collectivised economy" is inevitable, whether desirable or not. That the society of such an economy might be totalitarian had been proved in the Soviet Union and Nazi Germany; that it might be otherwise was uncertain. In 1947 Orwell praised the publication with which he was most identified, *Tribune*, on the grounds that it was "the only existing weekly paper that makes a genuine effort to be both progressive and humane— that is, to combine a radical Socialist policy with a respect for freedom of speech and a civilised attitude toward literature and the arts" (19: 38). Orwell's praise assumes that it was a unique accomplishment deserving special commendation to unite "a radical Socialist policy" with other attitudes that apparently were something other than radically Socialist, namely, "respect for freedom of speech and a civilised attitude toward literature and the arts."

On some occasions Orwell thought of socialism as an ideal that has been nowhere realized. In December 1943 he argued that "the real objective of Socialism is human brotherhood" (16: 42). Socialists, he asserted, "want a world in which human beings love one another instead of swindling and murdering one another" (16: 42–43). In 1945 Orwell wrote, "Socialism ought to mean the meek inheriting the earth" (17: 354). But in a December 24, 1943, column in *Tribune*, he had argued that the "real answer" to those who say socialism is impossible because "man is non-perfectible" is "to dissociate Socialism from Utopianism." (16: 35). At least once, Orwell compared the "hedonistic" morality of ordinary socialism unfavorably to the Nazi demand for sacrifice. In his March 21, 1940, review of *Mein Kampf*, Orwell gave Hitler credit for at least having "grasped the falsity of the hedonistic attitude to life." While "Socialism and even capitalism in a more grudging way, have said to people 'I offer you a good time,' Hitler has said to them 'I offer you struggle, danger and death,' and as a result a whole nation flings itself at his feet" (12: 118). On the other hand, Orwell sometimes speculated that perhaps socialism "in itself" did not necessarily have any particular human moral significance at all. He wrote to Humphry House in 1940 that "I don't believe that capitalism, as against feudalism, improved the actual quality of human life, and I don't believe that Socialism *in itself* need work any real improvement either. Hitler is perhaps a large-scale demonstration of this" (12: 141; italics in original).

In "Why I Write," Orwell significantly qualified his subordination of all else in his writing to the cause of "democratic socialism, as I understand it" by asserting that "I am not able, and I do not want, completely to abandon the world-view that I acquired in childhood" (18: 319). Orwell was eleven years old when World War I broke out. In his essays and journalism of the 1930s and 1940s he repeatedly caricatured those who clung to the political and social attitudes of the years before World War I as "Blimps"—a reference to the British cartoon character Colonel Blimp, a depiction of the British ruling classes as stupid, complacent, and bigoted. And yet when the Left intellectuals mocked or criticized not only the politics but also the underlying moral principles of that worldview, Orwell, almost alone in his milieu, spoke eloquently and insistently in defense of those principles.

In "Raffles and Miss Blandish," Orwell compares examples of popular crime fiction from the Victorian era and from the 1930s. He observes that Raffles, the fictional cricket-playing burglar of the Victorian era, is a thief but also a gentleman. Living in "a time when people had standards, though they happened to be foolish standards," Raffles, though a burglar, is still bound by certain restraints. He "will not commit murder, and he avoids violence wherever possible and prefers to carry out his robberies unarmed. He regards friendship as sacred, and is chivalrous though not moral in his relations with women" (16: 349). In the 1939 crime novel by James Hadley Chase, *No Orchids for Miss Blandish*, on the other hand, neither criminals nor police seem bound by any restraints at all. In the world of this best-seller, there is only "the triumph of the strong over the weak," and "if ultimately one sides with the police against the gangsters it is merely because they are better organized and more powerful, because, in fact, the law is a bigger racket than crime" (16: 351). Orwell finds some comfort in the thought that "the common people, on the whole, are still living in the world of absolute good and evil from which the intellectuals have long since escaped" (355), but the success of books like *No Orchids for Miss Blandish* is an ominous sign that this may be changing.

Orwell's great 1940 essay "Boys' Weeklies" focuses on two papers, *Gem* and *Magnet*, whose stories as late as 1940 presented a world in which "the clock has stopped at 1910. Britannia rules the waves, and no one has heard of slumps, booms, unemployment, dictatorships, purges or concentration camps" (12: 72). Although at the end of the essay Orwell muses about the possibility of "a left-wing boys' paper" (75), when he compares *Gem* and *Magnet* to "the more up-to-date papers which have appeared since the Great War" (67), the moral and even the political advantage is all on the side of the former. Orwell finds "bully-worship and the cult of violence" (69) in the later papers but not in *Gem* or *Magnet*. Similarly, the stories in *Gem* or *Magnet* do not revolve around "some single all-powerful character," as the more recent papers typically do; plots instead featuring "fifteen or twenty characters, all more or less on an equality" rather than one "central dominating character" may not have an explicit political message, but their ability to arouse dramatic interest despite the "absence of the leader-principle" has a greater political significance in the 1930s than it would have had in 1910 (69). The patriotism of *Gem* and *Magnet* is automatic and uncritical, but it "has nothing whatever to do with power-politics or 'ideological' warfare. It is more akin to family loyalty" (66).

It is akin, that is, to the kind of patriotism Orwell himself advocated in "The Lion and the Unicorn," where he insisted that English patriotism was compatible with socialism, claiming that his country was best thought of as "a family, a rather stuffy Victorian family," with "its private language and its common memories. . . . A family with the wrong members in control—that, perhaps, is as near as one can come to describing England in a phrase" (12: 401). And indeed, the arrival of war between England and Nazi Germany led Orwell, in the course of reviewing Malcolm Muggeridge's *The Thirties*, to the discovery that there was something to be said even on behalf of Colonel Blimp:

> It is all very well to be "advanced" and "enlightened," to snigger at Colonel Blimp and proclaim your emancipation from all traditional loyalties, but a time comes when the sand of the desert is sodden red and what have I done for thee, England, my England? As I was brought up in this tradition myself I can recognise it under strange disguises, and also sympathise with it, for even at its stupidest and most sentimental it is a comelier thing than the shallow self-righteousness of the left-wing intelligentsia. (12: 151–52)

Even as Orwell asserted that "every line of serious work" he wrote was written for a political purpose, he also said that "I could not do the work of writing a book, or even a long magazine article, if it were not also an aesthetic experience," adding that "So long as I remain alive and well I shall continue to feel strongly about prose style." Of course, Orwell also asserted in his 1950 essay on Charles Dickens that "all art is propaganda" (12: 47), a notion that might seem to leave little room for an aesthetic experience or style. And when Orwell's statement that "all art is propaganda" is quoted out of context, a strong interpretation of the statement might be that art is *nothing* but propaganda, and therefore the notion of art as something in itself is meaningless. In context, however, Orwell's meaning is very different. The absolute-sounding statement that "all art is propaganda" comes between two other sentences that clarify Orwell's meaning: "But every writer, especially every novelist, has a 'message,' whether he admits it or not, and the minutest details of his work are influenced by it. All art is propaganda. Neither Dickens himself nor the majority of Victorian novelists would have thought of denying this" (12: 47).

Orwell is not saying that Dickens or other major novelists were concerned only with politics, nor is he saying that the only aspect of Dickens's work worth considering is its politics. The "message" to which Orwell refers is simply the writer's view of the world and human life. In 1940 Orwell emphatically rejected the notion that his view of art as propaganda implied that any writer or artist should be seen only or even primarily as a "political propagandist":

> I have always maintained that every artist is a propagandist. I don't mean a political propagandist. If he has any honesty or talent at all he cannot be that. Most political propaganda is a matter of telling lies, not only about the facts but about your own feelings. But every artist is a propagandist in the sense that he is trying, directly or indirectly, to impose a vision of life that seems to him desirable. (12: 297)

Orwell not only believed that the "propaganda" aspect of art not is reducible to its political meaning, he repeatedly acknowledged and even emphasized that there is more to art and literature than propaganda, even if "propaganda" is taken in its broadest possible meaning, as Orwell himself used it. Exploring "the frontiers of art and propaganda" in May 1941, Orwell observed that "every piece of writing has its propaganda aspect, and yet in any book or play or poem or what not that is to endure there has to be a residuum of something that simply is not affected by its moral or meaning—a residuum of something we can only call art" (12: 493).

In a 1945 "New Year Message" to the readers of *Tribune*, Orwell defended the journal's willingness to discuss "even the most unpolitical book, even an outright reactionary book" by pointing out that such a book might have its "uses to the Socialist movement." He then went on, however, to explain and justify *Tribune*'s literary policy on grounds beyond the political: "But we also assume that books are not to be regarded simply as propaganda, that literature exists in its own right—as a form of recreation, to put it no higher—and that a large number of our readers are interested in it" (17: 10).

Orwell's very emphasis on the importance of aspects of literature beyond the political had a political implication—literature as he knew it was part of the world of liberalism, and it was a part he was not willing to give up. As a socialist, Orwell rejected liberalism's original belief that the rights of free speech and free thought were inextricably connected to the right to private property, but he recognized that it was liberalism, not socialism, that insisted on the primacy of the individual freedom that writers required in order to write. Whatever a writer's political opinions might be, "*as a writer* he is a liberal," Orwell wrote in his 1940 essay on Henry Miller, whose explicit political opinions, if any, were not liberal at all (12: 111; italics in original). Orwell was willing to criticize Charles Dickens for failing to recognize what seemed to Orwell so obvious, "that private property is an obstructive nuisance" (12: 31), but in his eloquent closing portrait of Dickens as "a nineteenth-century liberal" (56), it is hard to feel that the qualities Orwell admires so much in Dickens could have been expressed with the same force if Dickens's political opinions had been more up-to-date:

> When one reads any strongly individual piece of writing, one has the impression of seeing a face somewhere behind the page. . . . Well, in the case of Dickens I see . . . the face of a man who is always fighting against something, but who fights in the open and is not frightened, the face of a man who is generously angry—in other words of a nineteenth-century liberal, a free intelligence, a type hated with equal hatred by all the smelly little orthodoxies which are now contending for our souls. (12: 55–56)

In "Why I Write" Orwell declared that until he died he would continue "to love the surface of the earth, and to take a pleasure in solid objects and scraps of useless information" (18: 319–20), and surely his expression of this side of his character is one of the elements that gives his journalism and essays a significance beyond politics. One may disagree with some or many of the political judgments in *Homage to Catalonia* and still revere it as a classic of writing about war for Orwell's ability to convey the waste and brutality of war without surrendering to either cynicism or nihilism. When Orwell is wounded, he feels "a violent resentment at having to leave this world which, when all is said and done, suits me so well" (*Homage* 186). Defending Shakespeare against Tolstoy's attack, Orwell concedes that "Shakespeare was not a systematic thinker" (19: 61), but adds that if he "was not a philosopher or a scientist," Shakespeare did "have curiosity; he loved the surface of the earth and the process of life" (64). Both aspects of the characterization apply to Orwell as well.

One way Orwell evinces his love of "the surface of the earth" is in the lists that recur so frequently in his essays. While Walt Whitman's lists express an indiscriminate cosmic optimism, Orwell's lists convey his stubborn love for the surface of the earth, even when the particular part of the surface he remembers in all its concreteness might seem better forgotten. Writing an introduction for a now-forgotten novel, *The Position of Peggy Harper*, Orwell provides a list of specifics making up the life of a journeyman actor: "greasepaint and fish and chips, the sordid rivalries, the comfortless Sunday journeys, the lugging of suitcases through the back streets of unfamiliar towns, the 'professional' lodgings presided over by 'Ma,' the poky bedrooms with the rickety wash-hand-stand and the grim white chamber-pot under the bed" (18: 218). The "grim white chamber-pot," Orwell admits, is his own addition; it is not mentioned in the novel.

Looking back on his school days in "Such, Such Were the Joys," Orwell remembers "sweaty stockings, dirty towels, faecal smells blowing along corridors, forks with old food between the prongs, neck-of-mutton stew, and the banging doors of the lavatories and the echoing chamberpots in the dormitories" (19: 370). In "Looking Back on the Spanish War," Orwell counters the propaganda of both sides by grounding his reflections on specific memories, beginning with "first of all the physical memories, the sounds, the smells and the surfaces of things." He remembers, for example, "the huge cavalry barracks in Barcelona with its draughty stables and cobbled yards, the icy cold of the pump where one washed, the filthy meals made tolerable by pannikins of wine, the trousered militiawomen chopping firewood, and roll-call in the early mornings" (13: 497). The "special atmosphere of the time" is evoked by another list: "the shabby clothes and the gay-coloured revolutionary posters, the universal use of the word 'comrade,' the anti-Fascist ballades printed on flimsy paper and sold for a penny, the phrases like 'international proletarian solidarity,' pathetically repeated by ignorant men who believed them to mean something" (13: 502).

Orwell's stress on particulars known by personal experience provides implicit support for his commitment to what he called "objective truth." Writing at the height of World War II, Orwell argued that the most dangerous aspect of totalitarian regimes was not their violence but the threat they posed to clear perceptions of reality: "The really frightening thing about totalitarianism is not that it commits 'atrocities' but that it attacks the concept of objective truth: it claims to control the past as well as the future" (16: 89). In the same passage, Orwell linked the notion of objective truth with "the liberal habit of mind, which thinks of truth as something outside yourself, something to be discovered, and not as something you can make up as you go along" (16: 89). Looking over his collection of political pamphlets espousing almost every political perspective—"Conservative, Communist, Catholic, Trotskyist, Pacifist, Anarchist or what-have-you"—Orwell finds that "almost nobody seems to feel that an opponent deserves a fair hearing or that the objective truth matters so long as you can score a neat debating point"; nobody on any side seems to be "searching for the truth, everybody is putting forward a 'case' with complete disregard for fairness or accuracy, and the most plainly obvious facts can be ignored by those who don't want to see them" (16: 495).

From the mid-1930s to the end of his life, Orwell identified himself as a democratic socialist, not a liberal. He remained faithful, however, to the notion of truth "as something outside yourself, something to be discovered, and not as something you can make up as you go along." Even in the work where his political passions are most intense, *Hom-*

age to Catalonia, he repeatedly reports facts and incidents that tell against his own side and against himself. He reports feeling "a sneaking sympathy with the Fascist ex-owners to see the way the militia treated the buildings they had seized. In La Granga every room that was not in use had been turned into a latrine" (78). Refuting the "anti-Fascist papers" who reported that "churches were only attacked when they were used as Fascist fortresses," Orwell acknowledges that "actually churches were pillaged everywhere and as a matter of course" (52). Nor does Orwell spare himself. He confesses, for example, that "when you are watching artillery fire from a safe distance you always want the gunner to hit his mark, even though the mark contains your dinner and some of your comrades" (84). Near the end of *Homage*, Orwell warns the reader to "beware of my partisanship, my mistakes of fact and the distortion inevitably caused by my having seen only one corner of events" (231). Yet even those who disagree with many of the political judgments Orwell makes cannot help but recognize that *Homage to Catalonia* will retain its permanent value as a record of one man's attempt to tell the truth under almost impossible circumstances, even if the political events that are its subject are almost entirely forgotten. And one could make the same claim for Orwell's essays and journalism in their entirety.

The lasting importance of Orwell's work can be better understood if one sees his journalism, reviews, and essays not as an extended argument for socialism or even for "democratic Socialism, as I understand it" but instead as a plea for common decency in politics and society as well as in personal life. When Orwell criticized Charles Dickens for lacking "the vision to see that private property is an obstructive nuisance" (12: 31), he was saying nothing that any Marxist of the time could not have said with equal assurance. When, however, Orwell went on to explain why Dickens's implicit message "that 'If men would behave decently the world would be decent' is not such a platitude as it sounds," he was offering a message that was unique in the political discourse of his time and remains uniquely valuable today.

George Orwell was an intellectual who refused to believe that the theories of intellectuals on either the Right or the Left had succeeded in making traditional morality obsolete. Bookish, delighting in political-literary exchanges, always willing to tell unwelcome truths, Orwell was anything but a populist or demagogue; but he could not help observing that "the common man is still living in the mental world of Dickens, but nearly every modern intellectual has gone over to some or other form of totalitarianism" (12: 55). In "The English People" (1944), Orwell ascribed to the English people a stance close to his own: "They have the virtues and the vices of an old-fashioned people. To twentieth-century political theories they oppose not another theory of their own, but a moral quality which must be vaguely described as decency"(16: 209). More than fifty years later, Orwell's writings still stand out for the clarity and force with which they champion ideas and attitudes all too often ignored or discounted in the academic and political discourse of our time. He insisted, in season and out of season, that art is more than propaganda, that truth is "something to be discovered," not a mere construction of either individuals or governments, and, above all, that both personal life and politics should be guided by "a moral quality which must be vaguely described as decency."

Works Cited

Orwell, George. *The Complete Works of George Orwell.* Ed. Peter Davison. 20 vols. London: Secker, 2000.
_____. *Homage to Catalonia.* 1938. New York: Harcourt, 1952.

Animal Farm: Beast Fable, Allegory, Satire_____

John P. Rossi

Of George Orwell's writings, *Animal Farm* is second only to *Nineteen Eighty-Four* in terms of popularity and success. In the 1950s it became part of English literature curricula, making the story familiar to three generations of high school and college students, and it has appeared (along with *Nineteen Eighty-Four*) on many lists of the best novels of the twentieth century. Orwell's inspiration for *Animal Farm* arose from his experience in the Spanish Civil War, particularly how that conflict was distorted in left-wing political and literary circles in England. In Spain, he first saw how the truth could be distorted for political ends and how the very concept of historical truth was in danger of being lost (Crick 382).

In the preface to the Ukrainian edition of *Animal Farm*, Orwell told how the idea of using a beast fable came to him. "I saw a little boy, perhaps ten years old, driving a huge cart-horse along a narrow path whipping it whenever it tried to turn. It struck me that if only such animals became aware of their strength we should have no power over them, and that men exploit animals in much the same way as the rich exploit the proletariat." This inspired him to "analyze Marx's theory from the animals' point of view" (*Complete Works* 8: 113).

Animal Farm is the story of the how a revolution is betrayed and the idealism of the revolutionaries is corrupted. Instead of critiquing the failures of the Russian Revolution in a traditional history, Orwell, for aesthetic reasons, preferred the fable format to dramatize what happened in Russia between 1917 and 1944. Using a fairy tale enabled Orwell to show the absurdities of a failed revolution with irony and even humor. It would also give his tale a universality that a specific critique would lack.

Part of the effectiveness of Orwell's novella (at no more than thirty thousand words, he called it a "little squib") was its very spareness. There is hardly a wasted word in the story. Manor Farm, which stands for prerevolutionary Russia, is managed by an incompetent farmer, Mr. Jones, who represents the tsar, Nicholas II. Interestingly, when Orwell lived in Wallington, England, he had a neighbor named Mr. Jones, and there was a farm called Manor Farm near where Orwell grew up in Sussex. Throughout *Animal Farm*, Orwell uses names drawn from his past.

Manor Farm is, like Russia was, a potentially rich land that is poorly governed. Mr. Jones spends most of his time drinking with his cronies while complaining how lazy his animals are. In Russia, Nicholas II was an ineffective ruler for whom administering a great country was beyond his intellectual powers, though he was not an alcoholic.

One night, a twelve-year-old prize winning boar, Old Major, whose character is an amalgam of Marx and Lenin, calls the animals together and relates a dream that he had. The dream is the culmination of all that Old Major had learned during his long life. In essence, it is nothing less than Marx's theory of revolution from the animals' point of view. He tells the gathered animals of how he sees a day when they will take over the farm and run it for the benefit of themselves. Our lives are not ours, he says, and we are given just enough food to keep us alive and working. "Those of us who are capable of it are forced to work to the last atom of our strength: and the very instant that our usefulness has come to end we are slaughtered with hideous cruelty. No animal in England is free."

Manor Farm is rich enough to supply all our needs, Old Major tells the animals, but humans have exploited us and taken the fruits of our labor (eggs, milk, dung, etc.) for their own use. In his dream he sees a golden future when the animals will be free of human oppression and will live in "perfect comradeship." To realize this dream, the animals must become aware of who their enemies are. Eventually a rule is formulated so that the animals will know their friends: "Four legs good, two legs bad." When the birds protest, they are told that wings count as legs. Then Old Major teaches them a song to keep the idea of a "golden future time" alive. The song, "Beasts of England," resembles the communist anthem "The Internationale," with touches of "My Darling Clementine" and the Mexican revolutionary anthem, "La Cucaracha."

The first chapter sets the tone of the novella. The parallels with Russia on the eve of the revolution are obvious—a potentially rich land, badly governed, in which the ruling classes exploit the workers. Old Major's analysis of the animals' fate is similar to the position of the workers and peasants in Russia at that time.

The chapter also establishes Orwell's familiarity with agricultural life. Throughout his life he kept animals. He had a menagerie when he served in Burma and kept a goat when he lived in the English countryside. He and his wife also had a dog named "Marx" with which Orwell used to hunt rabbits. He knew great deal about farm animals, once telling a friend that pigs in particular were difficult to control: "They. . . are hard to keep out of anywhere because they are so strong and cunning" (*Complete Works* 19: 451). Thus, when it came time to give his animals human characteristics, he was usually on target. The cat of Manor Farm, for instance, was never around when there was work to be done. The big cart horse, Boxer, was powerful but mentally slow. Sheep were portrayed as dull, stupid, and easily led. Orwell's sense of humor also shows through in *Animal Farm*. After the overthrow of Mr. Jones, the animals find hams hanging in the kitchen. The animals reverently remove them and take them out for burial.

Three days after relating his dream, Old Major dies. In the second chapter, the animals eventually preserve his skull to remind them of Old Major's contribution to their revolution. Orwell's irony is apparent here, comparing the glorification of Old Major's skull to the embalming and preservation of Lenin's body in Moscow's Red Square.

When the drunken Mr. Jones neglects the animals, they rebel and drive him off the farm. The revolt is led by the pigs, particularly the two most intelligent, Snowball and Napoleon. The animals are surprised by the ease of their triumph, a detail that parallels the easy overthrow of the Russian tsar in 1917. After their triumph, Orwell has the animals investigate Mr. Jones's house, which they decide to turn into a museum to remind them how humans treated them. The pigs show their ingenuity by using their hooves to milk the cows, a further sign that they will be the leaders of the new regime.

Moses, Mr. Jones's pet raven, appears after the revolution, representing the Russian Orthodox Church, which was controlled by the state. He tells the animals that the revolution is a fraud and there is a wonderful place of rest and plenty called Sugarcandy Mountain where animals go when they die, reprising Marx's line about religion being the opiate of the people. The decision to turn Mr. Jones's farmhouse into a museum parallels what the Communists did with Orthodox churches after the revolution—turning them into museums dedicated to atheism.

The pigs, who can read and write, devise Seven Commandments of Animalism, which they write on the walls of the barn for all the animals to see. The laws are crafted in simple language so that the animals can understand them and unite around them. Only a few animals can read, among them a cynical donkey named Benjamin. In his skepticism about the revolution, Benjamin resembles Orwell. When the animals grow enthusiastic or optimistic, Benjamin voices his constant refrain: "Life will go on as it has always gone on—that is, badly." After the success of *Animal Farm*, some of Orwell's friends began calling him "Donkey George."

The key role played by the pigs parallels the Communist Party elite, the nomenklatura. Snowball, who is described as a "vivacious pig," is clearly modeled after Leon Trotsky, who combined revolutionary fervor and intellectual skills. Like Trotsky, Snowball is portrayed as brimming with plans for reforming Manor Farm, which the animals have renamed Animal Farm.

Orwell was fascinated by Trotsky. The character of Emmanuel Goldstein in *Nineteen Eighty-Four* was also based on Trotsky. When Orwell fought in the Spanish Civil War, he joined a faction that combined anarchist and Trotskyist ideals. Orwell admired Trotsky's literary skills but believed that he, like Stalin, was corrupted by power.

Orwell argued that while Trotsky and Lenin possessed admirable qualities, they bore some responsibility for the corruption of the revolutionary socialist movement.

Napoleon, a fierce-looking Berkshire boar, represents Joseph Stalin, the crafty and ruthless revolutionary more interested in power than ideas. A third pig, Squealer, is used by Orwell to show how Communist propaganda was used to distort the ideals of a revolution, themes which had concerned him since his experiences in Spain.

In chapter three, with the animals in control of the farm, they set to work to make it a success. Snowball draws up plans for modernizing the farm, which Napoleon reluctantly goes along with. Boxer plays a key role, encouraging the other animals with his slogan, "I will work harder." Boxer is Orwell's symbol for the working class, exploited by Mr. Jones and now, in his ignorance, being exploited by the pigs.

Committees are created to administer the farm. There is even an effort to teach the animals to read, though without much success. Boxer, for example, cannot learn the alphabet, never getting beyond the letter "D." Other animals can barely master a few words. With certain exceptions, chiefly Benjamin and Clover, the pigs have a monopoly on learning.

At this point in the story, Orwell introduces details that signal the beginning of the betrayal of the revolution. The dogs have puppies, whom Napoleon takes and secretly begins raising as his special protectors, a potential secret police. Then the animals discover that the pigs have been taking the milk and apples for themselves. When the animals protest, Squealer explains that the pigs as brain workers require the food. He begins a refrain that he will use throughout the story to justify special treatment for the pigs: "Surely, comrades, there is no one among you who wants to see Mr. Jones back?" The animals agree, the last thing they want is a return of Mr. Jones.

Orwell here was emphasizing the idealism of the early stages of the Russian Revolution. Everyone was a "comrade" and there was hope that a new era in history was unfolding. The pigs' gradual domination resembles how the Communist Party elite assumed power. By comparing the dogs to the secret police, Orwell was marking one of the first signs of the emergence of the totalitarian state. He also was delivering a warning: The utopianism of a revolution can easily be subverted.

Orwell knew that apologists for the Soviet Union would be furious at having the secret police portrayed as vicious dogs, as he had used a similar device before. In his study of poverty in England in the 1930s, *The Road to Wigan Pier* (1937), Orwell described the Soviet commissars as "half gramophones, half gangsters," which outraged Communist fellow-travelers. Orwell's publisher, the well-known leftist Victor Gollancz, called that remark a "curious indiscretion." It was anything but that, however; it was Orwell's arresting way of pointing out an unpleasant fact.

In discussing *Animal Farm,* Orwell pointed out that the revolution was corrupted when the pigs took the milk and apples (18: 318). He compared this to Lenin and Trotsky's crushing of the 1921 Kronstadt mutiny, which sought to revive the egalitarian spirit of the early days of the revolution. If the other animals had protested at this point, Orwell wrote, the revolution would have been saved. But now all privileges and luxuries were being reserved for the pigs. A new ruling caste was emerging.

Chapter four shows how Animal Farm's success worries the neighboring human farm owners. At first they ridicule the efforts of the pigs to make a success of Manor Farm, but they then grow anxious, because it might inspire their own animals to revolt. They spread false information that Animal Farm is a failure and that awful crimes are being committed there. Something similar happened after the Russian Revolution. Capitalist propaganda spread stories of gross immorality, free love, and other forms of depravity, which were exaggerations.

The pigs send out pigeons to tell the true story of Animal Farm, much in the way that the Communist International sent its agents throughout the world to tell the story of the revolution and its successes. The pigeons report back that Mr. Jones is organizing an army of humans to seize control of Animal Farm. Led by Snowball and Boxer, the animals fight off the humans and drive them off Animal Farm. The animals suffer only one fatality in the battle, a sheep who is given a hero's burial. Snowball and Boxer are awarded medals as "Animal Hero, First Class."

The Battle of the Cowshed, as the animals call their victory over the humans, is modeled on the defeat of the White Army in the Russian Civil War. Under Trotsky's leadership, the Communist forces, called the Red Army, won a dramatic victory. Trotsky's role made him the logical successor to Lenin in the eyes of many Communists—but not Stalin.

After the Cowshed victory, in chapter five Snowball draws up plans to build a windmill that will provide the animals with cheap electricity. Napoleon disagrees and shows his displeasure by urinating on the plan. Just as the animals are about to approve Snowball's plan, Napoleon whistles for his dogs, who appear and drive Snowball from the farm. Squealer tells the confused animals that Snowball was a secretly a traitor. Napoleon, he said, really supported the windmill project but pretended not to as a way of exposing Snowball's treachery. The animals are confused but accept Squealer's explanation, although some seem to remember that Snowball fought valiantly in the Battle of the Cowshed.

The ousting of Snowball follows closely what happened to Trotsky after Lenin's death in 1924. Regarded as Lenin's heir, Trotsky, the brilliant intellectual, fell victim to Stalin's machinations. First isolated from office and then banished, Trotsky became the symbol for all the enemies of the Soviet Union. Stalin eventually had him assassinated in Mexico in 1940.

The windmill project in chapter six stands for the Five Year Plans that Stalin inaugurated once he had solidified his power. Again, the parallels with the events in the history of the Soviet Union are remarkably close. Beginning in 1930, Stalin launched his plan to rapidly industrialize the Soviet Union. Despite huge losses of human life and many failures, he succeeded in completing an industrial revolution in the Soviet Union.

The work on the windmill is hard, and the animals are put on short rations, as Soviet citizens were during the Five Year Plans. Napoleon arranges a deal with a human, Mr. Whymper, to trade farm produce for things the animals can't produce, such as iron and oil. The animals are confused by these dealings with a human, because it contradicts "Four legs good, two legs bad," but Squealer reassures them that Napoleon is wiser than they. When some chickens refuse to turn over their eggs to Napoleon, he starves them into submission. This closely parallels Stalin's collectivization of agriculture in the early 1930s, when he seized foodstuffs to pay for needed manufactured goods from the non-Communist world.

Rumors spread that the pigs are sleeping in beds in Mr. Jones's house, which contradicts the rules of Animalism, but Squealer shows the animals that the commandment reads "No animal shall sleep in a bed *with sheets*." Again the animals are confused. They didn't remember the phrase "with sheets," but Squealer convinces them it was always there.

A storm destroys the windmill before it can be finished. Napoleon announces that Snowball had sabotaged the construction and was abetted by traitors in Animal Farm. In reality, the walls of the windmill had not been made sufficiently strong. The animals are shocked when four pigs are charged with aiding Snowball in his treason. When they confess their crimes, Napoleon sets the dogs on them and they tear open the pigs' throats. The dogs also attack Boxer, but he sends them sprawling with a savage kick. More confessions and executions follow, leaving the animals in shock. After pronouncing a death sentence against Snowball, Napoleon announces that the windmill will be rebuilt with walls twice as thick. Squealer tells the animals that Snowball is now working on Mr. Frederick's farm, Pinchfield, which stands for Hitler's Germany.

For chapter seven, Orwell took details from Stalin's bloody purges in the mid-1930s. More than a million Soviet citizens, mostly loyal Communist Party members, were murdered, and another two million were sent to gulags in the Arctic or Siberia. Many of them died also. By making this scene gruesome, Orwell was trying to show leftists how cruel Stalin's actions were—not exactly a popular point in 1944.

In the 1930s, Communist propaganda claimed that Trotsky was collaborating with the Nazis to sabotage the revolution. He was written out of histories of the Russian Revolution and even edited out of photographs with Lenin and Stalin, a point that Orwell would use with greater effect in *Nineteen Eighty-Four*. Orwell also foreshadows the rewriting of history, a theme that was central to him after the Spanish Civil War and would also be developed at greater length in *Nineteen Eighty-Four*.

The rebuilding of the windmill takes a terrible toll on the animals much in the way the Five Year Plans and the collectivization of agriculture did in the Soviet Union. With the work going slowly, Napoleon launches a reign of terror against animals whom he accuses of collaborating with Snowball. The animals are shocked by the bloodshed, but Squealer tells them it was necessary. When some remember a commandment against the killing animals, Squealer shows that they remembered it incorrectly. It reads: "No animals shall kill any other animal *without cause.*"

Squealer then introduces them to a new anthem that emphasizes patriotism and loyalty to Animal Farm and to Napoleon, who is now given the title "Leader." "Beasts of England" is outlawed as no longer necessary. The pig Minimus, the state poet, writes a eulogy to Napoleon that enables Orwell to poke fun at the glorification of Stalin, recalling the servile verse of Vladimir Mayakovsky and other Soviet poets. Napoleon is heralded as the father of the animals and the "Lord of the Swill Bucket," who provides his followers with fresh straw and a full belly. "Oh, how my soul is on fire / When I gaze at thy calm commanding eye / Like the Sun in the sky." This parallels what happened in the Soviet Union after Stalin killed off his rivals. Everything was done in the name of "Comrade Stalin." A work of art, a musical composition, a collection of poetry, any innovation was attributed to the inspiration of the genius of "Comrade Stalin." The mere mention of his name in a speech required a standing ovation. This bloodletting left the animals confused, but they swear to work even harder. Boxer proclaims, "I will work harder."

This scene touches on an issue that had long concerned Orwell—what he saw as a tendency toward power worship, especially prevalent among intellectuals. As he observed in one of his letters to the United States in *Partisan Review*, intellectuals worship Stalin "because they have lost their patriotism and their religious belief without losing their need for a god and a fatherland."

The parallel with events in Russia in the 1930s is almost perfect. The industrial and agricultural transformation took a terrible toll in human lives. According to a recent study of the period, Timothy Snyder's *Bloodlands*, between three and five million people died during these years. British historian Robert Conquest in his studies of this era even uses a higher figure, arguing that Stalin allowed mass starvation in parts of the Soviet Union as a way of solidifying his rule. Stalin instituted his bloody purges as a way of distracting attention from the Five Year Plans' failures and of destroying any potential rivals. Orwell's criticism of Stalin required political courage, as the Soviet Union was an ally of the West in the war against Hitler, and Stalin was portrayed favorably as a calm, pipe-smoking "Uncle Joe."

Chapter eight contains Orwell's treatment of the origin of World War II and the war itself, in one of the most brilliant satires of the book. While the animals are struggling in spite of food shortages and long hours of work to build the windmill, the pigs discover a store of valuable timber left over from Mr. Jones's time. Napoleon begins a series of complex negotiations with the nearby farms of Mr. Pilkington (representing England) and Mr. Frederick (representing Nazi Germany). As the negotiations progress, the pigs alternately single out the two farmers as a villain or a friend, depending upon who is closer to dealing with Napoleon, much as happened between 1936 and the outbreak of war in 1939. When it appears that Mr. Pilkington will be the trade partner,

Napoleon calls for "Death to Frederick." Squealer also informs the animals that Snowball is conspiring with both Pilkington and Frederick.

To everyone's surprise, a deal is struck with Frederick, but Napoleon demands cash in the form of bank notes. The notes are put on display as a sign of Napoleon's genius. It is then discovered that Napoleon had been cheated—the bills are forgeries. Napoleon is outraged, denounces Frederick for his treachery and predicts that soon he will attack Animal Farm.

Orwell's handling of this period in Soviet history is flawless, partly because it is a period he lived through and wrote about. Stalin's dealings with the West were complex in the years before World War II. In 1935 and 1936, he reversed the policy of "socialism in one country" in favor of collaborating with the West in a "popular front" of democratic countries. He was hoping to isolate Nazi Germany by forming alliances with the West. But at the same time, Stalin also was open to the possibility of striking a deal with Germany.

Napoleon's alternate dealings with Mr. Pilkington and Mr. Frederick follow closely Stalin's complex negotiations, including Soviet propaganda's alternate denunciations of the West and Nazi Germany. One can see in this section the foreshadowing of the shifting enemies in *Nineteen Eighty-Four* from Eastasia to Eurasia. It is clear that *Animal Farm* forms a close link to Orwell's later dystopia, as Bernard Crick argues in his biography of Orwell.

The timber arrangement stands for the Nazi-Soviet Nonaggression Pact of August 1939, a deal that shocked the world and freed Hitler to attack Poland and begin World War II. Stalin cooperated closely with Hitler for two years, living up to every detail of the pact, including sending a trainload of supplies to Germany on the day the Germans attacked the Soviet Union. Napoleon's anger when he discovers the forged bank notes parallels Stalin's sense of betrayal after the German attack on the Soviet Union in June 1941. We know that Stalin at first refused to believe the news of Hitler's treachery and even suffered something like a temporary nervous breakdown before regaining control.

Like Stalin, Napoleon rallied the animals to defeat Mr. Frederick's attack. The windmill was destroyed but the animals managed to drive Mr. Frederick from the farm. The destruction was terrible, the loss of animal life high. Even Boxer was seriously injured, representing the awful suffering of the Soviet peoples during the war, losses that exceeded twenty million deaths.

Orwell introduces other ingenious elements into the story at this point, in chapter nine. Moses the raven, representing the Russian Orthodox Church, returns to Animal Farm with his tales of Sugarcandy Mountain. The animals pay little attention to him, but Napoleon lets him stay. During the war, Stalin allowed the Russian Orthodox Church to reopen as a way of rallying patriotic memories among the people.

Two other developments at this time are crucial to Orwell's themes. After his injury, Boxer heroically tries to continue working for the good of Animal Farm, but he gradually grows weaker. In a scene bathed in pathos comparable to the death of Little Nell in Dickens's *The Old Curiosity Shop*, Orwell has Napoleon tell the animals that Boxer will be sent to the hospital to recover. As he is being driven away in an ambulance, the sign on the side of the vehicle reveals it to be from a glue factory where Boxer is to be slaughtered. The animals try to warn Boxer, who tries to kick the ambulance open, but he is too weak to do so. A short time later, Squealer announces that Boxer has died in the hospital, but that Napoleon was at his side the whole time. Soon thereafter, the animals see a van drive up and deliver a fresh supply of whiskey to the pigs.

Boxer's death represents not only the suffering that the Soviet people experienced during the war but also the betrayal of the working classes. The revolution that had begun with such promise had now degenerated to a point where the animals are no better off (and in some ways, worse off) than they were under the humans—a theme difficult for the Left to swallow in the 1940s.

Orwell introduces a new and disturbing element around the same time as the death of Boxer. When Napoleon's four sows give birth to thirty-one pigs, he orders that they be given special treatment, including education. The piglets are "the new class," the Communist elite, who are destined to become the future leaders of Animal Farm. Thus the revolution that began as an egalitarian struggle has now produced its own class system.

Orwell's arguments regarding the Soviet people being worse off under Communism, and the existence of a sharp class division between the elite and the workers, angered many on the Left. He insisted that this was inherent in totalitarian systems, a point most left-wing intellectuals couldn't accept, but one that Orwell would highlight again in *Nineteen Eighty-Four*.

In the last section of *Animal Farm*, Orwell brings the story full circle. The windmill is rebuilt, but instead of providing electricity to make the animals' lives more comfortable, it is used to mill corn that can be sold for a profit to buy the human goods to which the pigs have grown accustomed. Life remains hard for the animals, and there are few left who can remember the days before the revolution.

One day the animals are shocked to find that the pigs are walking upright, on two feet, led by Napoleon, who is also carrying a whip, the symbol of power and authority that Mr. Jones wielded. The pigs gradually take on characteristics indistinguishable from humans: using telephones, subscribing to magazines, and (in the case of Napoleon) smoking a pipe, an obvious reference to the pipe-smoking Stalin.

When the animals protest, Squealer marches out the sheep, to whom he has taught a new chant: "Four legs good, two legs better." The other animals can't believe their ears and ask Benjamin to check the rules of Animalism painted on the barn. All the commandments have been erased save one, which reads: "All animals are equal, but some are more equal than others."

In the concluding chapter in the novella, the pigs invite the humans to visit Animal Farm, now renamed Manor Farm, to see its improvements and to introduce a new period of harmony between pigs and humans. The humans are impressed by the changes the pigs have made, particularly how they have gotten their animals to work hard for so little food. At a dinner in their honor, the men congratulate Napoleon for his success. Mr. Pilkington proposes a toast, noting that while the pigs have "lower animals to contend with, we have our lower classes." One can almost see Orwell smiling as he wrote that line.

The last scene in the novella finds the pigs and humans playing cards. Suddenly a fight breaks out when both Mr. Pilkington and Napoleon play the ace of spades at the same time. The animals look through the window at the fight and discover that they cannot distinguish the pigs from the humans.

Orwell did not have a clear ending in mind when he wrote the book, and used the Teheran Conference of November 1943—where British Prime Minister Winston Churchill, U.S. President Franklin Roosevelt, and Stalin met—as his inspiration for the fight between the humans and the pigs. In fact, the Teheran Conference was a success that resolved several major issues among the Allies, such as establishing the date for the Allied invasion of Europe at Normandy.

In subsequent filmed versions of *Animal Farm*, Orwell's ending was changed. In the 1954 animated film, the animals attack the farm house and the pigs, implying that Communism will be overthrown by its own people. The 1999 version used the collapse of the Berlin Wall and the fall of Communism as its ending.

What Orwell did with *Animal Farm* was inspired. He told the story of the Russian Revolution and its aftermath between 1917 and 1943 in a way that could be understood as a powerful satire as well as a simple morality tale that even children could understand. In fact, when he was told by some of his friends that their children enjoyed *Animal Farm*, he was pleased. Orwell wrote in his essay "Why I Write" that *Animal Farm* was "the first book in which I tried, with full consciousness of what I was doing, to fuse political purpose and artistic purpose into one whole" (18: 320). He succeeded brilliantly.

Works Cited

Brunsdale, Mitzi. *Student Companion to George Orwell*. Westport: Greenwood, 2000.

Crick, Bernard. *George Orwell: A Life*. Rev. ed. London: Penguin, 1992.

Gross, Miriam, ed. *The World of George Orwell*. London: Weidenfeld, 1971.

Hitchens, Christopher. *Why Orwell Matters*. New York: Basic, 2002.

Orwell, George. *The Complete Works of George Orwell*. Ed. Peter Davison. 20 vols. London: Secker, 2000.

Rodden, John, ed. *The Cambridge Companion to George Orwell*. Cambridge: Cambridge UP, 2007.

_____, ed. *Understanding Animal Farm: A Student Casebook to Issues, Sources and Historical Documents*. Westport: Greenwood, 1999.

Of Communism, Censorship, Satire, and "Little Comrades": *Animal Farm,* Beijing, and the Problem of Genre_____

John Rodden

I

Shortly after the Chinese Communist Party's Sixteenth Congress end-ed in November 2002, and just weeks before the beginning of events commemorating the centennial of George Orwell's birth in 2003, a development occurred that not even the visionary author of *Nine-teen Eighty-Four* would likely have anticipated. Members of the Chi-nese Central Academy of Drama, the nation's most prestigious acting school, staged a public performance of Orwell's classic anti-Commu-nist satire, *Animal Farm* (1945). Ironically, this first-ever production of any work by Orwell in Communist China was permitted even though an English-language version of his beast fable—along with the rest of his oeuvre, including *Nineteen Eighty-Four*—remained on a black-list. Indeed, the only work of Orwell's ever published in China to that date was a Chinese-language edition of *Animal Farm* in the late 1980s, when Mikhail Gorbachev launched his programs of glasnost and per-estroika in the Soviet Union, and the zephyr of openness and reform briefly thawed out the Cold War deep freeze that the Chinese Commu-nist leadership had maintained.

The very fact that a theatrical production of *Animal Farm* was staged in the Chinese capital of Beijing in 2002 was a welcome surprise, if not a shock, to most Western observers. Communist Party leaders in Bei-jing had largely continued their policies of censorship and oppression into the new century, so that the *Animal Farm* production in the seven-hundred-seat Experimental Theater of the drama academy was initially heralded by Western observers as a possible sign of a major change in Chinese cultural policy. "When shrimps learn to whistle, the Cold War will end," Soviet leader Nikita Khrushchev had reportedly said, and the hope was that the *Animal Farm* performance might represent not just a thaw, but a rapprochement with the West.

The production ran two full months in Beijing and was witnessed by several thousand patrons. Director Shang Cheng Jun said he received official permission from the Ministry of Culture to stage the play. According to Shang's mentor, Beijing drama professor Su Yu, Shang decided to make the play child-friendly, with large animal costumes, to smooth the way for official approval. However, even though *Animal Farm* was inspired by events in the Soviet Union, with which the Chinese Communist leadership had sharp ideological disagreements, *Animal Farm* might strike the twenty-first-century Westerner as far more a fable about Chinese Communism than the long-defunct Soviet Union and its leader Joseph Stalin. Professor Su explained: "The problem of Stalinism and revolution is a very sensitive question. That is why the play is being presented as a show for children, very funny, with lots of animals and colorful costumes" ("Chinese Go Wild").

And therein lay the problem for director Shang and his acting troupe. They had been worried that Communist Party officials might censor their production, but they instead discovered a very different, almost equally distressing problem. "They don't get it," said Shang, reporting that playgoers seemed to find *Animal Farm* merely amusing and failed to grasp the political allegory altogether (McDonald). Some theatergoers said in exit interviews said that they had never before heard of Orwell's satirical fable.

Of course, in some respects, the public's confusion about the production and their ignorance of Orwell was fully understandable, given that this children's version—a festive *Animal Farm* for "little comrades"—deflected and obscured attention from the historical correspondences and political implications of Orwell's "animallegory." Moreover, his work had never been officially published except in an out-of-print translation appearing in a limited edition fifteen years earlier. More knowledgeable Chinese viewers were aware that *Animal Farm* satirized the Bolshevik Revolution and the history of Soviet Russia and that Napoleon the pig represented Stalin. They did not realize—or rather, they did not dare to mention publicly—that *Animal Farm* also possesses a striking relevance to Communist China's own revolution and history.

Shang's critics castigated him for having soft-pedaled Orwell's biting critique of Communism in order to appease China's censors. For instance, Napoleon's loyal dogs, who represent Lenin's Cheka or Stalin's NKVD (the Soviet secret police), kill only one character during the entire play—and the murder occurs off-stage. That is a very tame and misleading treatment of Stalin's mass purges of the 1930s, which in Orwell's book are depicted with Napoleon's dogs ripping out the throats of many of his perceived enemies. Moreover, the Beijing production was invested with a comic sensibility that featured slapstick, an eclectic mix of rhythm and music styles (ranging from klezmer to tango to the Irish singer Enya), and an odd assortment of puns and humorous asides referencing Chinese television personalities. On top of that, the actors themselves wore hilarious showboat costumes—as pigs, mules, horses, and chickens. One theater critic compared the effect of this staging to Disney's *Lion King*. All of this blunted or even effaced the force of Orwell's satire (McDonald).

Finally, as if to imply the Cold War has indeed really ended, Shang closed his adaptation of the fable with the penultimate scene from the book: Pilkington (the human owner of the neighboring farm, representing the Western capitalist countries) and Napoleon toasting each other. This celebration of their new business alliance thus stops before Orwell's actual ending in the fable, in which Napoleon and Pilkington engage in a card game, simultaneously playing the ace of spades, implying their coming rivalry—and thus predicting the impending start of the Cold War after the end of the World War II alliance between the Soviet Union and the United States and Great Britain.

III

The Chinese public's confusion about the staging of *Animal Farm* in Beijing is not, however, merely attributable to the four interrelated political and literary contexts that we have discussed: government censorship, public ignorance and anxiety, directorial self-censorship, and "kiddie glove" production decisions. Ironically, similar misconceptions arose from the moment of *Animal Farm*'s publication in August 1945—and indeed even before that, during its rounds of submission to publishers. For example, when Orwell's literary agent, Leonard Moore, sent Orwell's little fable to Dial Press in New York in 1945, their editors replied that "it was impossible to sell animal stories in the USA" (Orwell, *Collected Essays* 122). It may seem absurd to the knowledgeable present-day reader that American publishers of the 1940s could have read *Animal Farm* as a children's or animal story; how could editors and publishers mistake a sophisticated classic for a children's tale?

Whether funny or pathetic, the erroneous judgment of the editors at Dial Press was not an isolated case; many people in Great Britain misread the book too. Indeed, some British booksellers placed it in the children's sections of their shops. Like the Dial Press editors, these booksellers did not realize the story was a political allegory. They read *Animal Farm* much as did the young son of the art critic Herbert Read, one of Orwell's friends, who reported that his boy "insisted on my reading it, chapter by chapter, and he enjoys it innocently as much as I enjoy it maliciously" (qtd. in Crick 344).

These historical precedents should humble us when we read Western theater reviews that mock Beijing's *Animal Farm* production. If Anglo-American readers in 1945 and 1946 could so misread Orwell's fable—even with their advantages of historical proximity, cultural affinity, and relative freedom of speech and press—it makes the Chinese public's bewilderment seem not just eminently comprehensible but virtually inevitable. As we shall see, a prime cause of the bafflement, then and now, has much to do both with the tricky genres of the allegory and beast fable and with *Animal Farm* itself.

In my own classrooms, I often discover that today's American college students innocently commit some of the same errors as the Beijing theatergoers. So let us Westerners pause here briefly and hold up a mirror to ourselves before returning, perhaps mildly chastened, to the Beijing production. The recurring befuddlements and arresting historical parallels invite us to ponder how the stylistic and generic particulars of *Animal Farm* incite the puzzlements that have repeatedly occasioned its controversial reception scenes—whether literary, theatrical, or cinematic. Before examining those reception scenes in detail, however, the responses in 1945 of another young *Animal Farm* reader—and his father—warrant mention.

IV

Whereas the young son of Herbert Read misread *Animal Farm* for an animal story, the reaction of the son of the poet William Empson, one of Orwell's friends at the BBC and a sinologist who resided for many years in China, reflects another sort of misreading. It warrants mention here that Empson is also the author of a little-known, never-completed fable, *The Royal Beasts*, which he began to compose in China in 1937. From 1940 until his return to Beijing in 1946, he worked for the BBC in an office next to Orwell, who was a producer for the BBC's India broadcasts from 1941 to 1943, during World War II; Empson worked as the Far East producer and Chinese editor, chiefly responsible for broadcasting to the rest of Asia, including China.

Is it possible that Empson discussed his fable with Orwell and that it may have partly inspired Orwell's ideas in *Animal Farm*? Like Orwell's beast fable, *The Royal Beasts* is a satire in the tradition of Jonathan Swift. His plot features a tribe of African ape men. They are highly intelligent yet possess the physical features of subhuman primates and disdain being treated as "human beings." Empson shows the comical possibilities inherent in this situation via his protagonist Wuzzoo, a picaresque hero whose preference for a simian existence pokes fun at the assumptions of *Homo sapiens* and advances a serious social and even theological critique of the vanity of human wishes.

Moreover, just as Orwell's *Animal Farm* was written during World War II and is directly relevant to the European theater of the war, so too was *The Royal Beasts* composed during the Sino-Japanese War and richly pertinent to it. As BBC Chinese editor during World War II, Empson often spoke out against Japanese imperialism toward China. He was intimately familiar with Japanese life because he had taught as a professor of English in Japan from 1931 to 1934, when Japan had already started on its campaign of imperialism and military aggression. In 1937, the Japanese invaded Beijing and forced the major universities of northern China to combine into one institution, and exiled it to the Hunan province in the southwest, where Empson taught as the only foreign faculty member in any Chinese refugee university.[1]

According to Empson, his ten-year-old son, a Churchill admirer and a strong advocate for the Conservative (Tory) Party, was "delighted" with Orwell's fable and read it as "very strong Tory propaganda" (qtd. in Crick 444). Empson concluded his letter to Orwell about *Animal Farm*:

> I read it with great excitement. And then, thinking it over, and especially on showing it to other people, one realizes that the danger of this kind of perfection is that it means very different things to different readers. . . . I certainly don't mean that that is a fault in the allegory. . . . But I thought it worth warning you (while thanking you very heartily) that you must expect to be "misunderstood" on a large scale about this book; it is a form that inherently means more than the author means, when it is handled sufficiently well. (qtd. in Crick 444)

Empson was right: As we shall see, whether at the Cold War's outbreak in August 1945, or a decade later near its height in the winter of 1954–1955, or during the post-Communist era in 2002, Orwell's "little squib" came to mean many different things to different people (*Complete Works* 2421).

V

Let us now revisit the mid-1950s. Between the reading public's mis-conceptions about *Animal Farm* as the Cold War dawned and the Bei-jing theatergoers' confusions six decades later, cinema watchers also found themselves in a muddle when the famous film adaptation of Or-well's fable was released near the height of Cold War tensions, just days after the fall from power in late 1954 of U.S. Senator Joseph Mc-Carthy, the feared anti-Communist crusader. The 1954 Christmas sea-son brought to the screen an animated cartoon version of *Animal Farm*. The cinema posters screamed: "Pig Brother Is Watching You" (Rodden 282). As such scare ads suggest, moviegoers would soon witness a film marred by a form of Cold War cartooning similar in manifold ways to China's 2002 stage adaptation by its prestigious drama academy.

Created by the British husband-and-wife team of John Halas and Joy Batchelor, the 1954 animated *Animal Farm* was the first non-American feature-length cartoon and the first animated cartoon of a serious work of art. Halas and Batchelor were touted as cinematic pioneers. One critic wrote a book about the film's production; the film also received an award at the 1955 Berlin Film Festival (Rodden 282).

The sudden shift of opinion against Senator McCarthy made the politics of the *Animal Farm* film a subject of heated discussion in intel-lectual circles, particularly in America. McCarthy had been officially censured by the Senate in November 1954 for questionable financial dealings and persistent vilification of fellow senators. The move fol-lowed thirty-six days of televised hearings in 1954 on McCarthy's largely groundless charges that the U.S. Army "coddled Communists." McCarthy's fall from grace was as meteoric as his ascension. For many, the specter of McCarthyism had been "the Great Fear"[2]; now the media branded McCarthy's formerly popular anti-Communist crusade a "witch hunt."

The public's ambivalent attitude toward McCarthyism was reflected in the confused reception of the *Animal Farm* film. Perhaps because it portrayed Orwell's story as a general fable about the evils of power and lifted it clean from its historical context, the adaptation was assaulted in political organs from one end of the ideological spectrum to the other. On the far Left, Robert Hatch at the *Nation* reopened the attack on Orwell, judging the film a crude anti-Communist polemic. Conservative and anti-Communist critics, possibly still caught up in McCarthy's accusations about Communist control of Hollywood, implied that the British directors harbored "Trotskyite" sympathies. One reviewer suspected that Halas (an anti-Nazi war refugee from Poland) and Batchelor, who together had made numerous anti-Nazi propaganda films for the British government during the war, had engaged in leftist subversion of Orwell's message and deliberately redirected the fable's satire away from the Bolshevik Revolution (Brown 157). Noting the lack of any clear historical correspondences in the film to Russia under Lenin and Stalin, the reviewer asked, "Has truth become a luxury no longer available to liberals?" (Brown 157). Delmore Schwartz observed in *The New Republic*: "To a Rip Van Winkle or a Martian Man, the film might seem to be on the British Labour Party" (23) Another critic did mistakenly describe the film as "a bitter satire on the Welfare State" (Brown 157).

Admittedly, Halas and Batchelor made no attempt to remind viewers of the special relevance of Orwell's fable to Soviet history. One animated pig clearly resembled recently deceased Labour leader Ernest Bevin. In promotional ads, a fat-bellied pig wearing a string tie and smoking a cigar was clearly a caricature of a U.S. political boss, apparently a southern senator cut in the mold of Huey Long. Old Major was given a voice and face like those of British wartime prime minister Winston Churchill, and a pig with bushy eyebrows and a rude scowl resembled Joseph McCarthy. There was also a porcine version of the Nazi leader Hermann Goering, prompting at least one critic, in apparent ignorance of the book, to write that *Animal Farm* was a direct attack on fascism.

Other cinematic decisions by Halas and Batchelor were also read as ideologically motivated, and found questionable. Only the pigs talked, giving ammunition again to the Communist charge that *Animal Farm* (and Orwell) considered "the People" mere "dumb beasts" (Hatch 85). Widely deplored was the film's happy ending, implying that popular revolutions can succeed. The film closes with the donkey Benjamin leading animal revolutionaries from the far reaches of the globe in a triumphant march to oust the pigs from power. But I found that when Benjamin and the other animals join hands in the final frame, the film inadvertently evokes memories of the opening scenes and the solidarity of the first animal revolution led by the pigs—thus reawakening, rather than refuting, Orwell's doubts about the inevitable course of violent revolution.

Whatever the political motives of Halas and Batchelor, their adaptation served to confuse people further about Orwell's politics. For commercial reasons, rather than ideological factors stemming from censorship fears as in the Beijing production, *Animal Farm* was obviously also a film meant to cater to children—a production for, as it were, "little capitalists" rather than "little comrades." In effect, the film's directors transformed Orwell's political allegory into an ahistorical fantasy. For instance, the film's elimination of the characters of the neighboring farmers, Frederick and Pilkington, completely effaced the fable's origins in the events leading up to World War II and obscured its fierce lampooning of the Nazi-Soviet pact and other of Soviet Communism's "accommodations" with capitalism. The omission of certain minor characters like Clover, the mare who remains loyal to the revolution even after Boxer's death, and Mollie, the pretty dray horse who deserts the revolution for lump-sugar and ribbons, further robbed the fable of its historical moorings and its complexity. Politics aside, in light of the cuts and inverted ending, one could with justice object to what one reviewer called "the transformation of the prophet Orwell into the profit Orwell" (Weales 13).

VI

This returns us to our point of departure for this essay: the Chinese version of *Animal Farm* staged in Beijing in November 2002. As we have noted, the play's director—who fretted that Communist Party censors might forbid his production—encountered an apparently unexpected quandary in the public's incomprehension, even though his own production decisions appear to have ensured that his audience would not "get it." If playgoers failed to grasp the fable's immediate political relevance and satirical bite, wasn't that precisely director Shang's intention in his kiddie show for "little comrades"?

We live indeed in interesting times. So in the twenty-first century in Beijing, just as in 1945 in London and New York, we have yet another example of the paradoxical, even contradictory—and yet almost predictable—misunderstandings that Orwell's brilliant fable evokes: The book's reception is marked by a seesaw of twin ironies. On the one hand, it has been both the trigger and object of ideological contention; and on the other, it has been misread as a straightforward "animal story"—and Chinese audiences of our day are not alone in such misreadings. That fact should further remind us that in order to grasp the book, we need to understand its historical background and political context. And we need to be aware that more (outlandish) misconceptions about *Animal Farm* will likely arise with both the passage of time and the tendency of the mass public to watch adaptations rather than read books.

And let us not forget that Orwell himself judged *Animal Farm* to be his literary masterpiece. Did he therefore implicitly accept the risk voiced by William Empson? Did he consider the literary misinterpretations and ideological misconstructions a necessary and worthwhile, if regrettable and even politically hazardous, price to pay? Perhaps so. If so, his fateful decision reflects a final irony about the book's reception and influence. Probably *Animal Farm* would never have reached so many readers if it had been narrowly and transparently targeted at Stalin's Soviet Union: Its ambiguities are a major contributing factor to its immense circulation—and to the fame of its proud author, George Orwell, who groused jokingly to a friend after reading the early rave reviews: "But nobody said it's a beautiful book" (*Collected Essays* 73).

Notes

1. On these topics, see Empson's *The Royal Beasts and Other Works*, 130–81. For Empson's views on Orwell, see "Orwell at the BBC" in *The World of George Orwell*.

2. See David Caute, *The Great Fear: The Anti-Communist Purge Under Truman and Eisenhower*.

Works Cited

Brown, Spencer. "Strange Doings at Animal Farm." *Commentary* Feb. 1955: 157.

Caute, David. *The Great Fear: The Anti-Communist Purge Under Truman and Eisenhower*. New York: Touchstone, 1978.

"Chinese Go Wild for Animal Farm Play." *Scotsman.com*. Johnston Publishing, 23 Nov. 2002. Web. 29 Nov. 2011.

Crick, Bernard. *George Orwell: A Life*. London: Secker, 1980.

Empson, William. "Orwell and the BBC." *The World of George Orwell*. Ed. Miriam Gross. New York: Simon, 1976. 93–99.

_____. *The Royal Beasts and Other Works*. London: Chatto, 1986.

Hatch, Robert. Rev. of *Animal Farm*, dir. John Halas and Joy Batchelor. *Nation* 22 Jan. 1956: 85.

McDonald, Joe. "*Animal Farm* Struggles with Audiences in China." *Deseret News*. 28 Nov. 2002. Web. 29 Nov. 2011.

Orwell, George. *The Collected Essays, Journalism, and Letters*. Ed. Sonia Orwell and Ian Angus. Vol. 4. London: Secker, 1968.

_____. *The Complete Works of George Orwell*. Ed. Peter Davison. Vol. 16. London: Secker, 1998.

Rodden, John. *The Politics of Literary Reputation: The Making and Claiming of "St. George" Orwell*. Oxford: Oxford UP, 1989.

Schwartz, Delmore. Rev. of *Animal Farm*, dir. John Halas and Joy Batchelor. *New Republic* 17 Jan. 1955: 23.

Weales, Gerald. "Films from Overseas." *Quarterly Journal of Film, Radio and Television* (Fall 1955): 13.

Nightmares of History: *Animal Farm* and *Nineteen Eighty-Four*

Eugene Goodheart

Animal Farm was published in 1945, the year World War II ended; *Nineteen Eighty-Four*, Orwell's last and most famous work, appeared in 1949, a year before his untimely death at age forty-six. The publication dates are key to an understanding of why the books were written and how they were received. Nazi Germany, the most destructive totalitarian nation in history, had been defeated by an alliance of the United States, Great Britain, and the Soviet Union. The Soviet contribution to the war can be measured by the losses the country incurred, a staggering twenty million people, greater by far than those of its allies. The Allied victory was celebrated as the triumph of freedom and democracy over totalitarianism. But was it? Repressed in the consciousness of the Western members of the alliance (necessarily, because above all the war had to be won) was the totalitarianism of its Soviet ally. Germany's Adolph Hitler and the Soviet Union's Joseph Stalin, responsible together for the deaths of millions and the oppression of millions more, were cut from the same cloth.

Orwell never had illusions about Soviet Communism. He had fought against fascism in the Spanish Civil War in 1936 and witnessed at first hand the behavior of the Communists and Soviet emissaries who dominated the antifascist Republican side. Orwell tells the story of his experience in Spain in *Homage to Catalonia* (1938). If the Republican side had won, it is doubtful that the result would have been the socialist democracy that he and his comrades had fought for. The end of World War II became an opportunity for Orwell to warn the world in *Animal Farm* that totalitarianism had survived the war in the Soviet system.

Orwell's usual style is that of direct, plain-spoken confrontation. With the war hardly over, Western gratitude for the Soviet contribution to the war effort was strong. A direct assault on the Soviet system would be less effective than an animal fable, which makes it easier for the reader to focus on the tale and its message. Aesop is credited with inventing the animal fable, though animal fables existed long before him. Its primary audience being children, the fable has as its purpose moral instruction made pleasurable by the entertaining spectacle of animal behavior. *Animal Farm* is of course meant for adults, though children have read it for pleasure. At once fable and allegory, it requires of readers a sufficient familiarity with the events of the Russian Revolution to make the allegorical connection. As those events recede further into history, readers may need instruction in what was current knowledge for Orwell's contemporaries.

The setting of the fable is a farm owned by one Mr. Jones. Discontent among the pigs is rife; a prize-winning boar, Old Major (representing Karl Marx and Vladimir Lenin) has a "strange dream" (5) of rebellion against human tyranny that will end the slaughter, "the natural life of pigs" (8) under human rule. Believing that his death is imminent, he convenes the whole of the animal population in the neighborhood to rouse them to struggle against their oppressor and "remove Man from the scene, and the root cause of hunger" (6). By representing the laboring class as animals exploited by human beings, *Animal Farm* insinuates that in the class system, masters and servants belong to different species. The call to arms against the oppressor should bring to mind the Bolshevik Revolution in Russia in October 1917. The animal rebellion, led by pigs, succeeds, and the immediate aftermath is a shared sense of liberation and fraternity. "The animals were happy as they had never conceived it possible to be. Every mouthful of food was an acute pleasure, now that it was truly their own food, produced by themselves and for themselves, not doled out to them by a grudging master" (24). Mr. Jones recruits farmer friends to help him regain control of his farm. The effort fails, as did the counterrevolutionary efforts of the White Army of the overthrown Russian tsarist regime immediately after the Communists gained power. The most formidable enemy of the rebellion, however, is the enemy within. The sense of animal equality and fraternity is short-lived. The Communists preached a classless society of equals, but, like the Soviet Union, the farm, now controlled by the pigs, is anything but classless. Hierarchy reemerges and the pigs, the animals of highest intelligence, dominate the hens, the horses, the birds, and the rest of the animals. The leaders of the pigs, Napoleon and Snowball, assert their authority.

Readers familiar with the Russian Revolution will immediately recognize Napoleon and Snowball as Stalin and Leon Trotsky, respectively. The name Napoleon signals a connection that has been a prevailing view among historians: The Russian Revolution in its several stages was a reenactment of the trajectory of the French Revolution. Stalin is the Napoleon of the Russian Revolution, turning a revolution from below into another kind of authoritarian empire. Napoleon and Snowball have a falling out, as did Stalin and Trotsky, and Napoleon triumphs in the struggle. Fearing for his life, Snowball flees the farm, and Napoleon assumes the role of supreme leader. The expulsion and demonization of Snowball becomes a main strategy in Napoleon's consolidation of power. He eliminates all opposition to his rule, recalling Stalin's purges of his rivals for power. Napoleon's rule is the story of betrayal of the egalitarian promise of liberation.

Readers may be encouraged to think that since Napoleon seems to be replacing Mr. Jones in the role of tyrant that, in Orwell's view, there is nothing to distinguish Soviet Communism from capitalism. American literary critic Stephen Greenblatt draws the conclusion that, according to Orwell, "Communism is no more or less evil than Fascism and Capitalism" (Williams, 110). One has to have *Nineteen Eighty-Four* and other Orwell writings in mind to understand that this is not the case. Orwell declared himself to be a democratic socialist, and he was no admirer of capitalism, but he would have viewed the equation of totalitarian communism with capitalism, a system in which freedom actually exists, as a travesty. Is there any question that if he had had to make the choice between living in a democratic capitalist England and living in Communist Russia, he would have chosen England? *Animal Farm* is inadequate as a portrait of totalitarianism, because animal life and the limitations of the barnyard setting make it impossible to insert the elaborate technological apparatus on which totalitarian rule depends.

Animal Farm had its inspiration in Orwell's personal experience and his reading. He tells of observing a little boy whipping a huge cart-horse, which he came to see as comparable to the way the rich exploit the poor. He thought if only workers were aware of their power, they might end their exploitation rather than passively enduring it. In a little-known imaginary dialogue with Jonathan Swift (in Orwell's view the greatest English-language prose writer), Orwell says that Swift's *Gulliver's Travels* (1726) "has meant more to me than any other book ever written" (*Complete Works* 14: 157). Both *Animal Farm* and *Gulliver's Travels* are satires, and the fourth book of *Gulliver's Travels* is an animal fable. Its protagonists are the Houyhnhnms, a utopian community of horses, endowed with reason, who triumph over the disgusting Yahoos, Swift's version of degraded humanity. The horses in Swift's satire play a different role from that of Orwell's pigs. Swift's horses belong to the utopian imagination: They are moral and rational creatures that have no existence in the real world. In contrast, Orwell's pigs are fabulous translations of humanity. They suggest the animal origins of human need, desire, and ambition. (Given the enormity, in both senses of the word, of human desire and ambition, endowing pigs with human attributes may be unjust to the pigs.)

In the imaginary dialogue, Orwell brings Swift up to date on human progress made since Swift's time. Orwell asserts: "Surely you must admit that we have made a certain amount of progress since then?" Swift, already knowledgeable about the twentieth century, replies: "Progress in quantity, yes. . . . Whereas previously some petty tyrant was considered to have reached the highest point of human fame if he laid waste a single province and pillaged half a dozen towns, your great men nowadays can devastate whole continents and reduce entire races of men to the status of slaves." Orwell appears to support Swift: "Since your day something has appeared called totalitarianism" (*Complete Works* 14:

157–58). The dialogue, however, concludes with a rejection of Swift's misanthropy: "He was a great man, and yet he was partially blind. He could only see one thing at a time. His vision of human society is so penetrating, and yet in the last analysis it is false. He couldn't see what the simplest person sees, that life is worth living and human beings, even if they're dirty and ridiculous, are mostly decent" (14: 161).

What does Orwell's response to Swift tell us about *Animal Farm*? If the promise of the revolutionary pigs is to create a Houyhnhnm-like rational and decent society, it fails. The pigs, indeed the entire nonhuman animal world, turn out to be no different in their vices from human beings. Pride, power, greed, and cruelty are pervasive. After an attempt at reconciliation between pig and man, a quarrel breaks out between them. The concluding sentence of the tale says it all: "The creatures outside looked from pig to man, and from man to pig, and from pig to man again; but already it was impossible to say which was which" (118). There are decent creatures in the little world of *Animal Farm*, such as the horses Clover and Boxer, just as there are in the human world, but they are all too ready to accept authority. So what is the moral of Orwell's fable? Recall his reflection, occasioned by his witnessing of the beating of the cart-horse: if only the exploited were aware of their power, they might rid themselves of their oppressors. Well, the pigs are aware of their power; they rise up to overthrow their oppressor, only to become oppressors in turn. Orwell was not a misanthrope like Swift, but *Animal Farm*, perhaps despite his intentions, shares with Swift what appears to be despair about the human condition and, in particular, its political prospects. The horrors of the twentieth century were sufficient cause for despair.

Animal Farm can be read as a preface to *Nineteen Eighty-Four*, a far deeper exploration of totalitarianism than *Animal Farm*. (Though the Soviet model plays a role, the latter novel's conception of the totalitarian state is not confined to it.) Utopian fiction has been with us for centuries, its progenitor Thomas More, author of *Utopia* (1516), a Greek word that combines the meanings "no place" and "good place." In the nineteenth century, Samuel Butler titled his utopia *Erewhon* (1872), reversing the letters of *nowhere*. Utopia has no existence in the real world, nor will it ever have one. It is the dream of a rational and benevolent society, an ideal place from which the vices of society can be satirically observed and condemned. But what if utopia were realized? Enlightenment thinkers of the eighteenth century envisaged the possibility of a future in which liberty, equality, and fraternity would be triumphant. Beginning with the French Revolution in 1789, followed by a series of revolutions in the nineteenth century and culminating in the Russian Revolution of 1917, utopia came to seem a *somewhere*, a place possible to realize in the world.

Rather than utopia, however, these revolutions (the Russian Revolution is the prime example) brought into being monstrous perversions of the ideals that they affirmed. Utopia turned into dystopia, the dream into nightmare. Why and how this occurred became the subject of a subgenre of utopian fiction in the twentieth century, dystopian fiction; its most notable exemplars are the Russian Eugene (Yevgeny) Zamiatin's *We* (1924), Aldous Huxley's *Brave New World* (1932), and *Nineteen-Eighty Four*. Orwell was an admirer of Zamiatin's work. We see its influence, for instance, in Orwell's appropriation and translation of Zamiatin's Well-Doer in the character of Big Brother.

In *We*, Zamiatin, inspired by the episode of the Grand Inquisitor in Fyodor Dostoevky's *The Brothers Karamazov* (1880), lays out the logic of what was to become totalitarianism. In *The Brothers Karamazov,* Jesus returns to earth with the message of human freedom. The Grand Inquisitor, whose church rules in the name of Jesus, views the return of Jesus as a threat to his authority. He justifies his rule by declaring that freedom is a burden that ordinary human beings cannot bear. The church has assumed that burden and the power that goes with it in exchange for granting bread and security to the masses. Zamiatin reminds us that the exchange took place in the Garden of Eden. "There were two in paradise and the choice was offered to them: happiness without freedom, or freedom without happiness." Eve "chose freedom.

Naturally, for centuries afterward they longed for fetters," that is, for the fetters of security (Zamiatin 59). Late in *Nineteen Eighty-Four*, the protagonist Winston Smith, subjected to torture, seems to affirm the exchange, asserting that "men in the mass were frail, cowardly creatures who could not endure liberty or face truth, and must be ruled over and systematically deceived by others who were stronger than themselves. That the choice for mankind lay between freedom and happiness, and that, for the great bulk of mankind, happiness was better" (216). It is a deceptive and insidious exchange, for in giving up freedom, one gives up the promised security and happiness as well. Dystopian fiction is the story of the terrors of totalitarianism, the logical result of the surrender of freedom for an illusory security.

At the opening of *Nineteen Eighty-Four,* the revolution is already in the past. The Party that led the revolution is in power. Winston Smith is a minor clerk, an unhappy apparatchik, in Soviet parlance, in the bureaucracy of the totalitarian society of the fictional Oceania. His name is a somewhat surprising choice. Smith is Everyman, Winston the first name of Britain's great wartime leader. Orwell meant to associate his hero, who struggles for freedom, with Churchill's leadership in the fight for freedom against Nazi Germany. In coupling the ordinariness of Smith with the extraordinariness of the British leader, Orwell seems to be suggesting that in the totalitarian society of Oceania the spirit of freedom may reside in the ordinary person.

We find Winston on the first page climbing seven flights up to his flat (the electric current cut off, the lift is out of service), the climb made more difficult by the varicose ulcer above his ankle. As he passes through the hallway, he cannot escape the posters that hang everywhere on the walls: an enormous face with the caption below, "Big Brother Is Watching You." The hallway smells of cabbage and old rag mats. He is only thirty-nine, but appears to be forty-five. Life in Oceania has prematurely aged him. In less than a page, Orwell brilliantly evokes the atmosphere of oppression and squalor that will pervade the novel. Inside Winston's apartment, there is a "telescreen" that monitors the movements of the occupant, confirming the message of the poster. "Every sound you heard was scrutinized, and, except in darkness, every movement scrutinized" (7).

The reader should be alert to the irony: on the one hand, the Party that rules fails to make the lift operate efficiently, a service we expect from a benevolent and efficient government, and on the other hand, the Party proves to be remarkably efficient in its oppressive monitoring of the populace. Totalitarianism is not yet total. Darkness still eludes control, but we suspect that darkness too will be penetrated. We will learn that while the lives of the ordinary person are transparent to the government, the elite inner Party leaders who do the monitoring are hidden in darkness. Who they are and what they do remains a secret. Transparency and secrecy are arbitrarily distributed. Big Brother, the inaccessible leader of the Party, wants to control not only the movements of the populace, but also their thoughts and feelings. Privacy, family loyalty, intimate personal relationships are anathema to the state. Mind control falls to the Thought Police, who presumably will become unnecessary once every member of society internalizes the will of Big Brother.

The reader may at first be puzzled when he reads: "Nothing was illegal, since there were no longer any laws" (9). No laws in a totalitarian state? The reason is that state terror, the monitoring and punishment of all deviations from the will of the Party, is enough to enforce discipline. Consider too that the existence of laws would be a threat to the state, because even a law that the ruling Party created might have the unintended consequence of constraining it from doing anything and everything it wants to do. The combination of lawlessness and absolute power gives it license to change course arbitrarily and willfully at any moment. Totalitarianism is moral and legal anarchy.

The ambition of the totalitarian state, as distinguished from garden-variety authoritarian tyranny that has been with us for thousands of years, is to control the thought, indeed the inner life, of its subjects. To do so, external control is not sufficient. Each subject must learn to internalize the discipline. All thoughts and feelings that are potentially subversive are to be either extirpated or directed outward, away from the state. The state devotes a whole week to hatred of the enemy. Nothing makes for solidarity as much as collective enmity toward an adversary. Orwell has caught hold of truth that characterizes the citizenry even in our democratic societies. If there is no enemy, then the totalitarian conceit is to invent one. Oceania is always officially at war (either with Eastasia or Eurasia); "officially," because there may in fact be no war. (In dividing up the world among three powers, Orwell anticipated the rivalry for supremacy between the West and the Soviet Union that followed the end of World War II.) The enemy may be no more than an invention of state-controlled media. What is even more effective is to have the enemy personified: the official enemy of the state is Emmanuel Goldstein, modeled on Leon Trotsky (born Leon Bronstein), a Jew and Stalin's great rival for power. (Big Brother and Emmanuel Goldstein are also altered versions of Napoleon and Snowball in *Animal Farm.*) Throughout the novel, the question is raised as to whether Goldstein is still alive. It matters not: Dead or alive, the existence of Goldstein as anathema to Oceania is a political necessity for maintaining solidarity and paranoia.

In order to control the population, the state must have the power to say what passes for reality; that is, it must have the capacity to invent and reinvent "reality." Perhaps the greatest threat to the state is knowledge of the past. "Who controls the past," runs the Party slogan, "controls the future: who controls the present controls the past" (32). In order to control the past, the Party has to create a "memory hole" into which actual occurrences in the past, the knowledge of which might undermine its authority, are dropped. For instance, the heroic role of Goldstein in the revolution that brought Oceania into existence has to be forgotten or rewritten as treasonable. In Oceania, as on Mr. Jones's farm, the past is mutable. After they occur, events no longer have an existence apart from the Party's transcription of them. The idea of objective reality disappears. The reader, knowledgeable about the trajectory of the Russian Revolution, is immediately reminded of the way

Trotsky's heroic role in the Bolshevik Revolution of October 1917, as well as his subsequent contributions after the revolution, was either demonized or excised from the history books by Stalin.

The most powerful weapon in the arsenal of totalitarian states is language. Orwell invented a lexicon for describing the way in which government and media use and abuse language in order to instill obedience to the will of the state. The three slogans of Oceania are vivid examples of this abuse: "War Is Peace"; "Freedom Is Slavery"; "Ignorance Is Strength." In the first two instances, antonyms become synonyms and in the last instance, the effect is the same: not to know something, a sign of weakness, is declared to be a power. In an appendix to the novel, "The Principles of Newspeak," Orwell gives us a way of understanding the corruption of language and its consequences for the political life: "Newspeak," "doublethink," "thoughtcrime," "memory hole" and "Big Brother" are words and phrases that have entered into the English vernacular. Orwell's name is routinely invoked to describe language that deliberately or unconsciously distorts and betrays the truth to serve arbitrary power.

Consider, for instance, the most famous sentence in *Animal Farm*, the commandment that "All animals are equal, but some animals are more equal than others." It is a perfect instance of what Orwell characterizes as doublethink in *Nineteen Eighty-Four*. The language of equality is retained (the ideal of the revolution, after all, was equality), but the meaning is radically reversed. Doublethink is the perverse art of saying one thing, but meaning the opposite without acknowledging the contradiction. It is also the capacity for opportunistically taking one side or the other, depending on what furthers the gaining or retaining of power. A friend becomes an enemy, an enemy a friend when necessary. The perfection of doublethink, from the point of view of the state, occurs when it becomes a habit of the mind; those who think in this manner sincerely believe that they are uttering the truth. It is bad faith, not necessarily open hypocrisy. No longer does language represent reality; rather, language becomes an instrument of obfuscation, distortion, and repression. The word "Orwellian" is now promiscuously applied to every euphemistic expression that conceals the horrors of oppression and cruelty. To be Orwellian is the opposite of being Orwell, whose prose is a model of lucidity, honesty, and reason.

The drama of *Nineteen Eighty-Four* takes place in Winston's volatile mind, which shuttles back and forth between, on one side, a fascination with O'Brien, a member of the all-powerful inner Party and a factotum of Big Brother, and on the other, a revulsion at all that O'Brien represents. Anathema to Winston's deepest instincts, the state reveals itself in its ability take hold again and again of his mind in spite of every effort he makes to resist it. A strong counterforce to the state is sexual desire, as we see when Julia comes into Winston's life. Any desire or thought not sanctioned by the paranoid state is viewed as a threat to its very existence. In *We*, Zamiatin represents sexual desire as the most explosive force countering state control. Julia's promiscuity is similarly viewed as an uncontrollable force subversive of the state. Since Winston's deepest loyalty is to Julia, the state makes its ultimate task his betrayal of her as an enemy of the state. Arrested and subjected to physical and psychological torture, Winston proves his integrity by not betraying her—up to a point. Ever the psychologist realist, Orwell knows that human beings are not unbreakable, and that subjected to unspeakable torture and humiliation, even the most courageous among us will be broken. Winston has an insurmountable horror of rats, and in the dreaded Room 101, where the ultimate in torture occurs, he cannot resist their presence and betrays Julia. (Rats may have been Orwell's personal phobia, but he might have found a more horrible example for his story.)

Which brings us to Orwell's theory, or view, of human nature. In the tradition of British empiricism, he mistrusted intellectuals and their untested theories. He once said that he feared not the dictatorship of the proletariat, but rather the dictatorship of the intellectuals, who were given to abstract ideas about man and society. In this respect, he is implicitly closer to the great conservative writers Edmund Burke and

Alexis de Tocqueville, who mistrusted revolutions inspired by abstract ideas. Both Burke and Tocqueville viewed the French Revolution and its Reign of Terror as the unintended consequence of the ideas of the *philosophes*, the French intellectuals of the eighteenth century. A self-declared advocate of a decentralized democratic socialism, Orwell does not belong to the conservative camp. What is clear, however, is that he did not share the view of revolutionaries, who took progress for granted as the inevitable course of history. This should be clear from his deference to Swift's view in the imaginary dialogue. Moral and political progress, according to the theorists, assumes the malleability of human nature, which under totalitarian regimes means that human beings can be socially engineered, turned again and again into instruments of the State, and made to serve its changing purposes. Given his mistrust of theory, Orwell would not be expected to engage in metaphysical speculation about human nature. It is evident, however, that though he believed that human nature can change, he found the conception of an "infinitely malleable" human nature (*Nineteen Eighty-Four* 222) as repulsive as the idea that the truth of the past is malleable. The struggle in *Nineteen Eighty-Four* is between Winston's fundamentally decent nature and the coercive instruments of power, both physical and psychological, that ultimately overpower him. There are no limits to the power of coercion, but there *are* limits, Orwell seems to be saying, to the power of resistance.

Winston's capitulation at the end of the story is foreshadowed in the bizarre charade that O'Brien, Big Brother's servant, performs, pretending to be a leader of the Brotherhood, an illusory organization dedicated to the overthrow of Big Brother. In joining the conspiracy, Winston agrees to O'Brien's conditions that he would be "prepared to commit murder . . . to commit acts of sabotage . . . to betray [his] country . . . to cheat, to forge, to blackmail . . . to commit suicide," and more (142). The horrors of totalitarianism have been internalized even in those willing to overthrow it. In the spirit of doublethink, Winston's defeat is represented as a "victory over himself. He loved Big Brother."

We have other names for this achievement of doublethink: brainwashing and Stockholm syndrome, which Orwell would have had no trouble incorporating into his own lexicon.

I confess to having trouble finding Winston's love for Big Brother convincing. It is true that Winston had been drawn to O'Brien, but it is hard to believe that the torture O'Brien inflicts upon him can have been so easily transmuted into love. Abject capitulation yes, but love, whatever debased meaning it has acquired in Oceania? It is also hard to believe that during Winston's imprisonment O'Brien would demystify the official justification of Party rule, the exchange of freedom for happiness, when Winston appears ready to embrace it. O'Brien declares unexpectedly: "The Party seeks power entirely for its own sake. We are not interested in the good of others; we are interested solely in power" (217). Commenting in 1949, the year of the novel's publication, critic Philip Rahv wondered about Orwell's psychological realism, that is, whether "the party elite to which [O'Brien] belongs could live with this truth for very long" (qtd. in Howe 12). It seems as if Orwell is suspending psychological realism and delivering a lesson to the reader about the real truth of totalitarianism.

There is a long-standing controversy about the message the reader is to draw from Orwell's last two novels. Is he saying that we are doomed, or has he written in *Nineteen Eighty-Four* and *Animal Farm* cautionary tales that ideally should alert us to the threat in order to resist totalitarianism and prevent it from coming into being? Though *Nineteen Eighty-Four* was Orwell's last work before his death, there is good reason to believe he did not intend it as his last word about the present and the future. Orwell biographer Bernard Crick notes that the book does not end with Winston, but with Newspeak, which in effect is a cautionary statement about dangers that can be averted if we become sensitive to the use and abuse of language for political purposes. This may be evidence that Orwell did not think of himself as a prophet of doom. But what of the narrative itself, what does it tell us of the possibility of effective resistance?

Winston sees the proles, who remain relatively free of absolute control, as a possible source of resistance. They are the decent people who inspire Winston's (and Orwell's) faith in humanity. Is that enough? Orwell is famous for his clear-sighted realism and the candor with which he describes what he sees. But his blanket assertion of the decency of most people and their capacity to control their own destiny seems sentimental. What Orwell did not foresee—what he could not have been expected to foresee—was the implosion of the Soviet Union. At one point, Winston writes in his diary that "the Party cannot be overthrown from within" (60). However, the Communist Party and the Soviet state disintegrated amid great economic and political distress. The proletariat had no role in the demise of the Soviet Union. The reality is that totalitarianism is not as all-powerful as Orwell makes it out to be. It is fair to say that Orwell, who believed in human freedom, did not believe that the rise of totalitarianism was inevitable, but he was not hopeful about the possibility of avoiding it.

The reader may wonder why Orwell was so fixated on Soviet totalitarianism and paid so little attention to the Nazi version, the source of even greater terror and destruction. The reason is that the evil of Nazism, self-evident to anyone of decency, had been decisively crushed. Communism, however, survived and triumphed in the war. Because of its rhetorical idealism, it remained a dangerous temptation that needed to be demystified. Prominent and influential intellectuals were in its thrall, often disbelieving or downplaying the brutal reality of the Stalinist regime, even as incontrovertible evidence of it came to light. Orwell's focus on Soviet totalitarianism has endeared him to conservatives, who ignore or don't take seriously his commitment to democratic socialism; it has also troubled his relationship to those on the Left, many of whom have a history of sympathy with the Soviet Union. Orwell was a man of the Left who thought of himself as a critic of the illusions and stupidities of the Left. While other writers, such as Arthur Koestler in *Darkness at Noon*, may have given us a more incisive and persuasive insight into the ideology that buttressed Stalinism, Orwell doesn't provide Oceania with a clearly defined ideology; rather, he exposes the mindset that underlies all totalitarianisms: the desire in certain people for absolute power and control. Stalinism may be Orwell's main target, but his net is spread wide enough to include not only Nazism, but also tendencies in corporate capitalism.

With the demise of the Soviet Union and its satellites and the conversion of the Chinese Communist Party to state capitalism (only North Korea remains a dangerous, unreconstructed Stalinist state), what is the contemporary relevance of *Nineteen Eighty-Four*? Totalitarianism requires technological sophistication. Without the telescreen, the Party could not monitor the movements of people. And technology has made enormous advances since Orwell's time. Think of Facebook's capacity to invade the private lives of its subscribers. Some see in technological advance itself a totalitarian potentiality. I think such a view confuses means and ends. Technology can be used for totalitarian purposes, but in itself it is a neutral phenomenon. What persists, however, is the human susceptibility to mind control: in one version, susceptibility to the media when it passes lies or half-truths off as truths; in another version, susceptibility to the fanatical religious leaders who inspire followers to kill others and themselves for the greater glory of God. Authoritarian states still pose a threat. Perhaps the most dangerous contemporary manifestation of political power over the mind is not the state, but stateless political Islam.

Totalitarianism is not Orwell's exclusive target. He is the inveterate adversary of every kind of expression that distorts and conceals truth. In his essay "The Prevention of Literature," he writes: "In England the immediate enemies of truthfulness, and hence of freedom of thought, are the press lords, the film magnates, and the bureaucrats" (*Collected Essays,* 64). If Orwell were alive today, he might have mentioned the corporations and lobbyists who dominate our political life. In *Scenes from an Afterlife: The Legacy of George Orwell*, John Rodden shows in vivid detail the uses and abuses of the legacy of *Animal Farm* and *Nineteen Eighty-Four*. Radicals, liberals, and conservatives have all found support for their views in Orwell, some persuasively, others less so. Rodden succinctly summarizes the range of abuse of Orwell's legacy: "from hilarious ad campaigns spun off by carpet manufacturers and pro-gun lobbyists, to foreboding attack ads launched by regional Bell Telephone lobbyists and their adversaries, to the Soviet publication of *Nineteen Eighty-Four* in the dying days of the USSR and the reshaping of Orwell's renegade role there" (xvi). Orwell's reputation needs to be defended against those who twist it for their own ends. His greatest achievement is in his unequaled alertness to propaganda, that is, to the way in which those in power can manipulate language to make us accept lies as truth and illusions as reality, the effect of which is to make us passive and complicit with tyranny.

When I think of Orwell the person, a friend of Winston's named Symes comes to mind. Symes is "too intelligent. He sees too clearly and speaks too plainly. The Party does not like such people. One day he will disappear. It is written in his face" (47). Fortunately, Orwell is still with us in spirit.

Works Cited

Howe, Irving, ed. *Nineteen Eighty-Four Revisited.* New York: Harper, 1983.
Orwell, George. *Animal Farm.* New York: Harcourt, 1946.
_____. *The Collected Essays, Journalism, and Letters of George Orwell.* Ed. Sonia Orwell and Ian Angus. Vol. 4. New York: Harcourt, 1968.
_____. *The Complete Works of George Orwell.* Ed. Peter Davison. 20 vols. London: Secker, 2000.
_____. *The Lost Writings.* Ed. W. J. West. New York: Avon, 1985.
_____. *Nineteen Eighty-Four.* 1949. New York: Penguin, 1987.
Rodden, John. *Scenes from an Afterlife: The Legacy of George Orwell.* Wilmington: ISI, 2003.
Williams, Raymond, ed. *George Orwell: A Collection of Critical Essays.* Englewood Cliffs: Prentice, 1974.
Zamiatin, Eugene. *We.* 1924. New York: Dutton, 1952.

Literary and Scientific Perspectives on *Nineteen Eighty-Four*_____

Peter Davison

When the Soviet Union was at the height of its power and seemingly a threat to the Western democracies, Orwell's *Nineteen Eighty-Four* was especially timely. Many people read it as prophesying the future, and to such people, the passing of the actual year of 1984 would suggest the novel was past its sell-by date. But the novel has continued to be influential. This is not simply because of individual phrases that have stuck in the popular memory—Big Brother, Room 101—but because Orwell was not prophesying so much as warning. As a warning the novel is still potent, if for different reasons than in 1949, when it was published. Much has been written about what influenced Orwell in writing the novel (for example, William Steinhoff's 1975 *George Orwell and the Origins of 1984*), but one aspect has not, I think, received sufficient attention: Orwell's lifelong interest in science. Its importance to an understanding of *Nineteen Eighty-Four* is worthy of more consideration, especially the perversion of science, in which he took a particular interest at the time he wrote the novel, and which is still with us.

It is difficult to know precisely when Orwell took an informed interest in Soviet affairs. Various dates have been suggested, either from an examination of his life or directly by him—and he sometimes offered different dates. Thus, when Orwell returned from his service with the Indian Police in Burma and went to live in Paris in 1928 in order to try to become a writer, he would visit his aunt, Nellie Limouzin, her husband, Eugène Adam, and Adam's friend, Louis Bannier. Adam and Bannier had formerly supported the Soviets and had been witnesses to the October Revolution in Petrograd (Saint Petersburg) in 1917. However, they became disillusioned with Soviet Communism thereafter and went to live in Paris. About the time Orwell arrived in Paris, Adam and Bannier founded the Workers' Esperanto Association of the World in order to promote the use of Esperanto, an invented international language. Adam would only speak Esperanto. According to Bannier, Orwell would argue noisily with Adam *for* communism, proclaiming that "the Soviet system was the definitive socialism. So they were at each other's throats, despite the presence of the aunt" (Wadhams 42). Quite how the argument went with one man speaking only Esperanto and the other a combination of English and French is puzzling, even though Orwell had a natural gift for languages (he was conversant in eight and was learning a ninth, Italian, when he lay dying).

It is probably from this experience that Orwell began to take an interest in artificial languages, which would prove important in *Nineteen Eighty-Four.* Later, when working for the BBC in 1942, he arranged for broadcasts on Basic English, an artificial limitation of English to 850 words, designed to enable a learner to grasp its fundamentals easily and rapidly learn to converse in English. He was also an admirer of the novelist Evelyn Waugh (about whom he was writing at the time of his death), and it was probably from Waugh's novel *Scoop* (1938) that Orwell picked up the use of "cablese," the condensing of the English language by journalists to save the cost of sending news by cable, when creating Newspeak in *Nineteen Eighty-Four.*

In his preface to the Ukrainian edition of *Animal Farm,* Orwell makes it plain that, because he had never visited Russia, his "knowledge of it consists only of what can be learned by reading books and newspapers." He continues, indicating his disapproval of Soviet Communism, which was then fiercely admired by many on the Left: "Since 1930 I had seen little evidence that the USSR was progressing towards anything that one could truly call Socialism" (*Animal Farm* 111).

Writing to the author and social critic Richard Usborne, Orwell maintained he was "only intermittently interested in the subject [of Soviet Communism] until about 1935, though I think I can say I was always more or less 'left'" (*Life in Letters* xi). A major experience in Orwell's life that undoubtedly confirmed his social attitudes was his time in the north of England when he went to investigate the poverty and distress resulting from chronic unemployment, an experience that led to his writing of *The Road to Wigan Pier* (1937), the manuscript of which was handed in to his publisher on the eve of his departure to fight in the Spanish Civil War. Although he attended both Communist and Fascist public meetings in the north of England as part of his investigations, he was still relatively untutored politically. Thus we find that in Spain in 1937, Harry Milton, the only American in the British Independent Labour Party group of which Orwell was a member, thought Orwell "politically virginal." Milton and Orwell spent hours discussing politics in the trenches, so it is likely that Orwell learned much from him. (It was Milton who was standing by Orwell when Orwell was shot in the throat.) Yet another perspective on Orwell's political awareness at this time comes from another colleague in the trenches, Jack Branthwaite, whose father was a miner. He served with Orwell in Spain and told Stephen Wadhams that he thought Orwell inclined "slightly towards the communists when I first met him," adding, "I thought he was a wonderful man" (Wadhams 84).

After he returned to England from Spain in 1938, Orwell wrote that discovering "the truth about [Soviet leader Joseph] Stalin's regime . . . is of the first importance. Is it Socialism, or is it a peculiarly vicious form of State-capitalism? . . . It is difficult to go to Russia, once there it is impossible to make adequate investigations, and all one's ideas on the subject have to be drawn from books which are fulsomely 'for' or so venomously 'against' that the prejudice stinks a mile away" (*Complete Works* 11: 159). However, he found *Assignment in Utopia* by U.S. journalist Eugene Lyons, which Orwell reviewed on June 9, 1938, much more reliable than most books. Lyons was in the Soviet Union from 1928 to 1934 as a newspaper correspondent. These were years of appalling hardship for those living under the Soviet regime, as when some three million people starved to death in the Ukraine in 1933 as a result of a famine greatly exacerbated by Stalin's policies. Orwell concludes from Lyons's book that the Soviet system "does not seem to be very different from Fascism. . . . Everyone lives in constant terror of denunciation, freedom of speech and of the press are obliterated to an extent that we can hardly imagine. . . . There are periodical waves of terror," and "meanwhile the invisible Stalin is worshipped in terms that would have made Nero blush" (11: 159–60).

One can see in what Orwell learned from Lyons something of the tone that dominates *Nineteen Eighty-Four.* Lyons's book is almost certainly the source of the formula "two plus two equals five" so important in *Nineteen Eighty-Four.* In the Soviet Union, this formula symbolized the completion of a five-year state plan for national development in four years. However, Orwell might well have known it from the fourth volume of Laurence Sterne's *Tristram Shandy* (a copy of which Orwell had in his possession at his death), in which "Popish doctors" maintain that "God's power is infinite," so "he can do any thing," or Dostoyevsky's *Notes from Underground.*

On June 16, 1938, Orwell reviewed Jack Common's *The Freedom of the Streets.* Common, a friend of Orwell's, was a working-class writer who, in a series of connected essays, analyzed the attitudes of manual workers regarding socialism, remarking on how different their idea of socialism was from, in Orwell's words, "that of the middle-class Socialist who accepts Marx as his prophet" (*Complete Works* 11: 162). In his review, Orwell seems to have in mind events in the Soviet Union, doubtless influenced by his experience fighting in the Spanish Civil War and the animosity of Communists toward other socialist movements, especially the one for which he fought. Orwell goes on:

> Mr. Common writes all the while as though the dictatorship of the proletariat were just around the corner—a pious hope, but the facts do not seem to give much warrant for it. It would seem that what you get over and over again is a movement of the proletariat which is promptly canalised and betrayed by astute people at the top, and then the growth of a new governing class. The one thing that never arrives is equality. (11: 163)

Writing in 1945 to Michael Sayers (with whom Orwell had shared a flat in 1935 but who had lived in the United States throughout the war), Orwell says, "I don't think I could fairly be described as a Russophobe. . . . I think the Russian myth"—that is, the idealization of Soviet Communism—"has done frightful harm to the leftwing movement. . . . I thought all this as early as 1932 or thereabouts and always said so fairly freely" (*Life in Letters* 275).

Arthur Koestler's novel *Darkness at Noon* (1940) was written after its author (who was to become a close friend and ally of Orwell's) became disenchanted with Soviet Communism. It tells of a Bolshevik, Nicolai Rubashov, who had participated in the October Revolution of 1917 that brought the Soviets to power. Although instrumental in creating the Soviet Union, Koestler's protagonist nevertheless becomes one of tens of thousands of victims of Stalin's purges in 1938. He is tried, falsely convicted, and executed. Orwell reviewed the book in 1941 when it appeared in English, having appeared the previous year in German. The review is indicative not only of Orwell's reading in this field, but of his contempt for the "eagerness of Western intellectuals" to justify the Moscow show trials and to accept the confessions made by the accused. Orwell neatly gets to the heart of what is at issue in the book and in the Soviet state: Rubashov is "a composite picture having resemblances to both Bukharin and Trotsky"—Nicolai Bukharin and Leon Trotsky, both prominent leaders of the Russian Revolution and both victims of Stalin. Rubashov is also, Orwell continues,

> one of the last survivors of the original Central Committee of the Communist Party, is arrested, is charged with incredible crimes, denies everything, . . . and is shot in the back of the neck. The story ends with a young girl in whose house Rubashov has once lodged wondering whether to denounce her father to the Secret Police as a way of securing a flat for herself and her future husband. (*Complete Works* 12: 358)

Rubashov is persuaded to confess to crimes he did not commit by the apparatchik Gletkin, a "good Party man," the "almost perfect specimen of the human gramophone." Gletkin's argument is that the common people "cannot grasp that 'deviation' is a crime in itself; therefore crimes of the sort they can understand—murder, train-wrecking and so forth—must be invented" (12: 358). Orwell describes Koestler's book as "rather like an expanded imaginative version" of *Cauchemar en URSS* (*Nightmare in the Soviet Union*, 1937) by Boris Souvarine, a founding member of the French Communist Party who, following his time in the Soviet Union during the great purges and the fierce repression of ordinary Russians, was very critical of what he found there (12: 359).

Orwell returns to *Darkness at Noon* in a 1941 essay devoted to Arthur Koestler: "Naturally, the whole book centres round one question: Why did Rubashov confess?" Orwell argues that Rubashov and those like him "were actuated by despair, mental bankruptcy and the habit of loyalty to the party," a conclusion he says was also accepted by Souvarine in *Cauchmar en URSS*. "Justice and objective truth have long ceased to have any meaning" for Rubashov (*Complete Works* 16: 395–96). Orwell goes on later:

> If one writes about the Moscow trials one must answer the question, "Why did the accused confess?" and which answer one makes is a political decision. Koestler answers, in effect, "Because these people have been rotted by the Revolution which they served." . . . Really enter into the Revolution and you must end up as either Rubashov or Gletkin. It is not merely that "power corrupts": so also do the ways of attaining power. Therefore all efforts to regenerate society *by violent means* lead to the cellars of the Ogpu [secret police]. Lenin leads to Stalin, and would have come to resemble Stalin if he had happened to survive. (16: 397)

One other review is relevant for what it discusses as well as what it doesn't. On July 12, 1940, Orwell reviewed four books for *Tribune*: Jack London's *The Iron Heel* (1908), H. G. Wells's *When the Sleeper Wakes* (1910), Aldous Huxley's *Brave New World* (1932), and Ernest Bramah's *The Secret of the League* (1907; see *Complete Works* 12: 210–13). None is directly related to the Soviet system, but all are well-attested influences on Orwell—one, *The Iron Heel*, even referring to the year 1984. What is not mentioned in the review is a book that, it has been claimed, also influenced Orwell: *Swastika Night* (1937) by Katherine Burdekin (published under her pen name, Murray Constantine). Orwell may have received an edition of this book reprinted by the Left Book Club along with the other four (but see Davison 130–31).

Orwell was passionately keen on collecting pamphlets, especially political pamphlets. His collection is now held in forty-eight boxes by the British Library (for details see *Complete Works* 20: 259–96). On December 3, 1943, in his weekly personal column "As I Please" in the socialist journal *Tribune*, he says he had been collecting pamphlets since 1935 (16: 13). Ten years later, in his "Notes for My Literary Executor," he says he believes some of his pamphlets "must be great rarities" (17: 115). Between 100 and 150 pamphlets are devoted to anarchism and Trotskyism, and there are many more emanating from Communist writers. There are exceptions. Some were published by the National Labour Council and by the Independent Labour Party (of which Orwell was a member at the time). Two of the most significant pamphlets are *Why Did They Confess?* (published in the United States by Pioneer Publishers, 1937) and Souvarine's *Cauchemar en URSS.*

To many non-Communist observers, the confessions of so many in the Soviet Union to outrageous crimes against the state was deeply puzzling. There were three sets of show trials in Moscow, in 1936, 1937, and 1938; Orwell was particularly interested in the trial of Karl Radek, a close associate of Lenin's from before the 1917 revolution. Radek became secretary of the Communist International (the organization of world communist parties) in 1920, but then underwent a checkered career of expulsion from the party and later readmission. Eventually he was tried with sixteen alleged conspirators in January 1937. Although many of his colleagues were executed (the usual fate for those so accused), he was spared and sent to a forced labor camp, only to be murdered at the orders of the head of the secret police, Lavrenti Beria, in 1939. What Orwell found significant was the "fog of lies and misinformation" in the Soviet Union that "surrounds such subjects as the Ukraine famine, the Spanish civil war, Russian policy in Poland," yet Communist hardliners accepted the verdicts of the show trials without demur and were happy to gloss over what Orwell described in his important essay "The Prevention of Literature" as the "deliberate falsification of important issues" (*Complete Works* 17: 373).

It is one thing to derive facts from books and documents, and another to sense the atmosphere of what is at issue. Here one is on uncertain ground, but there are important clues. Orwell's close friend, the artist and editor Sir Richard Rees, who would later become Orwell's literary executor, arrived in Barcelona in April 1937 as a preliminary to his driving an ambulance during the Spanish Civil War. He went to see Orwell's wife, Eileen, who was working in the office of the Independent Labour Party. He wrote later that Eileen "seemed not so much surprised, as *scared*, to see me. . . . When she said she could not come out to lunch with me, because it would be too dangerous for me to be seen in public with her, I supposed I must have misheard and made no comment" (Rees, *For Love* 153). What Rees did not immediately realize was how tense relations were between the various left-wing parties. These would lead to a near-successful attempt by the Communists to wipe out their supposed allies, including the movement for which Orwell was fighting. Later Rees wrote:

> She seemed absent-minded, preoccupied, and dazed. As Orwell was at the front I assumed that it was worry about him that was responsible for her curious manner. But when she began talking about the risk, for me, of being seen in the street with her, that explanation no longer seemed to fit. In reality, of course, as I realised afterwards, she was the first person in whom I had witnessed the effects of living under a political terror. (Rees, *George Orwell* 147)

It is unbelievable that Eileen would not communicate these feelings to her husband. In *Homage to Catalonia*, describing the "May Events" of 1937 (the attempt by the Communists to dispose of their nominal allies, including Orwell's unit) Orwell refers to "the horrible atmosphere of suspicion and hostility" in their hotel and goes on to explain that "no one who was in Barcelona then, or for months later, will forget the horrible atmosphere produced by fear, suspicion, hatred, censored newspapers, crammed jails, enormous food queues and prowling gangs of armed men" (*Complete Works* 6: 129).

After having been wounded in the throat, Orwell returned to Barcelona, later writing:

> In Barcelona, during all those weeks I spent there, there was a peculiar evil feeling in the air—an atmosphere of suspicion, fear, uncertainty, and veiled hatred. . . . There was a perpetual vague sense of danger, a consciousness of some evil thing that was impending. However little you were conspiring, the atmosphere forced you to feel like a conspirator. (6: 148)

What we now know, though neither Orwell nor his wife could know at the time, is that three weeks after they had escaped from Barcelona, a report was made to the Tribunal for Espionage and High Treason in Valencia, accusing them of being *trotzquistas pronunciados*, "confirmed Trotskyists." Had they remained in Barcelona, they would doubtless have been arrested and tried for this crime. One can easily judge the seriousness of the charge from a similar document relating to one of their colleagues, Charles Doran, who was actually linked with Karl Radek, whose fate is described above (*Complete Works* 11: 30–31). One of Orwell's Spanish colleagues, Jordi Arquer, was caught and sentenced to eleven years imprisonment after being found guilty of precisely the charge leveled against Orwell and Eileen (20: 140).

Orwell's experience in Spain, what he had read about the Soviet Union—and even the atmosphere of his favorite Shakespearean play, *Macbeth*—would have been enough to suggest to him what he wished to depict in *Nineteen Eighty-Four*. Thus, in a broadcast he gave in 1943, he said of Macbeth that Shakespeare's king is "the typical figure of the terror-haunted tyrant, hated and feared by everyone, surrounded by spies, murderers, and sycophants, and living in constant dread of treachery and rebellion. . . . *Hamlet* is the tragedy of a man who does not know how to commit murder; *Macbeth* is the tragedy of a man who does" (*Complete Works* 15: 280–81).

But there were events nearer in time and place that greatly disturbed Orwell. As he states in his essay "The Freedom of the Press," intended as a foreword to *Animal Farm* in 1945 (but omitted by the publisher): "On one controversial issue after another the Russian viewpoint has been accepted without examination and then publicised with complete disregard to historical truth or intellectual decency. To name only one instance, the BBC celebrated the twenty-fifth anniversary of the Red Army without mentioning Trotsky" (*Complete Works* 17: 255; *Animal Farm* 100). At the end of World War II, the Poles were particularly oppressed by the Soviets, and Moscow put pressure on the Labour government in Britain to ensure that Polish troops were excluded from marching in the victory parade in London. Later, when a memorial to the wartime massacre of Poles by the Soviets at Katyn, Russia, was dedicated at Gunnersbury Cemetery in London in 1976, a later Labour government threatened to prosecute any British officer who attended in uniform. However, in September 1988, at a ceremony to mark the Soviet invasion of Poland, the government of Prime Minister Margaret Thatcher did allow British officers to attend in uniform. Only in 2010 have the Russians admitted that Stalin instigated the Katyn atrocity.

It was one thing for Orwell to recreate the political life of Soviet Russia in *Animal Farm*, but his real achievement was somehow to recreate the "tone" of life in Soviet Russia, but without ever having been there. One of the key moments in Orwell's understanding of Soviet life and attitudes was his meeting in Paris in March 1945 with Josef Czapski, a Polish painter and author who had studied in Saint Petersburg and witnessed the Russian Revolution. He fought with the Polish Lancers against first the Germans and then the Russians when they invaded Poland in 1939 and was one of the few prisoners who escaped the massacre by the Russians of prisoners at the Starobielsk prisoner-of-war camp. Having met Czapski, Orwell wrote to his publisher to ask that the text of *Animal Farm* be changed in the light of what Czapski told him. He kept in touch with Czapski and tried to get his memoir of Starobielsk published in English, and it was doubtless from Czapski that he learned much about the atmosphere of Soviet life.

From his childhood, Orwell had been interested in writing a book about the future. Jacintha Buddicom, his childhood friend, records that "we had in our house a copy of [H. G.] Wells's *Modern Utopia* . . . which was so greatly fancied by Eric that it was eventually given to him. He said he might write that kind of book himself" (Buddicom 39). What, however, prompted him to set about writing that book, the book that would become *Nineteen Eighty-Four*?

It was not until 1944, as a direct result of the Teheran Conference of November 1943, that Orwell thought of writing the novel. At Teheran, Stalin, U.S. President Franklin Roosevelt, and British Prime Minister Winston Churchill met to discuss the progress of the war, in particular the planned invasion of Normandy (D-Day) and plans for the postwar settlement. One contentious issue was what influence the Soviet Union would exert on its neighbors. The outcome was Soviet domination of Eastern Europe, leading to the Cold War. Although those Eastern European countries regained their independence at the end of the twentieth century, Orwell is still a figure of great importance to them, especially in Poland. When the Poles were desperately trying to regain their freedom from the Soviet Union, Orwell's face was shown on postage stamps issued by the Polish Underground State. He told his publisher that *Nineteen Eighty-Four* was intended "to discuss the implications [at Teheran] of dividing the world up into 'Zones of influence.'" He went on that, in addition to discussing these implications, he wished "to indicate by parodying them the intellectual implications of totalitarianism. It has always seemed to me that people have not faced up to these & that, e.g. the persecution of scientists in Russia, is simply part of a logical process which should have been foreseeable 10-20 years ago" (*Complete Works* 19: 487–88).

Although Orwell was now coming to see what it was that he wanted to write about, the novel was slow in gestation. One can see that physically. The manuscript of *Nineteen Eighty-Four* shows him changing the date of the opening of Winston Smith's diary as he wrote the novel. Thus, April 4, 1980 was changed first to 1982 and then to 1984 (*Nineteen Eighty-Four* 23–24). Had his progress on the book been faster, we might be talking about *Nineteen Eighty*, not *Nineteen Eighty-Four*!

As it happens, we can pinpoint just when and what it was that set in motion the composition of *Nineteen Eighty-Four*. What is apparent is just how very important a role science was to play in the composition of the novel. Orwell had been very interested in science from his school days at St. Cyprian's School in England. A friend of Orwell's from Eton College, Sir Roger Mynors, recalled how Orwell developed a passion for biology and got permission to do extra dissection in the biology laboratory. One day, Orwell, who had remarkable skill with a slingshot, brought down a jackdaw perched high up on the roof of Eton College chapel. He and Mynors (who would later become professor of Latin first at Cambridge and then at Oxford University) took it to the lab to dissect it. Recalled Mynors, "We made the great mistake of slitting the gall bladder and therefore flooding the place with, er . . . Well, it was an awful mess" (Wadhams 18–19). Orwell's interest in science continued after Eton. It is not always realized how much attention Orwell paid to science when he was working for the BBC and arranging programs to broadcast to India. Of twelve six-lecture courses that he organized for Indian university students chiefly based on Bombay and Calcutta University syllabi, five were devoted to science and one to psychology. Many of his speakers were leading figures in their fields, such as J. D. Bernal, Gordon Childe, James Needham, and Susan Isaacs.

It was clear that hearing British biologist John Baker speak at the 1944 PEN Conference for authors, in London, suggested to Orwell the line he could take in his new novel, and that the role of Soviet agronomist Trofim Denisovich Lysenko was very significant in prompting Orwell to begin writing (Orwell, *Lost Orwell* 128–33; *Life in Letters* 345–47). Baker was a founding member of the Society for Freedom in Science, and keen to expose the perversion of science under Stalin in the Soviet Union. In particular, he was concerned about Lysenko's manipulation of the theories of genetics. Lysenko rejected traditional hybridization theories and believed that he could thus vastly improve Soviet crop yields; he even believed he could make wheat become rye. His work was fallacious and even dangerous—many starved when his experiments failed. Stalin, however, had complete faith in him and decreed that any biologist opposing him should be dismissed and even sent to prison camps. One preeminent scientist, Nicolai Vavilov, president of the V.I. Lenin All-Union Academy of Agricultural Sciences, was arrested by Stalin's secret police for disagreeing with Lysenko and exiled to Siberia, where he died in 1943.

In the PEN lecture, Baker reiterated his objection to scientific planning, specifying the case of Lysenko and his appointment in place of Vavilov as director of the Academy of Agricultural Science. Baker concluded his talk by arguing that "the case of Lysenko provides a vivid illustration of the degradation of science under a totalitarian regime" (qtd. in Orwell, *Lost Orwell* 131). Lysenko's approach failed utterly, but he and his methods were not finally discredited in the Soviet Union until 1964.

Orwell's experience as a writer, in particular the way he wrote about the Spanish Civil War, was subjected to political attack. He therefore found it unsurprising that *Homage to Catalonia* and *Animal Farm* experienced difficulties in finding publishers, and that his reviews and articles about the Spanish Civil War were often rejected, accurate though we now know them to be. However, he was surprised that science, supposedly fact-based, should be subjected to political interference, even under Stalin. Surely science was "pure," factual, peer-reviewed? Hence, as he wrote in "The Prevention of Literature," "there are countless people who would think it scandalous to falsify a scientific textbook, but would see nothing wrong in falsifying a historical fact" (*Complete Works* 17: 374). But the case of Lysenko demonstrated otherwise. The fog of lies and misinformation that affected even the factual—the scientific—showed him only too clearly how destructive of truth was Soviet communism.

The role of science in *Nineteen Eighty-Four* is thus highly significant. It may seem a long way from dissecting a raven, but Orwell was always keenly interested in, and observant of, natural science—at St. Cyprian's, around where he lived in Wallington (on Jura), and in Morocco. Very obviously, the manipulation of even a simple arithmetical equation, $2 + 2 = 5$, illustrated how simply facts could be perverted. When Winston says, "In the end the Party would announce that two and two make five, *and you would have to believe it*," (emphasis added) the perversion of science is brilliantly and succinctly summed up. He goes on:

> It was inevitable that they should make that claim sooner or later: the logic of their position demanded it. Not merely the validity of experience, but the very existence of external reality, was tacitly denied by their philosophy. The heresy of heresies was common sense. And what was terrifying was not that they would kill you for thinking otherwise, but that they might be right. (*Complete Works* 9: 83–84)

Just as Lysenko's work depended on a denial of science, so is science denied in *Nineteen Eighty-Four* to such an extent that under Party control, "Science, in the old sense, has almost ceased to exist. In Newspeak there is no word for 'Science.'" Then, in an appendix titled "The Principles of Newspeak," he states: "There was no vocabulary expressing the function of Science as a habit of mind, or a method of thought, irrespective of its particular branches. There was, indeed, no word for 'Science', any meaning that it could possibly bear being already sufficiently covered by the word *Ingsoc*" (*Nineteen Eighty-Four* 323).

O'Brien denies that the earth is any older than those now living on it. As for the bones of extinct animals, "nineteenth-century biologists invented them" (*Nineteen Eighty-Four* 278). Furthermore, "when we are omnipotent we shall have no more need of science" (280). A few pages later: "Anything could be true. The so-called laws of Nature were nonsense. The law of gravity was nonsense. 'If I wished,' O'Brien had said, 'I could float off this floor like a soap bubble.' Winston worked it out. 'If he *thinks* he floats off the floor, and if I simultaneously *think* I see him do it, then the thing happens" (291).

What is particularly interesting is how well Orwell sensed the *atmosphere of life* under the Soviet regime without his ever having lived there. His insight into what motivated and what would eventually undermine Stalin's empire, coupled with his creative genius in offering a warning for all time rather than merely prophesying what might happen (but which also might not) has given *Nineteen Eighty-Four* its enduring power. It was also a mark of his genius that in highlighting the significance of scientific truth, and the dangers implicit in distorting that through the work of complicit scientists such as Lysenko, has made the novel enduringly relevant. It is possible to see how accurately Orwell hit the mark by examining the work of a contemporary Soviet novelist, Vasily Grossman. Grossman's novel *Life and Fate* shares with Orwell's the fearful atmosphere of life in that far-from-ideal socialist society. I am less concerned with the stories these novels tell, though they have much in common, than in the "atmospheres" they have in parallel and their shared interest in the perversion of science. Though neither author knew of the other, nor of what they each had written, they both saw the dangers of a society destroying genius and denying people their freedom and individuality. *Nineteen Eighty-Four* continues to be a powerful novel because it did not set out to be a prophesy of what 1984 would bring (a prophesy that, when that year passed, would have faded away), but because it offers a warning for all time.

Works Cited

Buddicom, Jacintha. *Eric & Us*. 2nd ed. Chichester: Finlay, 2006.

Davison, Peter. *George Orwell: A Literary Life*. Basingstoke: Macmillan, 1996.

Orwell, George. *Animal Farm*. Ed. Peter Davison. London: Penguin, 1989.

_____. *The Complete Works of George Orwell*. Ed. Peter Davison. 20 vols. London: Secker, 1998.

_____. *A Life in Letters*. Ed. Peter Davison. London: Secker, 2010.

_____. *The Lost Orwell*. Ed. Peter Davison. London: Timewell, 2006.

_____. *Nineteen Eighty-Four: The Facsimile of the Extant Manuscript*. Ed. Peter Davison. Weston: Harcourt, 1984.

Rees, Richard. *For Love or Money: Studies in Personality and Essence*. London: Secker, 1960.

_____. *George Orwell: Fugitive from the Camp of Victory*. London: Secker, 1961.

Wadhams, Stephen. *Remembering Orwell*. Harmondsworth, Ont.: Penguin, 1984.

Ideology Versus Psychology in *Nineteen Eighty-Four*: Dystopia Meets Modernism_____

Gorman Beauchamp

From its first appearance in 1949, *Nineteen Eighty-Four* divided readers between those who read the novel ideologically and those who read it psychologically. The ideological readings predominated, particularly as long as the totalitarian regimes against which the dystopian satire had been explicitly directed still loomed in Eastern Europe. The essence of the novel was seen as its historical-political analysis and its minatory warnings. "The moral to be drawn," Orwell said in a press release, replying to some reviews, "is a simple one: *Don't let it happen. It depends on you*" (152; italics in original). Most readers of the first persuasion would agree, then, with Orwell's first biographer, Bernard Crick, that his was essentially "a sociological rather than a psychological imagination" (397).

But there were always dissenting readers who stressed the psychological dimensions of the novel, not always as an aesthetic merit. In the well-known instances of Isaac Deutscher and Anthony West, the psychological "analysis" was directed at Orwell himself, with the anti-utopia offered as evidence of his personal irrational fascination with cruelty (Deutscher) or of "a hidden wound" that could alone "account for such a remorseless pessimism" (West 397). As the Cold War waned and fear of a real-world Oceania faded, interpretations of the book itself became less ideological, more literary, and consequently more psychologically focused. These analyses were less preoccupied with Orwell's psyche and more inclined to view the psychological motifs as consciously deployed narrative devices. The title of one influential essay of this period suggests something of this critical reorientation: "Masochism as Literary Strategy" (Fiderer).

At issue is the crucial function in the novel of the phenomenon called sadomasochism. Sigmund Freud originally believed that sadism and masochism were two sides of the same coin, a connection generally accepted by both professionals and laity. But for my purpose here, the two phenomena need to be treated as independent variables. Sadism functions centrally—and controversially—in *Nineteen Eighty-Four* as the motive for the Party's exercise of power. O'Brien's torture of Winston Smith mirrors microcosmically the rationale of Ingsoc, the Party's totalitarian ideology. "Power is not a means," O'Brien explains to Winston, "it is an end. . . . The object of persecution is persecution. The object of torture is torture. The object of power is power" (386). None of that I-must-be-cruel-only-to-be-kind pretense for O'Brien; he is cruel because he likes being cruel. The ultimate assertion of power, he professes, lies in making others suffer. "If you want a picture of the future," he declares in the most famous pronouncement in the novel, "imagine a boot stamping on a human face—forever" (390). And O'Brien, both as an individual and as a spokesman for Big Brother, enjoys having his foot in the boot.

This rationale for the exercise of power has seemed to most readers overwrought and fantastical, even in the face of the once-unimaginable enormities of twentieth-century totalitarianism—the Holocaust, intentional mass starvation in the Ukraine, the Moscow show trials, the Gulag—which Oceania was clearly meant to reflect. Much printer's ink has been expended debating the cause and cogency of Orwell's power-as-sadism thesis, a critical skirmish to which I have contributed a salvo or two myself. But here I want to make one further observation on the subject: The sadist's pleasure in his power must be significantly diminished if his victim *wants* to be hurt, if he *likes* having a boot stamping on his face. I am reminded of the joke where the masochist says, "Beat me!" and the sadist says, "No." The sadist, that is, does not need the masochist, who presents only minimal challenge to his will to dominate; but the masochist does need the sadist, to inflict the pain he craves.

Put in terms of the narrative of *Nineteen Eighty-Four*, O'Brien's sadism does not require Winston's masochism—it might, indeed, seem more terrifying if Winston were not so oddly complicit. Nevertheless, Orwell "masochizes" him: "At the sight of the heavy, lined face, so ugly and so intelligent," to adduce one typical example from the long, excruciating torture sessions, "[Winston's] heart seemed to turn over. If he could have moved he would have stretched out a hand and laid it on O'Brien's arm. He had never loved him so deeply as at this moment" (376). Gerald Fiderer in the essay cited above puts it this way: "The secret aim which informs his every defiant act is to arrive at the lovingly punishing hand of O'Brien" (17). All his resistance to Big Brother, the whole plot of the novel really, becomes then a series of pseudo-revolts designed, albeit unconsciously, to culminate in the torture chambers of the Ministry of Love. Whether Fiderer overstates the nature of Winston's masochism—he interprets the relationship between the two men as a homosexual one—the fact remains that Orwell has complicated his protagonist's personality in such a way and to such an extent that a pathological interpretation of his behavior seems not only possible, but plausible. And whether Winston's masochistic attraction to O'Brien represents an unconscious manifestation of elements in Orwell's own psyche or whether it serves some consciously chosen artistic purpose—or a combination of both—the result is that the psychology compromises the clearly stated purpose of the dystopia, opposition to totalitarianism in all its forms.

II

What accounts for this discrepancy between the stated purpose of the novel and the ambiguous, compromised nature of the protagonist? My suggestion is: modernism. This term denotes the aesthetic ethos and practice that emerged in the first decade of the twentieth century and that by mid-century had come to exercise near-hegemony over the serious—that is, highbrow—literary scene. Although the term *modernism* is a relatively late coinage to characterize the arts of that half century, all its great literary figures are now deemed modernists: Joseph Conrad, James Joyce, T. S. Eliot, W. B. Yeats, Marcel Proust, Andre Gide, Thomas Mann, Virginia Woolf, William Faulkner, Franz Kafka, to cite only the most prominent. As with any complex literary movement—the Baroque, say, or Romanticism—differences, sometimes even antipathies, exist among the practitioners who constitute the movement; but, of course, there must be certain assumptions and practices common to it.

One of the crucial distinctions, drawn by Virginia Woolf in her influential essay "Mr. Bennett and Mrs. Brown," is that between *pure* novels and *engaged* novels. Of the latter, she says, "They leave one with a strange feeling of incompleteness and dissatisfaction. In order to complete them it seems necessary to do something—to join a society, or, more desperately, write a cheque. That done, the restlessness is laid, the book finished," no need ever to read it again (105). Engaged writers, that is, look outside or beyond their fictional constructs to the external world with its specific problems; fictional characters serve as their messengers to or about that world and signify only as messengers, not as figures of interest in and of themselves. The dystopia is an engaged genre par excellence, and Winston, one would assume, ought to act so as to convey its antitotalitarian message about the real world.

The pure novel, the modernist ideal, would, among its other characteristics, focus on character as intrinsic, fascinating in and of itself. Modernism gave rise to what we now call the psychological novel and—to generalize barbarously, as I must here—characters in such works began to exemplify the kinds of behavior revealed and analyzed in the in-depth psychology studies of Sigmund Freud. While major modernist writers expressed varying and not always favorable responses to Freud, most literary and cultural historians now agree that he was the crucial codifier of the new view of human nature ushered in in the new century. "On or about December, 1910," Woolf famously, if a tad facetiously, declared, "human nature changed" (96). And Freud changed it. In his 1940 homage to Freud, the Anglo-American poet W. H. Auden wrote:

> To us he is no more a person
> Now but a whole climate of opinion
> Under whom we conduct our different lives . . .
> He quietly surrounds all our habits of growth (166)

The Freudian dynamic, according to which "man is not master in his own house"—people do not, that is, control or even understand their own motives or actions—came to inform modernism's fictive worlds, worlds of suppressed trauma and crippling neurosis, of unconscious desires and "the return of the repressed," of the Oedipus complex and the death instinct. The confidence of the preceding Victorian age, summed up in a line from William Ernest Henley's poem "Invictus"— "I am the master of my fate: / I am the captain of my soul" (114)— gives way to the confession of Brett Ashley in Hemingway's *The Sun Also Rises,* about to embark on yet another destructive affair: "I can't help it. I've never been able to help anything" (187). Brett speaks for her modernist cohorts.

In its fashioning of complex characters (and plots), modernism prized ambiguity, uncertainty, the oblique, and the problematic—that which is difficult, if not impossible to grasp and explain. The critic Philip Rahv lauded the nineteenth-century Russian writer Fyodor Dostoevsky as "the first novelist to have fully accepted and dramatized the principle of uncertainty or indeterminacy in the presentation of character" (598); this in reference to his protagonist Raskolnikov in *Crime and Punishment,* who murders an old woman for reasons that he himself never really understands. Black and white are "out" in modernism; infinitely nuanced shades of gray are "in." Within this intellectual-aesthetic milieu, then, Orwell fashioned Winston Smith.

Orwell accounts, obliquely, for Winston's masochism as stemming from the guilt he feels for having robbed his helpless baby sister of her bit of chocolate and his subsequent responsibility, at least in his own mind, for her and his mother's disappearance immediately thereafter. Scolded, he runs away, and when he returns, they are gone, never to appear again. The memory of this traumatic event, with all its echoes and ramifications, threads subtly through the novel, so that Winston's subconscious *need* for punishment appears psychologically plausible. And, I hasten to add, Orwell's complicating his character in this way, psychically wounding him, makes Winston a more intriguing figure and the book a more intricate and complex one than it would have been otherwise. But—to reiterate my thesis—aesthetic complexity is achieved at the expense of ideological concentration and cogency.

Consider a work the exact obverse of *Nineteen Eighty-Four*, Nikolay Chernyshevsky's *What Is to Be Done?* (1863), a Russian novel outlining, advocating, and predicting a utopian world soon to come. If, in sociopolitical terms, *Nineteen Eighty-Four* stands as the most significant novel of the twentieth century, *What Is to Be Done?*—challenged only by *Uncle Tom's Cabin*—holds that position in the preceding century. It became *the* classic of revolutionary literature, a bible for Europe's radicals: Lenin treasured his martyred brother's well-thumbed copy; Marx is said to have learned Russian in order to read it. "It was Chernyshevsky more than any other man," writes historian E. H. Carr, "who shaped the moral attitudes of two generations of Russian revolutionaries" (xvii). All this despite the fact that the book is awful as literature—wooden characters, flat plot, stilted dialogue, endless lecturing. Still, its protagonist, Rakhmetov, proved a powerful inspiration, the kind of hero whom you want to bring down the corrupt old world, the ideal "new man" who will transform Russia. Ruthlessly iron-willed and rigidly ascetic in his habits, he sleeps on a bed of nails to toughen himself for the coming revolution. In short, in Chernyshevsky's novel, ideological message and novelistic dramatization are in perfect sync.

Imagine, however, if near the end of the novel, Rakhmetov were arrested by the tsarist secret police and confessed himself relieved, since what he really relished was being beaten daily by big, brutal Cossacks.

Such a scenario would no doubt cast some retrospective shadow over the whole revolutionary project; and would, at a minimum, raise the question of why Chernyshevsky would have attenuated his message with an unnecessary personality quirk in his protagonist. Why, then, does Orwell? We know, of course, that under torture severe enough, almost anyone can be made to say or do almost anything, even cry, as Winston does when faced with a cage of hungry rats, "Do it to Julia!"—his one true love. His breaking under torture, while horrifying, is not surprising; anyone, if candid, would admit he or she would have been no braver in Room 101. What surprises, however, is Winston's complicity, the psychological undermining of his ideology, a hatred of totalitarianism.

By the mid-twentieth century, no aspirant to serious literary standing would have, except perhaps as parody, depicted a heroic figure like Rakhmetov, just as today no such aspirant would be guilty of a Fagan or an Uncle Tom. Each age imposes its own pattern of reality, what's possible and what's plausible, what rings true and what clanks false. Today superheroes exist only in comic books. "No man is a hero to his own valet," the saying goes; Orwell's age—and ours—is the age of the valet, artistically speaking, issuing in and reenforced by modernism, validated by Freud. In this intellectual milieu Orwell wrote his dystopia, with a protagonist seemingly brave enough to defy, at least mentally, the totalitarian system—"our man in Oceania," upholding our values—but who, inexplicably, reveals himself a cringing masochist welcoming his punishment. What poses a much more problematic— and presumably more interesting—character psychologically, generates ideological confusion.

III

That Aldous Huxley, when faced with a parallel challenge in crafting a credible protagonist for his dystopia *Brave New World* (1932), compromises him in the same ideologically unsatisfactory way suggests the subversive influence of modernism on the message novel.

True, *Brave New World* is a more amusing, playful work than *Nineteen Eighty-Four*, its projections more distant, less pressing than Orwell's. Years later, however, in *Brave New World Revisited* (1958), Huxley argued that the future would much more probably resemble his fictional one than Orwell's—and he was probably right. (An eventuality, by the way, that would have pleased Orwell, since he was trying to prevent his "future," not accurately predict it, a detail forgotten when his cogency as a prophet is assessed.) Whereas Oceania depended on force and fear, the telescreens and the jackboot, Huxley's London A.F. 632 (After Ford, that is) resembles a sybarite's paradise of promiscuous sex, escapist drugs, and constant consumption—"spending is better than mending"—a totally hedonistic life of perpetual unreflective adolescence, with benefits. Henry Ford, perfector of mass production, is worshiped (literally) as the deity of this world, where people are produced on assembly lines, like cars. Natural birth is obsolete, obscene to mention, and people grow as embryos in bottles, mentally and physically endowed by chemical means in vitro and psychologically conditioned in group nurseries. The five types so produced—from "Alpha pluses" to do the brain work to "Epsilon minuses," semi-morons for peonage—can be ordered in whatever numbers are needed for the jobs that need to be done.

In such a world—and, of course, I've barely sketched Huxley's here—the author wants a spokesman representing our own world to reject the values and practices of the fictional one. Huxley's manuscript revisions reveal him casting about to discover a dramatic counterforce to his dystopian future—first Bernard Marx, a somewhat stunted Alpha (something must have gone wrong in his bottling) who proved too feckless for the role; then, briefly, Helmholtz Watson, perhaps too clever to play the martyr; and finally John Savage. John is discovered on an Indian reservation in America, which is maintained something like a wild game preserve today, the accidental child of a Brave New Worldling woman who, visiting there, loses both her Malthusian belt and her way and is left behind, pregnant. John, raised among the Indians, is sui generis, neither a true savage like the Malpais, nor a properly conditioned Brave New Worldling like his parents. He is, instead, almost literally a Renaissance man, a creation of the Shakespeare canon, having learned to read and deduced his ethical principles from an old copy of *The Complete Plays* which somehow turned up on the reservation. In one sense, the character is a stroke of genius, with his perspective as Renaissance humanist autodidact occupying an ideal vantage point for observing and judging the hedonistic world of A.F. 632.

But, in fact, John proves an ambiguous creation, toward whom Huxley seems unable to maintain a consistent perspective. Not infrequently, John becomes the target rather the vehicle of the novel's buoyant satire. *Brave New World* reads in many ways as a funny book, the product, its author later recalled, of an amused, skeptical aesthete. Any satirist who can rechristen London's august Atheneum Club as the Aphroditium writes not wholly from despair. But making Savage ludicrous in the fierce maintenance of his chastity, as Huxley does in the hilarious scene where Lenina tries, aggressively, to seduce him, only undercuts, if it does not entirely subvert, the humanistic ethos he represents: a distillation of *The Tempest* that should serve to expose the value-sapping promiscuity of the Brave New World. Even worse, however, John's sexual reluctance emerges not as a matter of principle, but as a psychological neurosis, an hysterical prolongation of the Oedipus complex.

Huxley had small regard for Freud. A familiar story tells of his attending a convention of psychiatrists where he crossed himself piously every time Freud's name was mentioned. Still, Freud figures as one of the manifestations of Our Ford in A.F. 632—the form, that is, assumed by the divine Henry when pronouncing on matters psychological (although Huxley here often confuses Freud with Ivan Pavlov, who developed the techniques used in the Hatching and Conditioning Centres). And Huxley endows John Savage with a markedly Freudian psyche, perhaps even to the point of parody.

As a boy, John tries to murder his mother's Indian paramour—significantly named Popé—as the couple lie together "in the rank sweat of an enseamed bed," one of the lines from *Hamlet* that John quotes as he stabs. Indeed, John sees himself as Hamlet, Popé as Claudius, and the play itself as an Oedipal scenario of lust and guilt. For Freud, the Oedipal relation is the seedbed of all neuroses, and John Savage—insofar as naturalistic criteria apply to one of his provenance—certainly qualifies as a neurotic. The key scene occurs at his mother's bedside as she is dying:

> "Popé!" she murmured, and closed her eyes. "Oh, I do so like it, I do . . ." She sighed and let herself sink back into the pillows.
>
> "But, Linda!" The Savage spoke imploringly. "Don't you know me?"
> . . .
>
> He felt the faint answering pressure of her hand. The tears started into his eyes. He bent over her and kissed her.
>
> Her lips moved. "Popé!" she whispered again, and it was as though he had had a pailful of ordure thrown in his face. Anger suddenly boiled up in him. . . .
>
> "But I'm John!" he shouted. "I'm John." (204–05)

Only in his fury at this rejection does Savage finally direct his anger at the state apparatus, hurling away the hospital's supply of soma—the widely used hallucinogen distributed by the state—and causing a riot.

If *Brave New World* were only a science fictional comedy of the country mouse going to the big city, agog and perhaps sometimes aghast at the goings on of his more advanced cousins, then we would not be greatly concerned about the country mouse's psyche; his angst among all the special effects would be only part of the comedy. But *Brave New World* aspires to be something more serious than that: a dystopia, a warning against its world. And in the chapters immediately following Savage's meltdown appears the intellectual and ideological core of the novel, his debate with one of the World Controllers, Mustapha Mond, about the rationale and desirability of this brave new world. These chapters make for exciting reading, with Mond's provocative, audacious apologia for the superiority of his world over that which it replaced (ours), and John's Shakespeare-informed resistance. (So persuasive proves Mustapha Mond's argument that several critics contend that Huxley actually meant to show that he was right.) Their debate too long, complex, and multifaceted even to broach here, I'll note only its crescendo, John affirming the full nature of being truly human over the condition of always being comfortable and cared for:

> "But I don't want comfort. I want God, I want poetry, I want real danger, I want freedom, I want goodness. I want sin."
>
> "In fact," said Mustapha Mond, "you're claiming the right to be unhappy."
>
> "All right then," said the Savage defiantly, "I'm claiming the right to be unhappy."
>
> "Not to mention the right to grow old and ugly and impotent; the right to have syphilis and cancer; the right to have too little to eat; the right to be lousy; the right to live in constant apprehension of what may happen tomorrow; the right to be tortured by unspeakable pains of every kind."
> There was a long silence.
>
> "I claim them all," said the Savage at last. (240)

This affirmation has an undeniably heroic ring—Prometheus to Zeus, or something of that order. A confrontation between the spokesman for a paternalistic utopianism and the resisting advocate of a world less "perfect" and more free appears as a standard feature in most dystopias; but Huxley's, I think, is the most inclusive, the most finely honed, the most challenging. So—does the state of the speaker's psyche matter if his will is thus intact? (I am the master of my fate, I am the captain of my soul.) Does it matter that in the concluding chapter, immediately following, John is shown masochistically flagellating himself from a sense of guilt at experiencing sexual desire? Does it matter that his first sexual experience occurs in a sadomasochistic orgy that he incites, beating the woman with whom he copulates with a whip and denouncing her as a strumpet? Does it matter that the woman is Lenina, whom John has always associated with his own mother, Linda? Does it matter that the man who defended full humanness in all forms hangs himself out of sexual guilt? Does it matter that the despair from *personal* failure, not the state of the world as revealed to him by Mustapha Mond, drives John to suicide? How would it affect the reception of his sermon if a priest were discovered molesting the altar boys?

My point here is that John Savage emerges as so neurotic, so sexually conflicted, that his role as the sole surviving exemplar of human freedom and dignity is drastically undercut. If *he* stands as our exemplar, maybe Mustapha Mond wasn't so wrong about the pre-Fordian world. Simply as an entertainment, what the French call a *jeu d'esprit*, *Brave New World* probably gains from having such a protagonist—gains in psychological subtlety, in ironic juxtapositions, in amusing ambiguities. But do these features—complexity, irony, ambiguity—serve well a work with a serious warning to convey, a dystopia? From that standpoint, nothing is gained and much forfeited, the dramatization at loggerheads with the message. *Nineteen Eighty-Four*, as noted, is a much more dire, more insistent work than *Brave New World,* with none of its brio and playfulness, so that the compromising of Winston Smith matters more than Huxley's analogous send-up of Savage; but insofar as they meant their cautionary tales to be taken seriously, resorting to the modernist psychologizing of character for their protagonists was a mistake.

IV

In addition to the issues I have raised, much the best discussion of the psychological factors in and around *Nineteen Eighty-Four*, both in breadth and depth, is Alex Zwerdling's essay "Orwell's Psychopolitics" (1984), in which he brings to bear the great body of writing in the emerging field of social psychology in the 1930s, 40s, and

50s. In these decades, the phenomena of sadism and masochism were extended beyond their categories as sexual perversions of individuals to cover patterns of group behavior. "Social masochism," as the psychoanalyst Theodore Reik called it, "is everywhere, has become an attitude of life" (qtd. in Zwerdling 96–97). Erich Fromm, in the same period, in *Escape from Freedom* (1942), explored "the longing for submission" that fascism had uncovered and exploited. Even Freud himself came to see sadomasochism "as a universal tendency in human nature," as Zwerdling puts it, "neither primarily sexual nor entirely aberrant" (96). In the sociological study *The Authoritarian Personality*, published by Theodore Adorno and his colleagues a year after Orwell's dystopia, "the *potentially fascistic* individual" is identified as displaying "a general disposition to glorify, to be subservient to and remain uncritical toward authority figures" (qtd. in Zwerdling 99). The weight of such theory leads Zwerdling to conclude: "Winston Smith has many of the characteristics described in some social psychology written in the decade that produced Orwell's novel. He is of course a rebel on the surface and thinks he is joining a conspiracy to bring down a despotic regime. But Orwell makes it clear that at a deeper level, Winston wills his own degradation because of his wish to submit" (100).

One caveat about this conclusion seems tautological: social psychologists look at politics more or less exclusively through the lens of psychology, as a Marxist would view politics as the interplay of economic forces, or a theologian see God's providence at work—or as a cobbler might locate the appeal of fascism in a fascination with shiny black boots; this is what the French call a *deformation professionnelle*. But the case can pretty easily be made that Orwell, too, by this time shared the belief in the irrational nature of political dynamics: No system of rational explanation could account for the convulsive trauma that mid-century Europe had endured. He crafted his novel as this generation of theorists derived their theories: in the matrix and from the experiences of these terrible decades. One should not conclude from Zwerdling's discussion that Orwell knew all, or even more than a small fraction, of these psychological studies—some that Zwerdling cites were written after Orwell's death—but rather that the mid-twentieth-century zeitgeist engrossed him and them together.

Literary modernism and this mid-century social psychology developed independently, of course, without reference or relation one to the other, *except* for their common source in psychology, whether explicitly Freudian or not. Thus, character in the modernist novel and group behavior in social psychology share irrational, often self-destructive, motives, understood dimly, if at all, by the participants themselves. Both are, in Freud's metaphor, not even masters in their own house—not conscious, that is, of the dynamics of their own psyches. Orwell's attempt, as I see it, to make his dystopia aesthetically meritorious—with its confused, conflicted protagonist, in the true modernist manner—coupled with the collapse and slavish submission of entire nations to totalitarian rule, evidenced by recent history and explained by social psychology, combined to produce Winston Smith, the frailest of reeds upon which to prop a protest novel, easily broken.

If we grant the psychological interpretation of the novel—that Winston subconsciously desires and courts his punishment—where does that leave the antitotalitarian message that Orwell saw, consciously anyway, as its *raison d'etre*? The dystopian writer always faces the choice of how impermeable, how invulnerable to make his or her nightmare future: the more dire the forecast, of course, the more urgent the warning—but also the more pessimistic. Some offer a glimpse of hope, the possibility at least of a way out; and some actually show the evil order subverted by heroic resistance. Ira Levin's *This Perfect Day* (1970) is a good example of the latter type, a dystopic adventure story where a bright, brave young man—the Rahkmetov type—infiltrates and finally destroys Uni, another autocratic technocratic elite. *Nineteen Eighty-Four*, however, like *Brave New World*, offers no escape hatch, no way out of or beyond the nightmare. "Fight Uni!" was the cry of Levin's rebellious underground Brotherhood (228), while the Brotherhood in Oceania is (probably) an invention of the state, a trap to lure malcontents. The pessimistic hopelessness of *Nineteen Eighty-Four* accounts, no doubt, for the seriousness with which it was taken as a political warning and, at the same time, for the legitimacy of its claim as serious work of (modernist) literature. Modernism doesn't traffic much in happy endings.

Some have argued that to see the full dehumanizing effect of Ingsoc, Orwell necessarily had to offer a "normal" character—as normal, that is, as the dystopic circumstances allow—a flesh and blood character with flaws and failings and varicose veins, who serves, as I call it, as our man in Oceania, feeling the horror and hatred that we would feel in his place. True, but that is not quite what we get. In a naturalistic novel, a character constituted like Winston might present a fascinating study in the sadomasochistic interplay between him and O'Brien, a study in aberrancy. But *Nineteen Eighty-Four* is not a naturalistic novel, and Winston Smith is not a random naturalistic character. Rather, *Nineteen Eighty-Four* is the story of the fate of the world and Winston Smith is our one hope in it, the Last Man in Europe (as Orwell considered titling the book). While not strictly an allegory, the two major figures here loom large as symbolic figures, O'Brien embodying the totalitarian will to absolute power, Winston our own human desire for freedom, love, and personal integrity. So much is this the case that O'Brien is often taken as the disembodied voice of an abstract dynamic, Orwell's view of power as sadism, and debate rages over the nature and adequacy of that view, separate from the psychology of its fictive spokesman. But consider Winston as a corollary symbol. As a symbol of resistance to Big Brother, if only mentally, internally, he disappears in the Ministry of Love, his will and identity dissolved in the mind of O'Brien. Is he not then the masochistic submissive identified in the contemporary works of social psychology as the enabler of totalitarianism? But beyond that, if O'Brien is the true face of power for Orwell, then is not Winston the true face of mankind, for whom he stood as symbol—not only frail and fallible, but ultimately the willing victim of all the Big Brothers? Has our man in Oceania revealed us to ourselves?

We know from Orwell's other writings that this is not his consistent view of human nature, that he believed in the essential decency of the common man and hoped for the day when his exploitation would end. But the growing pessimism of his last years—the fear that only the cruel and unscrupulous attain and keep power—must have created doubts about the nature of the exploited as well as the exploiters. (As the bandit chief in the film *The Magnificent Seven* puts it, "If God had not wanted them shorn, he would not have made them sheep.") Winston Smith may have been a consequence of this pessimism. We know now, of course, that almost anyone can be made to say or do almost anything under torture or even certain kinds of relentless mental pressure. And in this sense, Winston is doomed from the first words he writes in his diary; we are horrified, but not surprised at what is done to him. But for him to *welcome* his doom, to *embrace* his torturer, to have loved Big Brother subconsciously *all along*—this not only horrifies but shocks, a revelation that compromises not only Winston but, to some degree, the book itself, as a dystopia. "Don't let it happen. It depends on you"—this the message Orwell meant his book to convey. And we (collectively, benefiting from the actions of our elders) didn't let it happen. Too bad Winston couldn't have been more help.

Coda

Commenting on this essay, the editor of this volume, John Rodden, pointed out an inconsistency between my acknowledging the extraordinary influence exerted by *Nineteen Eighty-Four* in the ideological world of the last half of the last century and my claim that "psychologizing" Winston Smith worked against the effectiveness of the novel as a dystopia. However, my claim here is not meant to be absolute, but relative. On the one hand, there is simply no question whatever of the sociohistorical centrality and importance of the novel; on the other, I want only to suggest that the fictive nature of the protagonist, in some ways and to some degree, unfortunately dilutes its ideological imperatives.

Let me be candid and personal. I had read *Nineteen Eighty-Four* any number of times without the "problem" that I identify above registering with me in any significant way. I must have noted Winston's bizarre behavior toward O'Brien, but it did not seem of prime import amidst the revelations and horrors of his ordeal in the Miniluv. Orwell's emphasis highlights the horrendous state apparatus crushing this one individual more than the individual's particular response to it, except, of course, for its complete success in destroying him: "Do it to Julia." Like me, earlier, the first-time or casual reader will remember and be affected by the horrors of Oceania—the dystopian writer's desideratum—far more than the quirks of the protagonist.

Works Cited

Auden, W. H. "In Memory of Sigmund Freud." *The Collected Poetry.* New York: Random, 1945. 163–67.

Carr, E. H. Introduction. *What Is to Be Done?* By Nikolay G. Chernyshevsky. New York: Vintage, 1961. ix–xviii.

Crick, Bernard. *George Orwell: A Life.* London: Secker, 1980.

Deutscher, Isaac. "*1984*—The Mysticism of Cruelty." *Heretics and Renegades.* London: Hamilton, 1955. 35–50.

Fiderer, Gerald. "Masochism as Literary Strategy: Orwell's Psychological Novels." *Literature and Psychology* 20 (1970): 3–21.

Hemingway, Ernest. *The Sun Also Rises.* New York: Scribners, 1954.

Henley, William Ernest. "Invictus." *Modern British Poetry*, 4th ed. Ed. Louis Untermeyer. New York: Harcourt, 1936. 114.

Huxley, Aldous. *Brave New World.* New York: Harper, 1998.

Levin, Ira. *This Perfect Day.* Greenwich: Fawcett, 1970.

Orwell, George. "Appendix G: Orwell's Press Release of 15 June, 1949." *Nineteen Eighty-Four*, ed. with critical introduction Bernard Crick. Oxford: Clarenden, 1984. 152–53.

Rahv, Philip. "Dostoevsky in *Crime and Punishment*." Fyodor Dostoevsky. *Crime and Punishment.* Ed. George Gibian. New York: Norton, 1964. 592–616.

West, Anthony. "George Orwell." *Principles and Persuasions.* New York: Harcourt, 1957. 164–76.

Woolf, Virginia. "Mr. Bennett and Mrs. Brown." *The Captain's Death Bed and Other Essays.* New York: Harcourt, 1978. 94–119.

Zwerdling, Alex. "Orwell's Psychopolitics." *The Future of Nineteen Eighty-Four.* Ed. Ejner J. Jensen. Ann Arbor: U of Michigan P, 1984. 87–110.

George Orwell's *Nineteen Eighty-Four* in the Twenty-First Century

Peter Stansky

Nineteen Eighty-Four was published in 1949 and was a great success from the very beginning. It has continued to be so and has sold millions of copies. One has the impression that reading it is a rite of passage in many high schools, and it is one of the few texts that many Americans have read in common. In many senses, texts are rather unstable entities. No doubt there are continuing elements in this particular novel. Yet there are others that may change as succeeding generations have read it. What are the elements of the book that remain the same? What are those that may change as we look at them more than a half century later?

To begin with, there is the comparatively stable element of its author, George Orwell. Was he as stable as all that? Who was he? For starters, he wasn't George Orwell at all. He was born and died Eric Arthur Blair. George Orwell was a pseudonym that he used for his first published book, *Down and Out in Paris and London* (1933), a work of reportage about living in poverty. He chose not to use his real name in part because he did not wish to run the risk of embarrassing his parents with a tale of being a dishwasher in Paris and a tramp in England. In any case, he didn't much like the name he was born with. He felt it was too upper class and pseudo-Scottish, and did not really reflect who he was: a member of "lower-upper-middle class," as he so precisely described it. For his pseudonym, he chose George, a deeply English name associated with the country's patron saint, Saint George, and Orwell, a river near where his parents were then living. The name is similar to that given to the central figure in *Nineteen Eighty-Four*, Winston Smith. Both names, particularly George and Smith, have an "everyman" quality. Yet Winston, of course, is an echo of Winston Churchill. Winston Smith was presumably born around the time of World War II, and that part of his name evokes an English hero. In his case, it is somewhat ironic, as he is nothing but a lower-level civil servant. Orwell wished to dwell on how an "ordinary bloke" of the middle classes reacts to the world that he finds about him.

Orwell himself never legally changed his name, remarking that if he did so he would then have to find another name to write under. All his books and, except for a very few early writings, his magnificent essays and his many reviews and shorter pieces were published under the name of George Orwell. (His collected works consist of twenty stout volumes, an amazing output for a man who only lived forty-six years.) He was known as "George" to those he met from the late 1930s on; he fully took on this persona at the time of the Spanish Civil War. Yet in the country churchyard at Sutton Courtenay where he is buried, he is simply identified as Eric Arthur Blair.

Orwell fought in the Spanish Civil War and wrote about it brilliantly in *Homage to Catalonia* (1938). Earlier in life he had been rather neutral, politically, but just before going to Spain, he had moved to the left, and committed himself to a socialist vision for the future of British society. He was driven to this point of view by the poverty he witnessed when he visited mining communities in the north of England, as recorded in *The Road to Wigan Pier* (1937). Then in Spain, overwhelmed by the egalitarian spirit he found in Barcelona, he declared himself a believer in democratic socialism, with the important qualification that it would be as he personally understood it. In Spain, he found his set of political beliefs, but also discovered what he considered socialism's greatest enemy: the Soviet Union and its version of communism. It was his conception of socialism and of its betrayers that shaped his two most famous books, *Animal Farm* (1945) and *Nineteen Eighty-Four* (1949). In Spain he had been a premature anti-Fascist. At the same time, he also became a premature anti-Communist, unfashionable on the Left in the 1930s and even more so during World War II, when the Soviet Union was an ally of Britain and the United States.

What story does *Nineteen Eighty-Four* tell? The world has been divided into three megastates. Winston Smith lives in Airstrip One, the former Britain that has become part of the western state, Oceania. Two of the states are generally at war with the third, but which two are allied changes periodically. Then history has to be rewritten to create a past that conforms to whatever happens to be the case at present. Orwell's vision of the future was not so inaccurate. Up until 1989, we had a world divided between West and East, with China as the third player. At the moment, one might say we have the West and China, with the volatile and unstable Middle East as the possible third factor. What will happen in the future is quite unclear.

Orwell sets his novel more than thirty-five years from the time he is writing. We know that the world is not quite right. The book opens with a clock giving the time in a modern way: "It was a bright cold day in April and the clocks were striking thirteen." Winston Smith, a resident of London, is a minor functionary in the all-powerful Party. His job at the Ministry of Truth (Minitrue) is to rewrite past stories in *The Times*, in Orwell's own time England's canonical newspaper, so that their contents conform to what might be the new Party line at the moment; Winston consigns stories that no longer conform to the Party line to a "memory hole." The past in *Nineteen Eighty-Four* is thus deeply unstable. The Party wishes to have it appear as always consistent when in fact it is modified all the time, particularly in the matter of which of the other two empires is Oceania's ally and which is its enemy. The news as printed in the past must conform to the "fact" that Oceania has always had the same ally. There is also the necessity either to eliminate or rewrite the story of particular figures as a new Party line dictates: certain individuals, once heroes, are now villains. How will this everyman cope with this situation? As Smith, he is everyman; as Winston, perhaps there is something heroic in him. He hates the conformist state in which he lives. The state demands that its inhabitants worship the head of state, Big Brother, and vehemently hate his enemy, Goldstein, modeled on Stalin's nemesis, Leon Trotsky. This is ritualized in the "Two Minutes Hate" that takes place each day in Trafalgar Square in the center of London.

It is this aspect of the novel—the rewriting of the past—that has the greatest resonance for the reader in the twenty-first century. As far as I know, Orwell had no inkling of the coming of the digital age. Documents from the past have always been unstable in one sense: they are interpreted in different ways and may well have different meanings for those who created them and those who interpret them at a later point. That is what historians do. They are also very much concerned with what might have been the "original intent" of the document. There is, however, a basic assumption that the document itself stays the same. Now, with the advent of digital documents, the situation is very different. This has even been shown in the case of an electronic version of *Nineteen Eighty-Four*: Online retailer Amazon.com issued a copy for its Kindle e-book reader, and then in 2009 recalled it without warning—deleting the novel, remotely, from all Kindles—saying it had gotten its version from a company that did not have the proper rights to it.

Now digital texts can be manipulated, changed, or destroyed with the greatest of ease. All trace of the original text of whatever length, if indeed it is the original, can be totally eliminated. Hence, the convention has arisen that when a digital text is cited as a scholarly source, the date of access needs to be given as well. This is in order to make clear that if the source is consulted later, there is the possibility that it may be different. The Soviets might well have set the pattern for this in their attempts to remove evidence showing that Leon Trotsky was a hero of the Russian Revolution—before he was identified as an enemy by Joseph Stalin. In a comparatively primitive way, this did exist in Orwell's time, as photographs of the Russian leaders reviewing May Day parades were doctored so that those who had been "purged" were no longer present. Similarly, the *Great Soviet Encyclopedia* was continually rewritten, not as other such compendia might be, on the basis of new information, but in order to make it conform to the new Communist Party line.

The past has always been subject to some alteration, particularly in the destruction and forgery of documents. Accounts of the past sometimes change drastically over time, as perceptions of what happened change. Events may be remembered in vastly different ways by different people. Or the past may be deliberately misrepresented. Orwell recognized the importance of having a past that is as accurate and stable as possible. At one point in *Nineteen Eighty-Four*, Winston and his lover Julia have a meeting in the apartment of O'Brien, a powerful member of the Inner Party who claims to be working for the overthrow of Big Brother. He will ultimately be Winston's torturer at the Ministry of Love. He will make Winston love Big Brother and accept that the Party can determine what reality is, even to the point of decreeing that two plus two equals five. Winston is attempting to subvert the system through being an inner rebel. At the same time, he wishes to appear to be a conformist. But the party knows that the essential point is for the individual to accept the perversion of the truth as the new truth with no reservation whatsoever. To control the past is an essential part of this operation. Orwell gives great credit to the power of history and believes that whoever commands the past can also control the present and the future. When O'Brien and Winston prepare to drink a toast in O'Brien's apartment, O'Brien asks if they should drink to the confusion of the Thought Police, or to the death of Big Brother, or to humanity, or to the future. "'To the past,' said Winston. 'The past is more important,' agreed O'Brien." When Orwell was writing the book, the ability to change the past to the degree that happened in the novel seemed highly improbable; in the twenty-first century it is quite feasible.

A continuing perplexing question about *Nineteen Eighty-Four* is whether it is a prophecy or a warning. Those on the Right, politically, tend to see it as a prophecy: This is what socialism inevitably leads to, an oppressive state where individuals are ground down and tyrannized. Certainly world history since the end of World War II provides much evidence for that point of view. Those on the Left are more likely to see it as a warning: This is what socialism *can* lead to if it is perverted and used as window dressing for a totalitarian state. On the whole, historical experience seems to favor the position of the Right. There does not appear to be, at least so far, any successful socialist state. The

Soviet Union clearly was a failure from quite early on, although for many it took some time to understand that clearly; in the 1930s, many remained hopeful about Soviet Russia as a force for good. At that time, the Western democracies were not taking a firm stand against Nazi Germany or Fascist Italy. The Soviet Union was a much stauncher opponent of Nazism than the Western powers—at least until the Nazi-Soviet Pact in 1939.

It was in the late 1930s that Orwell became a socialist and at the same time saw how easily a socialist society could be perverted. Consistent with his somewhat dour character, he believed in the dream— the egalitarian society he found in Barcelona at the time of the Spanish Civil War, the early vision in *Animal Farm*. But at the same time, he also became aware of how easily a potential utopia could be betrayed by the drive that powerful figures in society have to seek power—power for its own sake, power to control other people, power to acquire money, power as satisfaction—a drive that betrays the dreams of a better society. Orwell warns us that this is what is likely to happen, but unfortunately he does not tell us how to avoid it. One almost feels that he likes it—his fears have been realized—when he has an underdog to root for. Yet he hardly presents as a good thing the triumph of the pigs in *Animal Farm* or the broken Winston Smith sipping his Victory gin at the end of *Nineteen Eighty-Four*.

In terms of prophecy, it would appear that it is in the technical area that Orwell's dystopian nightmare is the most accurate and has the most resonance for the world in which we live now. This is true in three areas: language, surveillance, and, most important, the technical manipulation of records, the whole vast area summed up perhaps by the word "digital."

One of Orwell's greatest contributions was his intense awareness of the abuse of language, particularly in the case when a euphemism is used to suggest the exact opposite of the truth. The "memory hole" is to destroy memory, much as the "memory unit" at retirement homes is for people with Alzheimer's. The state is determined to force its members to accept contradictions. Orwell had an intense sense of the danger of jargon and cliché and how it can impede thought. Of course there is a splendid irony here. He himself in *Nineteen Eighty-Four* added terms to our language: Big Brother, Newspeak, doublethink, Thought Police— even his own name (though not by his choice) has entered the language, in the adjective "Orwellian." These are brilliant examples of Orwell's fecundity and imagination. However, they have almost themselves be- come jargon, so that he, a critic of language, created to some extent what he most detested: automatic and easy images that are short cuts in thinking.

Orwell was hence a fierce guardian of language. Most famously, in his essay "Politics and the English Language," he railed against the perversion of language, captured in *Nineteen Eighty-Four* by the term "Newspeak." He included in the novel an appendix on "The Principles of Newspeak." Its aim was to drain language of meaning and emotion, to make it as impersonal as possible, to allow horrible events to be neutralized through language, such as using "pacification" for the mur- dering of innocent civilians. As he wrote: "Countless other words such as *honor, justice, morality, internationalism, democracy, science,* and *religion* had simply ceased to exist. A few blanket words covered them, and, in covering them, abolished them. All words grouping themselves round the concepts of liberty and equality, for instance, were contained in the single word *crimethink*, while all the words grouping themselves round the concepts of objectivity and rationalism were contained in the single word *oldthink*" (Orwell 652–53).

The great drama of the book is the strength of the powers that be. The retention of power is the main purpose of the state, with no con- cern for ideology and ideas. There is no thought of improving the lot of anyone except the rulers, who live quite well. The aim is to take over the minds of significant members of the population. Orwell has made us vividly aware of the continual need to be vigilant about the perversion of language and the danger of politicians using anodyne terms, euphemisms, and "sound-bites" to hide their real intentions. He attempted, with limited success, to arm us against the protestations of politicians that their main concern is to improve the quality of life of everyone in the state. The more the leaders of states claim that their main interest is the good of the population, the more we are inclined to disbelieve them and to suspect that their main aims are profit and power. This is, for instance, ironically evident in the former Burma, written about by Orwell in *Burmese Days*, where there are ubiquitous billboards proclaiming that the chief concern of the ruling junta is the good of the people.

Orwell is not as concerned as one might have expected with the total population. The vast majority, the "proles," would appear to be so downtrodden that they do not present any sort of threat to the state. At some points in the book the "proles" might represent some hope, some of those who are older among them might remember a better world. Winston ventures into a pub in order to discover something about the past, but the man he speaks to is too befuddled by weak beer to tell him anything.

In many ways, Orwell failed to predict what has happened in the twenty-first century. He did not allow sufficiently for the positive aspects of technology, with particular reference to the activities of ordinary people. Recently events in the Middle East and elsewhere have demonstrated how the Internet, Facebook, and Twitter have allowed those who wish to change or indeed overthrow an existing regime to communicate and organize. On the other hand, of course, technology is a powerful weapon in the hands of the state, and in this Orwell is a major figure of warning. Nowadays we have a great degree of lip service paid to the idea of privacy, while at the same time we know that by technological means much information about us is available to far more people and institutions than in the past. Those with mobile phones can be tracked with the greatest of ease. More is known about us by more individuals, businesses, and government agencies than has ever been true in the past. There have been a slew of notices from companies informing us that their files have been hacked into, and that those intending to use the information to defraud us now have our personal details. We live in fear of identity theft. Our very persons, so to speak, can be taken away from us. There is more talk about "privacy" and "confidentially" than ever before, but never before has it less existed in practice.

We became particularly aware of this when the vast files of the Stasi, the East German secret police, were exposed at the time of the unification of Germany. When I visited the museum of the Stasi in Leipzig, I felt I was in a rather grubby Orwellian world. There was evidence of the rather primitive techniques to track people's smells! It would appear that practically everyone in East Germany was busy spying on each other, a phenomenon brilliantly captured in the 2006 German film *The Lives of Others.* I was more amused than shocked, though there were elements of both sensations, when recently I was using an automated teller machine, and the screen wished me a happy birthday! Who knows what information there might be available about all of us, including you, the reader of these words, as well as me, out there on the Internet, in corporations' data files, and in the hands of criminals, or to what purposes it could be put. These are dangers that we are facing in the twenty-first century that Orwell anticipated more than a half century ago.

Another aspect of the twenty-first century that Orwell predicted was the great growth of visual surveillance. In *Nineteen Eighty-Four* there is the ubiquitous telescreen, a two-way device that allows not only for the population to be continuously harangued, but also to be continuously observed. The novel opens with Winston climbing the seven floors to his flat, facing at each landing a large poster with the slogan, "Big Brother Is Watching You." Once in his flat, Winston's intent is to perform the forbidden act of writing in his diary and to position himself in such a way that he won't be observed by the telescreen. As the records of the Stasi made clear, there is no telling in the Orwellian state how many people are employed in observing their fellow citizens. Winston's subversive intention is to write in his diary, a deeply individualistic act. Rather surprisingly, contemporary Britain may well have more surveillance cameras than any other state. This is not what one expects in a country that claims to place such a high priority on privacy and individual rights. One might attribute it to a certain degree of British hypocrisy. It is both a democratic and a deeply hierarchical society. It is more dedicated than one might expect to keeping people in their place, to keep them well behaved. Having grown up in English society, Orwell was deeply aware of how almost everything about a person indicated his or her class position: accent, schooling, language. Surveillance in the novel is dedicated to keeping people in their place. The techniques are fairly primitive, but they anticipate the ever-growing capacity for surveillance that is available in this century.

Winston is a civil servant in the Ministry of Truth, which of course is the Ministry of Falsehood. The world has become divided into three superpowers—not quite what we have now, but what might have been true if the Soviet Union had survived. What is extraordinarily accurate is Orwell's picture of the role of conflict in the world. There are a series of endless comparatively small wars in the novel, much as we have experienced since the end of the World War II. We are quite legitimately terrified of the possibility of a major nuclear war, and the "small" wars, frequently marked by hate and ethnic violence, would appear to be a way to avoid that. In Orwell's novel, the population is trained to accept the situation through such slogans as "War Is Peace," "Freedom Is Slavery," and "Ignorance Is Strength." The physical ministry in the book is based on the large Senate House of the University of London, which served during World War II as the British Ministry of Information, whose purpose was to create propaganda to support the cause of the Allies. But for that purpose, a strict adherence to truth was not a primary concern. The depressing scenes in the Ministry's café were also based on Orwell's experiences of food scarcity during the war. The food situation was even worse in the years following the war and may well have been a factor in his and his wife's early deaths. Postwar austerity in Britain certainly help set the mood of the book.

The language and political aspects of *Nineteen Eighty-Four* are as relevant, if not more so, today as when the book was first published. What about the more personal elements of the book? Perhaps the love story, not too satisfactory originally, has not worn well. Winston falls in love with Julia, officially a member of the Anti-Sex League but in fact defying the state in her wish to make love as often as possible. She works in the Fiction Department in the Ministry. Through their love affair, Orwell introduces one of the great themes of English literature, love of the countryside. He also reveals his particular affection for where he grew up: the area along the Thames between London and Oxford, near Henley, which he calls in the novel the Golden Country. There, where they feel safe from omnipresent mechanical observation, Julia and Winston make love. Winston then finds a room over an antique shop in London where they believe they have the greatest of privileges—privacy—and can drink real coffee. Orwell certainly does not have an enlightened attitude toward women and in this respect is a creature of his times. He refers to Julia as a rebel from the waist down. While in bed, Winston reads to her from the banned work of Goldstein which, perhaps not surprisingly, sends her to sleep.

The antique shop turns out to be a trap, its owner an agent of the state. Julia and Winston are arrested. This is one of the most important moments in the novel, the crushing of hope in two ways: Winston thinks perhaps the proles, the vast majority of the country, in their natural resistance to authority, might be able to undo the state. Winston and Julia being arrested while he is listening to a woman sing outside his window seems to symbolize the crushing of the hope of any sort of rebellion by the proletariat. The arrest of Julia and Winston also means the destruction of their love. Winston ultimately betrays her. While he is being tortured, while he is being brainwashed, while he is threatened with what the state knows he fears most—being attacked by rats—he cries out, "Do it to Julia!"

Orwell's depiction of Julia was somewhat outdated in his own time, and it seems even more so now. Yet even though the love story ends very unhappily, it is still a testimony to what we dare to call a fact. Those two most private of activities, love and sex, attest to our individuality and in their ways are defiance of the public world, the world of the state. So too was the protest slogan of the 1960s, "Make Love, Not War." War is the most public of activities, while lovemaking is generally the most private. The sexual revolution of the 1960s supports a belief that the state had no business in monitoring what happens in the bedroom, a development that is still evolving in the twenty-first century. This is so dramatically contradicted in the novel when the Thought Police rush up the stairs and the wall opens up to reveal the telescreen. The Thought Police were continually observing what Julia and Winston thought was their very private domain.

What accounts for the great power of *Nineteen Eighty-Four* and its continuing popularity? At the time of its original publication, it was to a degree a Cold War document that pointed out, legitimately, the perversions of the Soviet system. But it was written by an author who considered himself a socialist. Particularly at the time of World War II and afterward, Orwell believed that England needed to be dramatically transformed and become more of a socialist society. At the same time, he was an intense patriot and adhered firmly to English values of individualism. England was a family, as he famously stated in his powerful wartime essay "The Lion and the Unicorn: Socialism and the English Genius" (1941), the title a reference to the heraldic beasts that support the royal British coat of arms. But for Orwell, it was a family with the wrong members in control. He felt, in fact incorrectly, that in order to win the war, England would need to become much more egalitarian and socialist. After the war, England, through the welfare state, did become a society that moved to the Left, but not as far as Orwell might have wished. At least England did not develop anything like Ingsoc, the official state ideology in *Nineteen Eighty-Four*.

But why does the book still have such a strong appeal, and why should it continue to be read in the twenty-first century? Orwell wrote it in his last years, partially spent living very austerely on the island of

Jura in the Hebrides. He was increasingly suffering from tuberculosis, which eventually killed him at the tragically young age of forty-six. He wrote in a strong, plain style without all that much elegance. The book is powerful and memorable. It is extremely grim and pessimistic, and it ends with Winston Smith as a physical and mental shell of his former self. The very last line of the book is "He loved Big Brother." Winston is totally broken; he is almost the walking dead.

The book continues to live and in some ways seems almost more relevant today than it ever was. It was very much a product of its time, of Orwell's experiences in the Spanish Civil War and of the austerities during World War II at home and in the years immediately after. Yet it also captures the poverty and deprivation of so much of the world today. It presents the brutality that the powers that be can demonstrate toward those whom they dominate. To a surprising degree, it depicts the world as we now know it. We are not destroying ourselves with atomic bombs, but all over the world small wars are going on. Regimes are replaced by new rulers that would appear to be better but generally in short order become as bad as those they have replaced. The world is full of the rhetoric of freedom that frequently masks oppression. Language is used to hide the real horrors that are taking place. Torture is used in the name of freedom. Orwell's insights into the reality of power are extremely acute.

Yet perhaps strangely, there is an optimistic message, I believe, buried in the book that communicates to readers, perhaps particularly young and idealistic ones. Winston's and Julia's rebellions are totally unsuccessful, even though they made love and were in love for a time. O'Brien reduces Winston to a shadow of his former self, which was fairly dilapidated to begin with. But Winston did try to fight for truth. He kept a diary, keeping it out of the sightlines of the telescreen. He tried as hard as he could to maintain the truth that two plus two equals four. His rebellion totally failed. And the tale would seem to say that such individual protest is doomed. But somehow, that is not the subtext of the book. *Nineteen Eighty-Four* does communicate to the reader the message that it is necessary to try to hold on to what you think of as the truth, and that one must not give in to a tyrannical society.

One element of the book seems to be even more vivid in the twenty-first century than before: the ability of technology to change not only how we live, but also to tamper with the very past itself. This makes the work *both* a warning *and* a prediction. There is no doubt that George Orwell's *Nineteen Eighty-Four* is still an exciting and important book to read so many years after its first publication. Long may that continue.

Works Cited

Crick, Bernard. *George Orwell: A Life*. Boston: Little, 1980.

Cushman, Thomas, and John Rodden, eds. *George Orwell: Into the Twenty-First Century*. Boulder: Paradigm, 2004.

Gleason, Abbot, Jack Goldsmith, and Martha Nussbaum, eds. *On Nineteen Eighty-Four: Orwell and Our Future*. Princeton: Princeton UP, 2005.

Howe, Irving, ed. *Orwell's Nineteen Eighty-Four*. New York: Harcourt, 1982.

_____, ed. *1984 Revisited*. New York: Harper, 1983.

Orwell, George. *Nineteen Eighty-Four*. Boston: Houghton, 1987.

Rose, Jonathan. *The Revised Orwell*. East Lansing: Michigan State UP, 1992.

Slater, Ian. *Orwell: The Road to Airstrip One*. New York: Norton, 1985.

Stansky, Peter. *Nineteen Eighty-Four Ten Years Later*. Austin: Humanities Research Center, 1995.

_____, ed. *On Nineteen Eighty-Four*. New York: Freeman, 1983.

Stansky, Peter, and William Abrahams. *The Unknown Orwell; Orwell: The Transformation*. Stanford: Stanford UP, 1994.

Taylor, D. J. *Orwell: The Life*. London: Chatto, 2003.

Veiled Autobiography: George Orwell, Winston Smith, and *Nineteen Eighty-Four*_____

Henk Vynckier

Ever since *Nineteen Eighty-Four* was published in 1949, scholarly commentators, as well as millions of ordinary readers, have acknowledged the central position of George Orwell's novel in contemporary discussions about politics, ideology, human rights, surveillance technology, and the mass media, and *Nineteen Eighty-Four* has been variously read as dystopia, satire, political fable, futuristic fantasy, allegory of reading, modernist fiction, and autobiography. My aim in this essay is to offer a fresh reading of the novel that elaborates on the last-mentioned approach: *Nineteen Eighty-Four* as a work of autobiography. I attempt here a psychological reading of the novel based on a forceful, idiosyncratic author-character identification, that is, between George Orwell and his fictional protagonist, Winston Smith. Thus, the purpose of this essay is twofold: first, to illustrate how deeply rooted the novel's political vision is in the author's private interests as a student and collector of printed materials, books, and artifacts; and second, to thereby enable a new psychological/autobiographical reading of one of the most influential texts of the twentieth century.

In his oft-quoted essay "Why I Write," published in 1946, Orwell had called attention to the "world-view" he acquired in childhood, and he confessed his lifelong passion for "solid objects and scraps of useless information" (*Complete Works* 18: 320). Elsewhere, Orwell commented on his collections of boys' weeklies, comic postcards, political pamphlets, and other collectibles. *Nineteen Eighty-Four* mirrors these passions, as the protagonist Winston Smith appears as a collector who, not unlike his creator, responds to inner voices and endeavors to restore a sense of the past and reclaim his humanity with the help of "scraps of beautiful rubbish" from a junk shop (9: 104). Throughout *Nineteen Eighty-Four*, Smith delves into bibliophile terminology, the antiques trade, and other aspects of "oldthink" material culture as a

---

reservoir of images to reconstruct an earlier civilization now shattered and replaced by a totalitarian order based on propaganda, Newspeak, the telescreen, and memory holes.

Tragically, however, Smith overlooks the innate tendency of the collecting project to strip objects of their historical essence and capture them in a timeless classification. In consequence, his collecting effort, though heroic, is ultimately doomed to fail. The Party's collectivist ideology and mastery of practices of classification and collection far outstrips his solitary project of collecting and he is captured, tortured, and brainwashed by the Thought Police. At last, like the "I" in the title of Stanley Kubrick's film *Dr. Strangelove or: How I Learned to Stop Worrying and Love the Bomb* (1964), Winston Smith learns to stop worrying and love the thing he feared most, Big Brother. In doing so, he surrenders all his former loves: the girl from the Fiction Department, Julia, his love of the truth in a world dominated by lies, mathematical certainty, his childhood memories, and the scraps of beautiful rubbish he had so cherished. Thus, the following reading of the novel, which focuses on private pleasures and obsessions shared by the protagonist and author, sheds further light on Orwell's lifelong struggle against totalitarian ideologies and helps to answer a question that has preoccupied not only his biographers but also millions of admirers of this great novel: What inspired Orwell to write this searingly unforgettable fictional masterpiece, *Nineteen Eighty-Four*?

One early indication of the questions the novel would raise can be gathered from the in-house memorandum Orwell's publisher Frederic Warburg wrote upon receiving the finished typescript of the novel in December 1948. Warburg noted that *Nineteen Eighty-Four* was "amongst the most terrifying books I have ever read" and expressed the hope not to have to read anything similar for many years after. He surmised that it would be "worth a cool million votes to the Conservative Party" and envisioned Winston Churchill, the prime minister of wartime Britain and a leading anti-Communist elder statesman, as the potential author of a preface for the novel. He was also keenly aware of the book's commercial potential and noted, tongue-in-cheek, that if his publishing house failed to sell fifteen to twenty thousand copies, "they ought to be shot" (Taylor 401–02; Bowker 383–84). Warburg's confidence in being able to avoid the firing squad was justified, as *Nineteen Eighty-Four* sold close to twenty-three thousand copies in Great Britain by the end of October 1949, and twenty thousand copies in the United States by the end of June 1949.

At this point, the story of *Nineteen Eighty-Four* becomes the stuff of legend. Orwell saw his novel picked up as a selection by the Book-of-the-Month-Club in the United States, and it sold 190,000 copies in this edition by March 1952. Soon, a variety of inexpensive and pocket editions appeared, and sixty years later the book remains in print in any number of editions, both in the original English and translations into dozens of languages, including not only the major European languages, but also Persian, Indonesian, Vietnamese, and Chinese. The raw bibliographic data concerning this global publishing phenomenon can be studied in detail in Gillian Fenwick's *George Orwell: A Bibliography* (1998). The story does not end with the coming of the twenty-first century, however, as *Nineteen Eighty-Four* has continued to migrate into new media and publication formats. In 2005, for example, an opera adaptation called *1984*, by American composer Lorin Maazel, premiered at the Royal Opera House in London, and in recent years e-book versions of *Nineteen Eighty-Four* have become available from Amazon, Barnes and Noble, and Apple's iTunes Store. Clearly, Orwell's "terrifying" last novel refuses to die and reemerges time after time to confront modern people and evoke their deepest fears, anxieties, and hopes. Big Brother is coming to an iPad near you.

One explanation for the staying power of this novel, which became apparent in the 1960s and 1970s, is that, with many millions of readers profoundly influenced by it, *Nineteen Eighty-Four* was a "game-changing" book that had altered the course of history. William Steinhoff's *George Orwell and the Origins of 1984*, published in 1975, is a representative example of this view. Steinhoff hailed *Nineteen Eighty-*

Four as a book that "changed the world," arguing that Orwell had seized upon "momentous events in the actual world" and "so remarkably crystallized [them] . . . that literature and the world since then have been different." The end result was that people had been "compelled to think again about what it means to create a society deserving to be called decent" (222).

Steinhoff's tribute to *Nineteen Eighty-Four*, however, is indebted to Orwell himself and to an early interpretive community of critics who had been close to Orwell. The term "crystallized," for example, echoes the title of a 1966 book by a personal friend of Orwell's, George Woodcock, called *The Crystal Spirit: A Study of George Orwell*; and the word "decent," with which Steinhoff ends the last sentence of his book, is a key word in Orwell's vocabulary. The phrase "compelled to think," too, reflects the view of Orwell as a combative critic and debater, as a scan of the backs of the two major collected editions of Orwell's writings will reveal. For example, the fourth volume of *The Collected Essays, Journalism and Letters of George Orwell*, edited by Orwell's widow, Sonia, and Ian Angus, is entitled *In Front of Your Nose*; and several volumes in Peter Davison's *The Complete Works of George Orwell* carry titles such as *Facing Unpleasant Facts* (vol. 11), *Keeping Our Little Corner Clean* (vol. 14), *I Have Tried to Tell the Truth* (vol. 16), and *It Is What I Think* (vol. 19).

Much has been added, though, to our understanding of the Orwell legend since Steinhoff offered his somewhat one-sided or even naive congratulatory analysis in 1975, and it is now clear that there is more to being a game-changer than just speaking the truth and keeping your own little corner clean. To achieve real historical change, even the most talented and driven game-changers need the right historical platform, a proper supporting cast and an occasional bit of luck. As John Rodden has argued in numerous books and essays, most notably *The Politics of Literary Reputation: The Making and Claiming of "St. George" Orwell* (1989) and *Scenes from an Afterlife: The Legacy of George Orwell* (2003), Orwell did not achieve the kind of reputation attributed to transformational figures without a specific historical context, and in Orwell's case this meant political and governmental sponsors, literary canonization and educational policy initiatives, and mass media adaptations.

As Warburg predicted, *Nineteen Eighty-Four* sold well in Britain and the United States in 1949 and 1950, but its rise to global popularity following the author's death in January 1950 was partially powered by secret, but strong, governmental sponsorship. The U.S. Central Intelligence Agency (CIA) and the British Information Research Department (IRD)—a propaganda arm of the British Foreign Office that existed from 1948 to 1977—launched a covert global sponsorship program resulting in dozens of translations, newspaper serializations, and radio adaptations of *Nineteen Eighty-Four*. Germany, Holland, Denmark, Finland, and other countries in Cold War Europe threatened by Communism were obvious targets of this campaign and proved receptive, but so was Occupied Japan, the newly independent Indonesia, and even Taiwan, still called Formosa by many in the West in those years. One dimension of this fluid migration of *Nineteen Eighty-Four* into different languages, media, and continents during the early years of the Cold War is that its specific genre characteristics encouraged such fluidity and adaptability. More than other anti-Communist works, *Nineteen Eighty-Four* traveled well because a dystopia (that is, a work of imaginative fiction about a dehumanized totalitarian society that appears under the guise of a perfect utopian society) could be easily applied to or reinterpreted for diverse political situations and cultural contexts. The same can be said of *Animal Farm*, which as an outwardly naïve fable could be applied in defense of any number of different agendas.

A second factor Rodden documents in the transformational history of Orwell's *Nineteen Eighty-Four* and, for that matter, *Animal Farm* concerns the broad acceptance of Orwell's final two novels by educational policy-makers and course instructors. Both *Animal Farm* and *Nineteen Eighty-Four* became required reading for large numbers of students and were included in the curricula of schools and colleges, especially in the United States, Britain, and throughout the British Commonwealth. Two aspects of these works fueled this development: Orwell was perceived to be politically correct in terms of the domestic and international politics of that time—here was a man of the Left who had a reputation for honesty and telling the truth and who was asking everybody loud and clear to keep an eye on the commies; and in addition, Orwell championed a clear style and "prose like a window-pane," and this led to the inclusion of the two novels and essays such as "Shooting an Elephant" and "Politics and the English Language" in the curricula of high school and college composition courses. Not only in English-speaking countries, however, was Orwell pressed into pedagogical service. Generations of German students growing up in the western half of divided Germany became familiar with the name Orwell, as both *Animal Farm* and *Nineteen Eighty-Four* were included in school curricula and remained best-sellers throughout the second half of the twentieth century.

The resilience of *Nineteen Eighty-Four* was further enhanced by early British and American radio, television, and film adaptations, which attracted large audiences and kept the novel in the news. Already in August 1949, NBC Radio produced a version starring the respected English actor David Niven, and the same company broadcast a second radio adaptation in 1953. The first television adaptation was seen on CBS-TV in 1953, and the second on the BBC in 1954. The latter starred Peter Cushing as Winston Smith and witnessed the biggest British audience for a television show up to that time—an audience reputed to be bigger than that for that year's coronation of Queen Elizabeth II.

The same television show casts an interesting light on the historical factors required to create "game-changers." In Britain, sales of *Nineteen Eighty-Four* had slowed to 150 copies per week in 1954, and as a sales phenomenon, the novel was slowly fading. The BBC production, however, reignited fascination with the story for a new generation; other trends, such as the release of a full-length British animated film version of *Animal Farm* by the Halas and Batchelor animation studio, and the publication of a number of books about Orwell in the mid-1950s, converged with the television phenomenon to keep *Nineteen Eighty-Four* as popular and relevant as ever. It remained for Columbia Pictures to produce the first feature film adaptation of the novel in 1956; as Rodden comments, "The Orwell ascension had become the Orwell cult and, by 1956, the Orwell industry" (*Politics* 46).

Ascension, cult, and industry; these are the words that mark the politics of this particular literary reputation. Pleasure, urban adventuring, and collecting; those are the words that mark the psychology of the man behind the reputation, as I now return to the notion of *Nineteen Eighty-Four* as an autobiographical work. An incident recorded by Bernard Crick, Orwell's first biographer, suggests an interesting avenue for looking into Orwell's private pleasures and collecting habits. In February and March of 1936, Orwell traveled in the industrial north of England to research poverty and unemployment for his documentary book *The Road to Wigan Pier*, which would be published the following year by Victor Gollancz's newly founded Left Book Club. At one point, Orwell spent several days in Liverpool, and his local hosts drove him around the city to visit the docks and slums. Orwell saw 250 hungry and ragged men waiting for work while a company agent offered a job to 50 men only; he saw the police patrolling the docks after a fight; and he was struck by the sight of some slums being cleared. As Crick reports, Orwell and his hosts also stopped "at several antique-cum-junk shops at his request, and he bought two brass candlesticks and a ship in a bottle." He also told his hosts that "he was thinking of trying to set up a small antique shop in a cottage or shop he was about to rent down in Hertfordshire" (Crick 186). Orwell would, indeed, soon move into a cottage in Hertfordshire that dated back to the sixteenth century and was known as the "Stores," as it had been the location of the village grocery store.

This anecdote offers glimpses of two Orwells: Orwell the leftist writer and Orwell the antiques collector and dealer. Orwell visited Liverpool and other cities and towns in the north to research working-class life, and *The Road to Wigan Pier* faithfully depicts a desolate world of coal mines, slag heaps, foundries, filthy lodging houses, and nineteenth-century workers' slums. In one of the most striking passages of the book, he describes going down a coal mine and spending a couple of hours crawling back and forth to the coal face to experience personally what coal miners go through every day. Everything about this undertaking, therefore, suggests that Orwell was very serious about this socially driven writing project. As Gordon Bowker, Orwell's most recent biographer, claims, this journey, together with the subsequent journey to Spain in late 1936, were "journeys of discovery" that shaped the author's personal and political values for the rest of his life. Yet we also see that there were times during this journey of discovery when some inner urge would overcome Orwell, and he would busily hunt for such objects of middle-class desire as brass candlesticks and ships in bottles. Orwell may have pursued an overt literary-political program much of the time, but as a private individual he was obviously also fond of a cultural practice that celebrates intimacy, the family circle, nostalgia, childhood, authenticity, and personal eclecticism, and therefore contradicts his political program. An additional hint of this private Orwell is seen in "*The Road to Wigan Pier* Diary" in the tenth volume of *The Complete Works*. In the entry for February 2, 1936, Orwell records a long talk with a hostel warden who collected "glass and pewter" and told him about some "priceless glass" that he had looted in France in 1918 while on the heels of the retreating Germans. The warden also showed him "nice pieces of pewter and some very curious Japanese pictures . . . looted by his father in some naval expedition about 1860" (10: 419).

The cultural practice of collecting, which is clearly what Orwell is engaged in in the above snapshots from his life, has attracted a lot of attention in recent decades—much of it critical. The French sociologist Jean Baudrillard, for example, proposed in his *The System of Objects* (1968) that collecting is a capitalist value system designed to feed "the voracious appetite for nostalgia and primitivism of the Western world's bourgeois interiors" (89); and Susan Stewart, another critic of consumption, commented that the collector's hunt for souvenirs, knick-knacks, curios, and other collectible objects suggests a kind of false labor. The collector creates a "smaller economy," which, "although dependent upon and, a mirroring of, the larger economy of surplus value . . . is self-sufficient and self-generating with regard to its meanings and principles of exchange." (159) In other words, the collector who explores urban neighborhoods and rummages through junkshops and flea-markets may not seem like a hard-charging capitalist engaged in the pursuit of money, but he too experiences what the German culture critic Walter Benjamin identified in his 1931 essay "Unpacking My Library: A Talk About Book Collecting" as "the thrill of acquisition" (60). The comments of these critics are pertinent. Orwell did not just visit one store in Liverpool, but several, and when he acquired objects, he offered a rationale centering on a rather fantastic scheme of opening an antiques shop in a village of hardly one hundred inhabitants.

The biggest irony in this story is that Orwell, indeed, seems to have practiced two modes of labor during his travels. On the one hand, he was a courageous public intellectual who dedicated much of his literary output to criticizing what Stewart calls "the larger economy of surplus value," i.e., capitalism. On the other hand, he was a collector, and a pretty obsessive one, who loved rummaging through the junk stores and flea markets of the smaller economy. When he concentrated on the social landscape in *The Road to Wigan Pier*, the clarity of his vision was such that his contemporary Edith Sitwell compared him favorably to Friedrich Engels, whose *The Condition of the Working Class in England* had sketched an unforgettable portrait of the industrial hells of the mid-nineteenth century. When his collector's instinct took over, though, Orwell's critical gaze would abandon the public realm and plunge into a microcosm of delightful objects that could be seized, fondled, and carried away for inclusion in his personal collection. Thus, the open-ended, liberating project of cataloguing social injustice existed alongside a more private and limited, yet also very open-ended, project of pursuing personal obsessions.

As for the origin and history of the Orwellian collecting project, with the publication of Bernard Crick's *George Orwell: A Life* in 1980 and four more major biographies since then, as well as the completion of Peter Davison's edition of *The Complete Works*, plenty of evidence is available. As is typical for many collectors, family history seems to have been important. Orwell's real family name was Blair, and the Blairs, who had a heraldic crest, had been a prominent family with aristocratic and colonial connections dating to the seventeenth century. Bowker calls attention to Orwell's inheritance in the first chapter of his biography, noting that Orwell was "keenly aware of his family ancestry—the procession of ghostly forebears" whose names were "inscribed in the family Bible inherited from his father." Orwell also inherited an oil painting of Lady Mary Blair, a mid-eighteenth-century aristocratic ancestor, and "a set of leather-bound volumes once owned by his great uncle Captain Horatio Blair, to which he became sentimentally attached" (Bowker 4). In addition, his father had served in the Indian colonial service and his mother had artistic interests, and this meant that the family home was full of embroidered stools, bags, cushions, boxes full of sequins, wooden needle-cases, small boxes from India and Burma, and many other items.

Orwell would recreate this family atmosphere in the third extract from "The Autobiography of John Flory," a collection of sketches that Peter Davison ranks among Orwell's earliest attempts to create fiction. In this fragment, the narrator recollects his father's library with its many books, pieces of Indian furniture, tiger skins, old photographs, eastern weapons, and assorted "rubbish," and recalls the time he spent there leafing through books or listening to his father's stories (*Complete Works* 10: 97). A similar vignette of an Anglo-Indian family can be found in the novel *Coming Up for Air* (1939), a comic masterpiece that indicates that over time Orwell learned to mock the ancestral lineages and Anglo-Indian connections that had shaped him as a child (7: 139). Nevertheless, as he acknowledged himself, that same family background had instilled in him once and for all "the sort of mind that takes pleasure in dates, lists, catalogues, concrete details, descriptions of processes, junk-shop windows, and back numbers of *Exchange and Mart*" (12: 232). Endowed with that sort of mind, over time Orwell became an avid collector of boys' weeklies, political pamphlets, seaside postcards, beer tankards, Victorian trinkets, and all sorts of objects with a curiosity value.

To be sure, Orwell would sometimes take pains to differentiate his own collecting habits from traditional practices such as, for example, bibliophilia, which had been popular in England for centuries and was often viewed as a rich man's game. In 1934 and 1935, just before he journeyed to the north, Orwell was employed as a shop assistant at Booklovers' Corner, a secondhand bookshop in London, and some of the writings that resulted from this experience, such as the novel *Keep the Aspidistra Flying* (1936) and the essay "Bookshop Memories" (1936), are critical of the secondhand and antiquarian book business and the bibliophiles, snobs, and other odd characters who frequent such businesses. As Crick comments, however, the time spent in Booklovers' Corner was productive for the young author and "fortified Orwell's interest in popular culture" (160), and Orwell would continue to frequent such stores and buy books and other printed materials all his life. In 1945 and 1946, while living in London, for example, Orwell spent much time "browsing in second-hand bookshops, indeed second-hand shops of all kinds" (Crick 348).

Crick's observations are supported by an Orwell essay from 1946 with the telling title "Just Junk—But Who Can Resist It?" Here, Orwell reflects on his personal obsessions and suggests that the appeal of the junk shop is to "the jackdaw inside all of us, the instinct that makes a child hoard copper nails, clock springs, and glass marbles out of lemonade bottles" (*Complete Works* 18: 19). He also catalogues some of the objects worth looking for in the junk shops of London, concluding with a story about a particularly rubbishy shop that he has known for years, in spite of the fact that it sells nothing he would ever be tempted to buy; however, at the same time he admits, "It would be all but impossible for me to pass that way without crossing the street to have a good look" (18: 19). This, clearly, is the mark of the true collector who goes by instinct rather than intellect. Noteworthy also is the inclusion of glass paperweights with pieces of coral enclosed in them on the list of objects worth looking for in these shops, as a similar paperweight will play a prominent role in *Nineteen Eighty-Four.*

Another aspect of Orwell which remained constant throughout his life and intersected with his collecting hobbies was his love of nature. At different times when he lived in the country he would conscientiously record in his domestic diary the number of eggs, cups of goat milk, and quantities of other produce he gathered each day—another instance of the jackdaw instinct of the collector at work. Whether in the city or the country, Orwell could never resist the pleasures of accumulation and inventorying; in an essay on the novel *Foul Play* (1869), a desert island story by the late Victorian adventure novelist Charles Reade, he observed: "A list of the objects in a shipwrecked man's possession is probably the surest winner in fiction, surer even than a trial scene" (12: 233).

All of these themes—writing, naturalizing, collecting, and listing—are enumerated in one key sentence in his programmatic essay "Why I Write," when Orwell claims, "What I have most wanted to do throughout the past ten years is to make political writing into an art." At the same time, he admits that, due to the "world-view" that he acquired in childhood and is unable and unwilling to abandon as adult, he could not do the work of writing "if it were not an aesthetic experience." He then asserts: "So long as I remain alive and well I shall continue to feel strongly about prose style, to love the surface of the earth, and to take a pleasure in solid objects and scraps of useless information." Thus, Orwell's love of objects was one aspect of his character and of the "ingrained likes and dislikes" that enabled him to invest his writing with aesthetic quality (18: 319–20).

Orwell's love of objects and the collecting practices that resulted from this love, indeed, frequently inspired his writing and resulted in such classic Orwell essays as "Boys' Weeklies" (1940), "The Art of Donald McGill" (1941), and his introduction to the first volume of Reginald Reynolds's *British Pamphleteers*. William E. Cain sums up the position of many critics when he calls "Boys' Weeklies" "a pioneering foray in cultural studies" (78), and the same can be said for "The Art of Donald McGill," an essay based on Orwell's collection of mildly obscene seaside postcards. Orwell, observed Jeffrey Meyers, "took comic postcards seriously, and explored the meaning and purpose of the genre" (Meyers 268). As for *British Pamphleteers*, Orwell's collection of pamphlets was extensive, numbering close to two thousand items, and his introduction to the volume was described by its editor Reynolds as "characteristic and provocative" (Meyers 182). In all of these instances, therefore, Orwell's writing is thoroughly supported by lifelong research and collecting interests, and it is evident that over time Orwell's collecting practice moved beyond the sort of awkward expeditions he engaged in in Liverpool. The false labor of those junk shop expeditions clashed with the literary and political project he was undertaking at that time, but the essays on boys' weeklies, comic postcards, junk shops, secondhand bookstores, pamphlets, and so on of later years indicate that Orwell was developing an identity as a collector that supported his writing program and political views.

A final and coherent articulation of Orwell's collecting interests can be found in *Nineteen Eighty-Four*, and, as in the anecdote about Orwell in Liverpool, the story begins with a commercial transaction in a junk-shop in a proletarian neighborhood. The protagonist Winston Smith, a Party member and employee of the Ministry of Information, has bought a book. While exploring a proletarian neighborhood, he had seen this obscure object of desire in the window of a little junk-shop and "had been stricken immediately by an overwhelming desire to possess it" (*Complete Works* 9: 8). So he buys the book, without being conscious of any specific purpose for which he might have wanted it, and commences the guilty journey home, knowing that what he carried with him was "a compromising possession" (9: 8). During later inspections of the "thick, quarto-sized blank book with a red back and a marbled cover" in his flat, he notices how special this compromising object is: "It was a particularly beautiful book. Its smooth creamy paper, a little yellowed by age, was of a kind that had not been manufactured for at least forty years past. He could guess, however, that the book was much older than that" (9: 8). Smith, it seems, is captivated by the book's combination of beauty and age, and Orwell, for all his sneering at bibliophiles, applies the correct book collector's terminology when he uses terms such as "quarto," "red back," "marbled cover," and "creamy paper" to describe the material characteristics and condition of the book. Bibliophiles call books that are old, beautiful, and still in excellent condition "collectible," and they highly prize such books for inclusion in their collections. Smith's book is, clearly, such a collectible item, and helps him reconnect with an older civilization predating the regime of Ingsoc and Big Bother.

What could have driven a Party member and government employee like Smith to transgress in this manner? Winston Smith's job at the Ministry of Truth is to rewrite newspaper articles in order to maintain the illusion that the Party's vision of history has always been entirely accurate. As he does this, he is fully aware of the gigantic historical fraud thus perpetrated and reflects, "All history was a palimpsest, scraped clean and reinscribed exactly as often as was necessary" (9: 35). Smith's familiarity with the word "palimpsest" and his willingness to consider its implications for the world in which he lives indicate a restless inner self that has not been fully subjected to thought control. He believes in truth, yearns for his long-lost mother and younger sister, dreams of a Golden Country beyond the reach of the Party, and hates rather than loves Big Brother. Such is the man who wanders around proletarian sections of town like some kind of urban flaneur and who brings home compromising possessions like old books.

An old Latin saying holds that things that please will be repeated— *bis repetita placent*—and the restless Smith soon pays a second visit to the junk-shop, which is run by one Mr. Charrington. Such are the pleasures of transgression in the fictional world of Oceania, and this time Smith finds an antique glass paperweight with a bit of red coral embedded in its core. Struck by its beauty and "the air it seemed to possess of belonging to an age quite different from the present one," he purchases the paperweight and listens to the proprietor's musings that the trade in antiques is dying out, as there are no customers anymore and no stock either: "I haven't seen a brass candlestick in years," says Charrington (9: 98–99). That the disappearance of brass candlesticks should be associated with the passing of an age comes as no surprise to readers familiar with Orwell's interests as a collector. Smith finally examines some furniture and an old steel engraving in a bedroom upstairs and resolves to make future visits to this fascinating shop in order to buy more "scraps of beautiful rubbish" (104), thereby indicating the continuation of an open-ended collecting project and Smith's ongoing personal and political awakening.

Peter Davison comments in a footnote to the "Just Junk" essay that Charrington's shop clearly reflects Orwell's familiarity with the London junk shop scene. Expanding on this, I would argue that Orwell's extensive knowledge of collecting, junk shops, secondhand bookstores, and other aspects of material culture thoroughly informs all of the first two parts of *Nineteen Eighty-Four* and enabled him to sketch below the surface of Winston Smith's daily existence an older English civilization now irredeemably shattered and replaced by a new totalitarian order. This older civilization, though thoroughly ransacked and difficult to reconstruct, seems to beckon the wandering hero to a journey of self-discovery and political awakening, and he eagerly responds to the call. Yet, as Samuel Johnson warned, "In the purchase of old books, let me recommend to you to examine with great caution whether they are perfect" (qtd. in Carter and Barker 69). Smith, however, is unable to do so, and lacks the necessary caution. He has many longings but insufficient expertise and does not realize that Charrington is really a member of the Thought Police, the antique shop a police trap, and the beautiful old book a lady's keepsake, which in a previous age would have been used by young women as a diary, but is now made available by the Party as a medium for Smith to incriminate himself. It was once a precious and antique implement for collecting oneself; now it is but another device of social control similar to the telescreen.

A similar irony exists in the excitement with which Smith receives *The Theory and Practice of Oligarchical Collectivism* by Emmanuel Goldstein, a former founding Party official now accused of treason, whose book is officially reviled as the inspiration for a shadowy dissident organization known as the Brotherhood. It is "a heavy black volume, amateurishly bound, with no name or title on the cover. The print also looked slightly irregular. The pages were worn at the edges, and fell apart, easily, as though the book had passed through many hands" (9: 191). In the language of book collecting, such a book would be described as "a poor copy" or "a reading copy," meaning that its deteriorated condition from having passed through many hands would prevent any serious book collector from buying it, unless he or she despaired of ever finding a decent collectible copy, or just wanted a cheap copy to read. Yet that is specifically what this particular book is all about. It is an ugly book in comparison with the antiquarian lady's keepsake, but its amateurish manufacture and worn pages are the guise necessary to convince Smith of its authenticity as a very rare and forbidden book produced by a shadowy underground organization and secretly passed from one conspirator to another. As such, it is even more of a compromising possession than the antique diary, and whoever reads it is guilty of treason and subject to arrest.

Summing up, we see that throughout the first two parts of *Nineteen Eighty-Four*, Smith searches for a way to restore history as a viable dimension of the human experience, and he turns to collectible objects and other scraps of the past as his best media. The methods he uses are those of the private collector as he deploys opportunistic, low-tech tactics in a struggle with the strategically mobilized forces of the Party. The authenticity of his awakening is real, and the effort is heroic. Tragically, however, Smith overlooks the innate tendency of the collecting project to strip objects of their historical essence. As Susan Stewart states, "The collection replaces history with *classification*, with order beyond the realm of temporality. In the collection, time is not something to be restored to an origin; rather, all time is made simultaneous or synchronous within the collection's world" (150). This analysis of the politics of collecting matches the Party slogan: "Who controls the past, controls the future: who controls the present controls the past" (9: 37). Moreover, in the bleak world of *Nineteen Eighty-Four* the collectivist, not the collector, triumphs, and everything Orwell loved and stood for and had nurtured deep within his inner self is appropriated, mocked, and perverted by Big Brother types dressed in party uniforms and clad with leather boots.

In "Why I Write," Orwell asserts his resolve to stand up for things like prose style, the surface of the earth, solid objects, and scraps of useless information. One last element of idiosyncratic author-character identification that may be suggested here is that Winston Smith, too, offered a sort of "Why I Write" statement when he described his job in the Ministry of Truth as that of rewriting history as if it were "a palimpsest, scraped clean and reinscribed exactly as often as was necessary." The beauty of palimpsests, though, is that the scholars who inspect them invariably discover evidence of surface scrapes and rubs and of reinscription. In addition, while most of the *scriptio inferior*, that is, underlying texts that have been scraped away or rubbed out, are irretrievably lost, it does happen sometimes that the erased text is still partially legible or reappears after the passage of time. Time, in this case, is indeed the one element of hope in *Nineteen Eighty-Four*. The appendix on "The Principles of Newspeak" ends with a statement that "the final adoption of Newspeak had been fixed for so late a date as 2050" (9: 326). Thus, as powerful as the Party already is in the year 1984, when Winston Smith purchases his diary and begins the journey of descent that will lead him to love only Big Brother and betray all his former loves, total mind control is not expected to be established until more than sixty years into the future. This is an immensity of time in the historiography of *Nineteen Eighty-Four*. The collectivists may have been able to move swiftly in their conquest of geographical space, but the inner realms take much longer to yield. And in that lies the hope, and the call to resistance, in Orwell's great final novel.

Works Cited

Baudrillard, Jean. *The System of Objects*. Trans. James Benedict. London: Verso, 2005. 1996.

Benjamin, Walter. "Unpacking My Library: A Talk About Book Collecting." *Illuminations: Essays and Reflections*. Trans. Harry Zohn. New York: Schocken, 1969. 59–67.

Bowker, Gordon. *George Orwell*. London: Little, 2003.

Cain, William E. "Orwell's Essays as a Literary Experience." *The Cambridge Companion to George Orwell*. Ed. John Rodden. Cambridge: Cambridge UP, 2007. 76–86.

Carter, John, and Nicolas Barker. *ABC for Book Collectors*. New Castle, Del.: Oak Knoll, 2004.

Crick, Bernard. *George Orwell: A Life*. London: Secker, 1980.

Fenwick, Gillian. *George Orwell: A Bibliography*. Winchester: St. Paul's Bibliographies, 1998.

Meyers, Jeffrey. *Orwell: Wintry Conscience of a Generation*. New York: Norton, 2000.

Orwell, George. *The Collected Essays, Journalism, and Letters of George Orwell*. Ed. Sonia Orwell and Ian Angus. London: Secker, 1968.

_____. *The Complete Works of George Orwell*. Ed. Peter Davison. 20 vols. London: Secker. 1998.

Rae, Patricia. "'Just Junk': Orwell's Real-Life Scavenging and *Nineteen Eighty-Four*." *English Language Notes* 38.1 (September 2000): 73–79.

_____. "Mr. Charrington's Junk Shop: T. S. Eliot and Modernist Poetics in *Nineteen Eighty-Four*." *Twentieth Century Literature* 43.2 (Summer 1997): 196–220.

Rodden, John. *The Politics of Literary Reputation: The Making and Claiming of "Saint George" Orwell*. Oxford: Oxford UP, 1989.

_____. *Scenes from an Afterlife: The Legacy of George Orwell*. Wilmington: ISI, 2003.

Steinhoff, William. *George Orwell and the Origins of 1984*. Ann Arbor: U of Michigan P, 1975.

Stewart, Susan. *On Longing: Narratives of the Miniature, the Gigantic, the Souvenir, the Collection*. Durham: Duke UP, 1993.

Taylor, D. J. *Orwell: The Life*. New York: Vintage, 2004.

Woodcock, George. *The Crystal Spirit: A Study of George Orwell*. London: Fourth Estate, 1984.

The Intellectual as Critic and Conscience: George Orwell and Albert Camus_____

John Rodden

I

Leading European intellectuals recently commemorated the deaths of two great men of letters of the twentieth century: the Englishman George Orwell and the French Algerian Albert Camus. The month of January 2010 marked the sixtieth anniversary of the death of Orwell in 1950 and the fiftieth anniversary of the death of Camus precisely a decade later in January 1960. British and French writers in particular celebrated the heritage that Orwell and Camus represent, a legacy of intellectual integrity, moral courage, and literary excellence.

Both of these men exemplified a rare honesty in speaking truth to power and voicing a cry against oppression and injustice. They did so not only against the malfeasance of government officials and the cowardice of the establishment, but even against their own immediate reference group, their fellow intellectuals on the Left, what the New York social critic Harold Rosenberg called "that herd of independent minds" stampeding together in the same direction.[1] Rosenberg was referring to his own group of New York intellectuals, but he was also merely echoing what Orwell had repeatedly said three decades earlier in London and Camus shortly thereafter in Paris. Yet in order to appreciate fully the heritage that Orwell and Camus represent, a short history lesson is in order.

II

The very word "intellectual" was not even part of the Western lexicon until the late nineteenth century. Yes, there were men of letters, essayists, journalists, and gentleman scholars. But not an identifiable class—"the intellectuals"—as we have come to understand the term. It arose after the trial in 1894 of Alfred Dreyfus, a captain in the French

258

Critical Insights

Army who had been convicted of treason on trumped-up charges. The truth was suppressed by both the French military and the French government. Dreyfus, a Jew who was the victim of vicious anti-Semitic prejudices during his military trial, was packed off to prison. However, some writers, especially Emile Zola in *J'accuse!* (*I accuse!*), could not and would not remain silent once they had discovered the truth. In his explosive manifesto, Zola wrote, "I accuse the government, I accuse the military, I accuse the powers that be of lying and corruption and deception of those whom they would proclaim to serve, the public" (52). Published in 1898, *J'Accuse!* caused a firestorm of controversy in Paris. Plenty of Parisian writers and men of letters wanted to suppress the truth: "Let this French Jew take the blame," they felt. There were others, however, who agreed with Zola. And thus was born the "intellectual"; that is, the thinker who insists that the truth be proclaimed in language clear and direct and simple and concrete—and, wherever possible, fluid and euphonious.

And so, the role of the intellectual as a critic of power began, first in France and then throughout the Continent and elsewhere. But what happens when, soon thereafter in the twentieth century, the intellectuals themselves begin to demonstrate that they are corrupt and deceptive, when they begin fully collaborating with power, such as during the occupation of France by the Nazis during World War II? Or for a much longer period shortly thereafter with Soviet Russia? The Western intellectuals' betrayal of their calling continued even after Joseph Stalin occupied all of Eastern Europe—partly because "Uncle Joe" was an ally of the West against the Nazis, even if only beginning in June 1941, and not before then or after the war.

It is much more difficult, and it requires much greater intellectual integrity and moral courage, to be a critic *of your own side*, of your fellow intellectuals. Yes, it's easier to speak truth to power if the powerful are in faraway places like the White House or 10 Downing Street or the Palais de l'Élysée, where they ignore you like an elephant does a fly, as you declaim and breast-beat in your academic publications and your ephemeral newspaper columns.

But what happens when you brush shoulders with colleagues and friends and even family members day after day because they are the writers and editors of the journals and magazines to which you would like to contribute? Then it's not so easy to criticize because then you pass from merely being a critic of power to a "conscience."

A conscience is a critic *from within*. Yet a conscience criticizes not in order to weaken but to strengthen his or her own side, to hold it to the highest possible standard, even higher than those whom it opposes. A critic who is also a conscience insists that truth comes before beauty, power, or any other value or attribute. That is not so easy to uphold faithfully, which is why we seldom find writers of the caliber of George Orwell and Albert Camus.

III

On the three great issues that faced them in the mid-twentieth century, Orwell and Camus took unorthodox, indeed heterodox, stances toward their respective intelligentsias, both of which were largely Left-dominated. Both men suffered greatly as a result, but they have been vindicated by history. The first issue was fascism and Nazism; the second was colonialism and imperialism; and the third was Communism and Stalinism.

On the first issue, as the Spanish Civil War broke out, Orwell was not content, like most of his fellow writers and intellectuals, to stay home safely in England, or even to venture to Spain as a journalist and report on events. No, he decided to go and fight as a soldier, alongside a Spanish militia. He didn't do what almost all the other foreign writers and intellectuals do. If they came to Spain in support of the Republic, they joined the Stalinist-backed and Communist-dominated International Brigade, financed straight from Moscow, which was also in the process of trying to suppress and even annihilate the independent, quasi-Trotskyist militia that Orwell had joined. Orwell had a reflexive allegiance to neither the fascist Right nor the Stalinist Left; he took neither easy ideological position. Instead he got a bullet through his windpipe, almost died as a result, and as he attempted to flee from Spain—as the files of Stalin's secret police have shown, now that scholars have access to them—a warrant was issued by the Stalinists for his arrest and murder, and he managed to escape simply by good fortune. He lost his voice for almost two years, but later was able to speak, if softly. But he did not write softly. His indignant pen was loud and clear.

His memoir, *Homage to Catalonia* (1938), describes what happened. Orwell insisted on intellectual integrity, and so the book was "ruined," he later wrote, by the necessity of introducing many long passages from various newspaper columns ("Why I Write"). He felt he had to document, chapter and verse, the lies of the British press that had supported Stalin's version of what was happening in Spain and how the International Brigades collaborated with it. Of course, the fascist leader Francisco Franco won the Spanish Civil War. The fascists dominated Spain for decades thereafter, and *Homage to Catalonia* thus represented an elegy for a socialism that Orwell believed he momentarily saw from his sickbed in Barcelona, but which was never capable of full realization. The book sold only nine hundred copies during his lifetime.

Camus faced an even more direct and difficult challenge: documenting the Nazi occupation of France. Camus became the editor-in-chief of *Combat*, the French Resistance newspaper, which as an underground publication reached a circulation of more than a quarter million. Camus thereby exerted an enormous, if clandestine, intellectual and moral influence within the French Resistance. Meanwhile, of course, many intellectuals became collaborators and made their peace with the Vichy government and with the occupation. Others, like Jean-Paul Sartre and Simone de Beauvoir, assumed a quietist stance. Sartre spent most of the occupation completing his dense, nine-hundred-page philosophical treatise, *Being and Nothingness*, published in 1943, which was his reply to Heidegger's *Being and Time*, published sixteen years earlier. Sartre had briefly attended some of Heidegger's lectures in the 1930s.

Needless to say, *Being and Nothingness* was not read by many people in the French underground who were trying to get rid of the Nazis. So here too, like Orwell, Camus did not take the easy ideological stance: fascist or Stalinist, collaborationist or internal exile.

IV

And what about the second issue, imperialism and colonialism? Both Orwell and Camus lived in exile, one could say. Orwell was born in 1903 in Bengal, in what was then part of British India. As an infant, Orwell returned to Britain with his family. But in his twenties, after graduating from Eton, the elite public school, he ventured back and spent five years as an officer with the Indian Imperial Police in various stations in Burma, where he began to hate part of himself as an oppressor of the Burmese natives, for doing what he later referred to as "the dirty work of imperialism." Coming home to England in 1927, he struggled as a writer for several years, then wrote *Burmese Days* (1934), a novel that is a worthy successor to E. M. Forster's *Passage to India* (1927). Orwell's rebel hero, John Flory, is in some respects remarkably like Orwell himself. Throughout the last quarter-century of his life, despite an abiding affection for Rudyard Kipling's verse and prose, Orwell consistently opposed British imperialism, including the vanities of empire and the idea of White Man's Burden. He supported Indian independence and even expressed equivocal support for Mahatma Gandhi—despite Orwell's own outspoken atheism and opposition to what he saw as Gandhi's political naïveté and anachronistic spirituality.

Here again, Camus faced perhaps an even more vexed and harrowing dilemma. Born in 1913 in Algeria, of French parentage, his father died in World War I. However, his mother, his brother, and the rest of their family remained in Algeria their entire lives. When the call for Algerian independence arose in the mid-1950s, Camus was torn. He was famously quoted as saying that if it was justice for revolutionaries to plant bombs in the trolleys his mother rode in Algiers, then he would choose his mother over justice.

For that statement, he was widely condemned not only by the Algerian revolutionaries, but also by the entire Left—not only the Marxist or Communist Left, but the so-called fellow-traveling Left led by Jean-Paul Sartre and Maurice Merleau-Ponty. As Sartre later wrote in his preface to Frantz Fanon's famous anti-imperialist treatise of the 1960s, *The Wretched of the Earth*: "To kill a European is to kill two birds with one stone. In the end, one is left with the oppressor dead and the oppressed liberated. And so a dead man and a free man" (xlvi). Camus, of course, was both a European and an Algerian; the choice was not so easy for him. For him to support Algerian independence and the concomitant anti-Americanism of the Algerian revolution meant that one day his mother might be blown to smithereens on a trolley.

No, it is not an easy choice when you decide to criticize your own side, your fellow intellectuals. For the herd of independent minds stampeding in the same direction may set their sights on *you*. Still, in historical hindsight, it is a modest consolation for us to know that during the recent brutal civil war in Algeria, which began in the early 1990s and lasted more than a decade, it became quite common in Paris to state that Camus had been vindicated by history, in that Algeria would have been much better off if it had evolved into a multi-ethnic state with limited self government, closely linked to France. If Orwell had been a prophet about the geopolitics of the late twentieth century and the lure of leader worship, Camus was judged to have been proven correct about the future of Algeria.

V

And what about the last and greatest of the three issues—Stalinism and Communism? We have already mentioned Orwell's outraged memoir addressing the Stalinist betrayal of socialism in Spain, *Homage to Catalonia*. Orwell actually preceded that book with *The Road to Wigan Pier* (1937), his first courageous statement against the "smelly little orthodoxies," as he referred to them, practiced through obedience to those in power ("Charles Dickens" 56). In fact, in one famous anecdote, when he was lunching with a friend, Orwell spotted the editor of the *New Statesman*, Kingsley Martin, at a table across from them. Orwell told his friend that he had to move and asked if they could change places. The friend asked him why. And Orwell said, "I can't bear throughout the lunch to look at Kingsley's corrupt face." Martin had commissioned articles from Orwell about the Spanish Civil War and rejected them because they would "give ammunition to the enemy," he said. Truthtelling would hurt "our own side." Thereafter, Orwell rarely wrote for the leading left-wing newspaper of his day in Britain (Muggeridge 166).

As the 1940s progressed, Orwell instead increasingly turned his attention to the specter of totalitarianism, which he feared might prevail worldwide. He realized presciently that it signaled a new form of dictatorial tyranny, and that its manifestations on the Right (in the guise of fascism and Nazism) and on the Left (in the shape of Stalinist Communism) actually represented mirror images of each other. In *Animal Farm* (1945) and *Nineteen Eighty-Four* (1949) above all, Orwell spoke truth to power, voicing his warnings about a totalitarian future with uncompromising fierceness and frightening clarity. *Nineteen Eighty-Four* is justly read as a fictional blueprint that combines the key elements of totalitarianism in its right- and left-wing versions, whereby it contributed significantly in the decade that followed to the birth of the academic subfield in comparative government of totalitarian studies. In fact, when I think of the landmarks in scholarship addressing totalitarianism during the 1950s and 1960s—celebrated books such as Hannah Arendt's *The Origins of Totalitarianism* (1951), Richard Löwenthal's *World Communism* (1964), and Carl Friedrich and Zbigniew Brzezinski's *Totalitarian Dictatorship and Autocracy* (1956), I am reminded of Alfred North Whitehead's famous, if hyperbolic, remark in *Process and Reality* that "the safest general characterization of the European philosophical tradition is that it consists of a series of footnotes to Plato" (63). For one could make the same claim about the debt of the early post–World War II literature on totalitarianism to *Nineteen Eighty-Four*—and with far less exaggeration.

Nonetheless, it bears emphasizing that Orwell devoted no more than intermittent attention to fascist Spain and Nazi Germany. His pen was typically pointed in the direction of Stalinist Communism, particularly the twisted rationalizations and hypocrisies of his fellow intellectuals on the British Left. He became the "conscience" of the Left because he invariably directed his main energies against the moral and political vices of "our own side," insisting that the Left hold itself to the highest standard of intellectual integrity. The prime target in *Animal Farm* and *Nineteen Eighty-Four* is Stalinism and its "duckspeaking" intellectual defenders in the Anglo-American world.

Orwell was especially outraged by the Left's mindless sloganeering and "quacking" of the ever-shifting Soviet party line, and he satirized these habits with gusto. Today, part of our Western literary heritage consists of the catchwords Orwell launched permanently into the political lexicon and the social imagination via *Nineteen Eighty-Four*: "Big Brother Is Watching You," Newspeak, and thoughtcrime, to name a few. And also from *Animal Farm*: Sugarcandy Mountain (representing Heaven, or the illusory promise of an afterlife offered by religion) and the slogans of Animalism, such as "All animals are equal, but some are more equal than others." Orwell was castigated and derided by the British Left for casting the Soviet leaders as pigs and "Uncle Joe" Stalin as Big Brother.

Orwell paid a high price among British radicals for his audacity. Yet Camus, here again, confronted arguably an even more painful challenge on the issue of Stalinism in his relationship with the French Left of the 1950s. The Communists, along with their fellow travelers led by Jean-Paul Sartre, acknowledged the existence of the Soviet gulag, but they subscribed not only to *tiers mondisme* ("third-worldism"), but also to its corollary, anti-Americanism—and those dogmas forbade public criticism of Stalin's genocidal labor camps. If criticism about the gulag was brought up, leftist French intellectuals immediately referred to McCarthyism in the United States and proclaimed them equivalent. What we now know as the mass murder of tens of millions of people under both Stalin and his successors was compared to a truly awful, though modest by comparison, persecution of American Communists by Senator Joseph McCarthy during the early 1950s.

Camus was unwilling to accept that easy equivalence. He refused to indulge in the cynical illusions and double standards of Stalinism, the Marxist-dominated French intelligentsia's drug of choice throughout most of the postwar era, which the conservative French intellectual Raymond Aron famously referred to as "the opium of the intellectuals" in his 1955 book of that title.[2] Yet already Camus had issued a similar warning—as a leftist addressing fellow leftists—and been ostracized by erstwhile friends and political comrades such as Sartre and De Beauvoir. Camus was vilified especially when he wrote *The Rebel* (1951), in which he analyzed the history of Marxism, concluding that even revered French figures on the Left such as the French Revolutionary Robespierre were guilty of simplistic politics whereby they yielded to "the lure of profundity" (as Orwell titled a 1937 essay), or murder for an idea.

VI

So that is the valuable legacy of George Orwell and Albert Camus, both of them principled critics of their own sides and "consciences" within the intelligentsias of the two leading Western European capitals of their day. These comparisons are illuminating, for the contrasts between the two men are so overwhelming and arresting that these striking similarities of political stance and moral probity are readily obscured and have been widely overlooked by historians.

Orwell was sometimes compared by his friends to a Saint Francis, an ascetic, a secular saint who in the end actually came close to killing himself for the sake of truth and art. Suffering tuberculosis, going in and out of sanatoria throughout the late 1940s, he insisted on remaining on the bleak island of Jura in the Scottish Hebrides and finishing *Nineteen Eighty-Four*; his lungs hemorrhaged as he concluded the final chapters of the novel in early 1949. He entered his last sanatorium and never re-emerged. What he left us was his masterwork, *Nineteen Eighty-Four*. He died for that book, and in a sense, he died for us. That was his final gift.

Camus, by contrast, though also tubercular as a young man (he suffered a severe bout of tuberculosis when he was seventeen and never fully recovered from the disease), was an extraordinarily dashing and romantic figure, sometimes called even during his lifetime "the Humphrey Bogart of French letters." He looked remarkably like Bogart, especially when he wore his trench coat. After winning the Nobel Prize at the age of forty-three in 1957, an award that brought him anguish rather than pleasure, he proclaimed on getting the news, "No no! It should be Malraux, Malraux!" Then he sent a telegram to Andre Malraux, a distinguished elder man of letters, saying the same thing. Malraux immediately wrote back, "Camus… your telegram does you honor." Malraux was not congratulating him, but rather more or less acknowledging, "You're right! I deserve it."[3]

As a result of receiving the Nobel Prize, Camus was posthumously dubbed the "Jack Kennedy of literature" in Paris in the early 1960s. Kennedy himself at the age of forty-three had been elected president of the United States in 1960. But Camus had died tragically, just months before Kennedy's election. It was Camus's fatal encounter with the Absurd, the existential specter depicted in his great novels such as *The Stranger* (1942) and *The Plague* (1947). Traveling with his publisher Michel Gallimard in Provence, France, Gallimard's speeding car crashed. When Camus was found on the roadside, the manuscript of his unfinished new novel, *The First Man*, lay in his hands. (Next to the manuscript of the *The First Man* was also a copy of Nietzsche's *The Joyful Wisdom*.) To add to the absurdity and sense of tragedy, Camus had intended to take a train home to Paris; an unused ticket was found in his pocket. And so another romantic myth arose: Albert Camus, the "James Dean of French literature," forever the rebel, per the title of his celebrated study of historical radicals.

Intellectual integrity, moral courage, and literary excellence: George Orwell and Albert Camus. We are as much if not far more in need of those virtues and their standard bearers in the twenty-first century—and doubtless long hereafter.

Notes

1. See Rosenberg, "The Herd of Independent Minds."
2. See Aron, *The Opium of the Intellectuals*.
3. On this anecdote, see Lottman, *Albert Camus: A Biography*.

Works Cited

Aron, Raymond. *The Opium of the Intellectuals*. Princeton: Transaction, 2001.

Camus, Albert. *Camus at "Combat": Writing 1944–1947*. Ed. Jacqueline Lévi-Valensi. Princeton: Princeton UP, 2007.

Lottman, Herbert R. *Albert Camus: A Biography*. Berkeley: Gingko, 1997.

Muggeridge, Malcolm. "A Knight of the Woeful Countenance." *The World of George Orwell*. Ed. Miriam Gross. London: Weidenfeld, 1972. 166.

Orwell, George. "Charles Dickens." *The Complete Works of George Orwell*. Ed. Peter Davison. Vol. 12. London: Secker, 20–57.

_____. "The Lure of Profundity." *New English Weekly*. 30 Dec. 1937.

_____. "Why I Write." *The Complete Works of George Orwell*. Ed. Peter Davison. Vol. 18. London: Secker, 316–21.

Rosenberg, Harold. "The Herd of Independent Minds: Has the Avant-Garde Its Own Mass Culture?" *Commentary* 6 (Sep. 1948): 242–245.

Sartre, Jean-Paul. Preface. *The Wretched of the Earth*. Frantz Fanon. New York: Grove, 2005. xlvi.

Whitehead, Alfred North. *Process and Reality*. New York: Torch: 1960.

Zola, Emile. *The Dreyfus Affair: J'Accuse and Other Writings*. New Haven: Yale UP, 1996.

George Orwell and Jacintha Buddicom: A Memoir_____

Dione Venables

On June 25, 1903, a son, Eric Arthur, was born to Ida and Richard Blair.

Emphasis is sometimes given to the location of the birth of Eric Blair in Motihari, a remote town in northern India where Richard Blair was a sub-deputy opium agent. It is not clear why this natural event should generate a particular interest in Motihari. Eric's mother, Ida Blair, fled India in the face of an epidemic to return to England with her daughter Marjorie and Eric, when he was just a few months old. There are, however, stirrings among those who like to guess at the unguessable, suggesting that the fact that George Orwell, who was Eric Blair at that time, had been born in such an isolated corner of the British Empire may well have influenced his later discomfort and eventual disgust at the way the Empire was being run. So much sudden interest in Orwell was being generated in the 1970s, with journalists, biographers, and international academics vying with each other in describing the forty-six years of Orwell's short life, and implying that his formative years had been grey and unhappy, that my cousin Jacintha Buddicom decided, in exasperation, to write her own memoir on the subject.

Few could have been better qualified.

The Blairs, having lived in Henley-on-Thames since their return to England in 1903, decided, after ten years, to move a couple of miles out of this old market town to the village of Shiplake-on-Thames and lease a house, Rose Lawn, whose garden backed onto the grounds of Quarry House, home of the Buddicom family. Young Eric, a solitary child by nature according to his younger sister Avril, would not have failed to hear the sounds of laughter and rambunctious play with which the three Buddicom children occupied themselves when the weather was fine, with outdoor sports and hunting games from one end of the property to the other. There were trees to climb and lawns for ball games, vegetable gardens and even an old stone quarry in which to hide, to dig a cave, to camp out in. Curiosity must have overcome him on one such day when the children were playing French cricket with their stepfather, Freddy Norsworthy. Jacintha suddenly noticed a boy in the field adjoining the garden, standing on his head and grinning at her upside-down. She climbed onto the five-barred gate between their garden and the field, and her stepfather asked him what he was doing.

"You are noticed more if you stand on your head than if you are right way up," was the response. Eric was eleven years old at that time. The year was 1914 and the storm clouds of war were gathering momentum.

Eric had, it seems, worked out the first of many diversions by which he would ensure that he and his activities would always be noticed. Jacintha Buddicom's book *Eric & Us* (1974) is clear and quite specific about the way the relationship developed from that day forward. By the end of the summer holidays in 1914, Eric, sometimes with little Avril in tow, had become a daily fixture in the Buddicom family.

War was declared between Britain and Germany on August 4, 1914, while the Blairs were on holiday in Cornwall. Eric seems to have seized upon the situation with fervour and, according to Avril, spent much of the time trying to discover the sequence of events that had led to this tragic outbreak of war. The daily newspaper headlines stirred the children into excitement and speculation, especially when recruitment began and the railway stations became blocked with eager young men, gathering together to join their regiments. Jacintha was two years older than Eric, but, as he had warmed to her sharp and perceptive mind early in their acquaintance, it was her company rather than her brother Prosper's that Eric usually sought to discuss the latest situation on the political front. Prosper Buddicom was born in July 1904, a year after Eric. He was smaller and blonder, and not inclined to settle down to talk of war, debate the situation, and consider the consequences, as were Eric and Jacintha. They wrote stirring war poetry together, and Eric, being the apple of his mother's eye, allowed Ida to submit his most successful effort, "Awake! Young Men of England," to the local newspaper. The *Henley and South Oxfordshire Standard* published Eric's first poem in October 1914, shortly after he had returned to school for the winter term. He was eleven years and four months old, but enflamed with patriotic zeal, when he wrote this inspiring image:

Oh! give me the strength of the lion,
The wisdom of Reynard the fox,
And then I'll hurl troops at the Germans,
And give them the hardest of knocks.

Oh! think of the War lord's mailed fist,
That is striking at England today;
And think of the lives that our soldiers
Are fearlessly throwing away.

Awake! oh you young men of England,
For if, when your Country's in need
You do not enlist by the thousand,
You truly are cowards indeed.

Jacintha was also busy with her pen, though her work was not shown around, remaining instead between the worn covers of an old exercise book. Hers were not nearly as stirring a rallying cry as that of St. Eric the Ready!

As the years slid by, the children grew and learned and wrote together. Eric announced on one of their fishing trips on the river Thames, above Shiplake Lock, that one day he was going to be "a famous author." The children took this in their stride, but he repeated this intention several times as the years drew them toward the end of childhood. The Buddicoms paid a visit each holiday to their grandfather William Squire Buddicom at his home at Ticklerton, near Church Stretton in Shropshire, a far-removed and magically remote place in the depths of a deeply rural country area. From about 1915, Eric was included in their holiday invitations, and it was at Ticklerton that he shot his first rabbit, and where he first discovered the English poet A. E. Housman.

William Buddicom had a remarkable collection of first editions in his library, most of which had been collected by his father: These included a Second Folio of the *Complete Works of William Shakespeare.* What made this calm and kindly man unique is that he not only permitted the children to handle these precious volumes, but he actively encouraged them to read and absorb their contents. He liked nothing better than to ask them what they were reading at any time, and then go over the pages, explaining difficult words and describing the building-up of sentences and textual refinements. When Eric became glued to the first illustrated edition of Housman's *A Shropshire Lad*, Grandfather Buddicom lent it to him to take home, knowing that it would be in safe hands, and returned during the following holiday visit. The fact that this book is now in my own library, undamaged, apart from one or two lightly pencilled-in indications of his approval, shows that Eric Blair's devotion to books was well developed by the time he was thirteen.

Eric was fifteen by the time the Great War raged its way into 1917 and the first tanks rolled and rumbled menacingly over the muddy battlefields of the Somme in France. He had a growth spurt in 1916 and was now the tallest in their group. A photograph taken at Ticklerton during the summer holidays that year shows how Eric's spurt had already made him a head taller than Prosper, who was also growing fast at this time and was himself already taller than Jacintha. She stopped growing after her fifteenth birthday and remained a tiny, petite, and elegant figure into old age.

Jacintha in 1918, when she was seventeen, shows her sitting with her friend Joan Horn, whose family also lived in Shropshire. The two girls were the same age. The difference in their builds illustrates Jacintha's compactness, since Joan Horn's stature was considered to be attractive and normal. This picture also goes some way to explaining how it was that, two years later, after Jacintha and Eric had whiled away many sunny holiday afternoons lying among the bluebells in a certain dell that was their favorite "private" place, Eric, by then over six feet tall and entirely devoted to Jacintha, and enjoying a certain amount of intimacy with her, attempted to "go the whole way" while the two families were on holiday together at Rickmansworth. This momentary madness of a callow youth permanently destroyed their relationship.

He must have known by then that he would always love her and wanted them to be engaged. However, he would not be going to university. He had not worked hard enough at Eton College, and had been content to enjoy life at his own pace in this ancient and charismatic seat of learning. His closest friend there was Cyril Connolly, whom he had known since their preparatory school days at St. Cyprians, Eastbourne, where both boys had won scholarships to Eton. "CC," the name by which Cyril was known, worked hard and achieved the required scholarship to ensure a university entrance, but Eric's term reports had not impressed either his tutors or his father, whose income would not have been able to support Eric through his university years without the assistance of a scholarship. So, despite the pleas of both Ida Blair and Laura Buddicom that Eric was too intelligent to be refused the chance of at least taking the scholarship exam, his future was decided: After his last school term he would be entered for the Civil Service Examination, as his father was before him. When the time came, Eric passed this exam, was accepted into the Indian Imperial Police, and, filled with anguish over Jacintha's anger at his momentary madness with her, sailed away to Burma without Jacintha's promise of betrothal. Returning to the continent of his birth, he had in a way come full circle. The spark of his genius was only in its first stage. There were, however, the first signs of literary passion in his boyish love poems to Jacintha.

The sea voyage to India marked the end of childhood for Eric Blair and began the metamorphosis which would result in the gradual emergence of George Orwell. He put his head down and concentrated on filling his mind and memory with everything he experienced. Five years of policing in Burma saw him returning for his first leave and losing no time in visiting Ticklerton, where there was no Jacintha. He eventually spoke briefly with her on the telephone in London, and she was short and polite with him, polite but cool. The spark had gone, and he must have decided that she was still angry with the memory of his teenage indiscretion.

When they put the phone down, a line was drawn under their relationship and he told his family that he never wanted to hear the name Buddicom again. What he had not known was that he had arrived home just as Jacintha, having at last fallen in love, had given birth to her daughter Michal. The father of Jacintha's child left England for Australia as soon as he learned she was pregnant, and Jacintha had been left to withdraw from her friends and home, and to have her baby in a home for unmarried mothers, devastated that she had shamed her family. How could she have shared that with Eric at that time?

In the summer of 1948 Jacintha discovered that George Orwell, the writer of *Animal Farm*, was none other than her first and deepest love, who, by then, no longer called himself Eric Blair. She wrote to him via his publisher and the response stayed with her for the rest of her life. The strong and devoted knight in shining armor of their youth had become a wheezing, decimated husk of a man; his voice, once charmingly modulated, was now oddly high-pitched and shot through with the cobweb-thin whisper of tubercular lung disease. They exchanged a few poignant letters, snatched three short but revealing conversations on the telephone, and Jacintha, unable to make herself go to Cranham Sanatorium to visit Eric, stayed away until she read in the October 1949 newspapers of George Orwell's sickbed marriage to Sonia Brownell.

Part of Jacintha was never able to forgive herself for shying away from Eric's deep concern for the future of his small son Richard. He had wanted so very much for her to take him and bring him up, supported by his father's literary earnings—and warmed by the gratitude of the boy who had been Eric Blair and who had become the *famous writer* George Orwell. How could she take his unknown child and bring him up with love and wisdom when she had had to give up her own loved and cherished baby daughter? When he died in January

1950 something in her died with him. She went to his London funeral and sat in the back of the church, a small unnoticed figure, mourning the loss of someone she later described as "less imperfect than anyone else I ever met" (qtd. in Orwell 9). In her forward to the second edition of *Eric & Us*, Jacintha wrote: "I never met George Orwell . . . but . . . I knew Eric Blair very well indeed."

Works Cited

Buddicom, Jacintha. *Eric & Us*. 2nd ed. Chichester: Finlay, 2006.

Orwell, George. *Orwell: A Life in Letters*. Ed. Peter Davison. London: Secker, 2010.

RESOURCES

Chronology of George Orwell's Life_____

1903	Eric Arthur Blair is born on June 25 in Motihari, Bengal.
1904	Returns to England and settles at Henley-on-Thames, Oxfordshire.
1911–16	Boards at St. Cyprian's School, a private preparatory school at Eastbourne, Sussex.
1917–21	Secondary education as a King's Scholar at Eton College. Contributes to *The Election Times* and *College Days*.
1922–27	Officer with the Indian Imperial Police in Burma.
1927–28	Tramping expeditions to East End of London.
1928–29	Lives in working-class district of Paris. Begins early drafts of *Down and Out in Paris and London* and *Burmese Days*.
1930–31	Returns to England.
1932–33	Teaches full time at The Hawthorns, a small private school for boys, in Hayes, Middlesex.
1933	*Down and Out in Paris and London*, by "George Orwell," published by Victor Gollancz. First appearance of his pen name.
1934	*Burmese Days* published by Harper & Brothers, New York.
1934–36	Part-time assistant at Booklovers' Cove, 1 South End Road, Hampstead.
1935	*A Clergyman's Daughter* published by Gollancz.
1936	In north of England for a book on unemployment conditions.
1936	Publication of *Keep the Aspidistra Flying* by Gollancz.

1936	Marries Eileen O'Shaughnessy at parish church in Wallington, Hertfordshire.
1936	"Shooting an Elephant" published in the literary magazine *New Writing*.
1937	Sees fighting in the Spanish Civil War, serving with Independent Labour Party contingent in a militia of the POUM (Partido Obrero de Unificación Marxista, or Workers' Party of Marxist Unification).
1937	*The Road to Wigan Pier* published by Gollancz in trade and Left Book Club editions.
1937	Shot in throat by Fascist sniper at Huesca, Spain. Escapes with Eileen from Spain into France by train.
1938	*Homage to Catalonia*, having been refused by Gollancz, is published by Secker & Warburg.
1938–39	In French Morocco (mainly at Marrakech); writes *Coming Up for Air*.
1940	*Inside the Whale and Other Essays*.
1941	*The Lion and the Unicorn* published by Secker & Warburg (first of "Searchlight Books" edited by Orwell and T. R. Fyvel).
1941–43	Takes position as talks assistant, later talks producer, in Indian section of BBC's Eastern Service.
1943	Resigns from BBC and joins *Tribune* as literary editor (until 16 February 1945).
1945	Eileen Blair dies.
1945	Publication of *Animal Farm* by Secker & Warburg in an edition of 4,500 copies.
1946	*Critical Essays* published by Secker & Warburg.
1946	*Animal Farm* published in the United States.

1947	*Such, Such Were the Joys* completed about May 1948. First draft composed as early as 1946.
1947	Patient in Hairmyres Hospital, East Kilbride (near Glasgow), suffering from tuberculosis; stays seven months.
1948	At Barnhill, Jura, a quiet island off the coast of Scotland, for five months.
1949	Patient in Cotswold Sanatorium Cranham, Gloucestershire, with serious case of tuberculosis.
1949	Publication of *Nineteen Eighty-Four* by Secker & Warburg. It quickly appears as a Book-of-the-Month-Club selection.
1949	Marries Sonia Brownell.
1950	Dies of pulmonary tuberculosis on January 21 at the age of 46. Funeral follows at Christ Church, Albany Street, London. Buried, as Eric Arthur Blair, at All Saints Cemetery, Sutton Courtenay, Berkshire.

Works by George Orwell

Long Fiction

Burmese Days, 1934
A Clergyman's Daughter, 1935
Keep the Aspidistra Flying, 1936
Coming Up for Air, 1939
Animal Farm, 1945
Nineteen Eighty-Four, 1949

Nonfiction

Down and Out in Paris and London, 1933
The Road to Wigan Pier, 1937
Homage to Catalonia, 1938
Inside the Whale and Other Essays, 1940
The Lion and the Unicorn: Socialism and the English Genius, 1941
Critical Essays, 1946 (U.S. edition: Dickens, Dali, and Others, 1958)
Shooting an Elephant and Other Essays, 1950
Such, Such Were the Joys, 1953
The Collected Essays, Journalism, and Letters of George Orwell, 1968 (4 vols.)
Orwell: The War Broadcasts, 1985 (U.S. edition: Orwell: The Lost Writings, 1985)
Orwell: The War Commentaries, 1986

Miscellaneous

The Complete Works of George Orwell, 1986–1998 (20 vols.)
The Lost Orwell: Being a Supplement to The Complete Works of George Orwell,
2006

Bibliography

Bounds, Philip. *Orwell and Marxism: The Political and Cultural Thinking of George Orwell*. London: Tauris, 2009.

Bowker, Gordon. *Inside George Orwell: A Biography*. London: Macmillan, 2003.

Brunsdale, Mitzi. *Student Guide to George Orwell*. Westport, Conn.: Greenwood, 2000.

Crick, Bernard. *George Orwell: A Life*. 1980. Rev. ed. New York: Penguin, 1992.

Cushman, Thomas, and John Rodden, eds. *George Orwell: Into the Twenty-First Century*. Boulder: Paradigm, 2004.

Davison, Peter, ed. *The Complete Works of George Orwell*, 20 vols. London: Secker, 1987–2000.

_____. *George Orwell: A Literary Life*. New York: St. Martin's, 1996.

_____, ed. *The Lost Orwell*. London: Timewell, 2006.

_____, ed. *Orwell: A Life in Letters*. London: Secker, 2010.

Gross, Miriam, ed. *The World of George Orwell*. London: Weidenfeld, 1971.

Hitchens, Christopher. *Why Orwell Matters*. New York: Basic, 2002.

Howe, Irving. *Politics and the Novel*. New York: Meridian, 1957.

Meyers, Jeffrey. *Orwell: Wintry Conscience of a Generation*. New York: Norton, 2000.

Newsinger, John. *Orwell's Politics*. New York: St. Martin's, 1999.

Orwell, Sonia, and Ian Angus, eds. *The Collected Essays, Journalism, and Letters of George Orwell*. 4 vols. London: Secker, 1968.

Patai, Daphne. *The Orwell Mystique: A Study in Male Ideology*. Amherst: U of Massachusetts P, 1984.

Rodden, John, ed. *The Cambridge Companion to George Orwell*. Cambridge: Cambridge UP, 2007.

_____. *Every Intellectual's Big Brother: George Orwell's Literary Siblings*. Austin: U of Texas P, 2007.

_____. *The Politics of Literary Reputation: The Making and Claiming of "St. George" Orwell*. New York/Oxford: Oxford UP, 1989.

_____. *Scenes from an Afterlife: The Legacy of George Orwell*. Wilmington: ISI, 2003.

_____, ed. *Understanding Animal Farm: A Student Casebook to Issues, Sources, and Historical Documents*. Westport, Conn.: Greenwood, 1999.

_____. *The Unexamined Orwell*. Austin: U of Texas P, 2011.

Saunders, Loraine. *The Unsung Artistry of George Orwell: The Novels From Burmese Days to Nineteen Eighty-Four*. Aldershot, England: Ashgate, 2008.

Shelden, Michael. *Orwell: The Authorized Biography*. New York: Harper, 1991.

Taylor, D. J. *Orwell: The Life*. New York: Holt, 2003.

CRITICAL
INSIGHTS

About the Editor_____

John Rodden teaches English and German in the Department of Foreign Languages and Literature at Tunghai University, Taiwan. He has taught rhetoric and intellectual history at the University of Texas at Austin and the University of Virginia. Among his books dealing with George Orwell's work and heritage are the following: *Understanding* Animal Farm: *A Student Casebook to Issues, Sources, and Historical Documents* (1999), *The Politics of Literary Reputation: The Making and Claiming of "St. George" Orwell* (2001), *Scenes from an Afterlife: The Legacy of George Orwell* (2003), *George Orwell: Into the Twenty-First Century* (2004), *The Cambridge Companion to George Orwell* (2007), and *Every Intellectual's Big Brother: George Orwell's Literary Siblings* (2007).

Rodden has also written four books that deal with the history and politics of modern Germany, especially with issues of human rights in the former East Germany: *Textbook Reds: Schoolbooks, Ideology, and Eastern German Identity* (2006), *The Walls That Remain: Western and Eastern Germans Since Reunification* (2007), and *Dialectics, Dogmas, and Dissent: Stories of East German Victims of Human Rights Abuse* (2010).

Rodden has also published four books of American intellectual and cultural history focused on the New York intellectuals, and he is presently completing a study of how and why selected members of that group were the object of decades-long surveillance by American intelligence agencies. Rodden's most recent book is *The Intellectual Species: Prospects in the Post-Gutenberg Age* (2012).

Rodden's scholarly and intellectual activity has centered for more than a quarter-century on the contingencies of reputation-building in modern history. His first book, *The Politics of Literary Reputation*, conceptualizes a theory of reputation-formation—which he terms "the rhetoric of reception"—that treats Orwell's reputation as a case study for exploring the vicissitudes and dynamics of the reputation process generally.

Contributors_____

John Rodden teaches English and German in the Department of Foreign Languages and Literature at Tunghai University, Taiwan. He has taught rhetoric and intellectual history at the University of Texas at Austin and the University of Virginia. Among his books dealing with George Orwell's work and heritage are the following: *Understanding* Animal Farm: *A Student Casebook to Issues, Sources, and Historical Documents* (1999), *The Politics of Literary Reputation: The Making and Claiming of "St. George" Orwell* (2001), *Scenes from an Afterlife: The Legacy of George Orwell* (2003), *George Orwell: Into the Twenty-First Century* (2004), *The Cambridge Companion to George Orwell* (2007), and *Every Intellectual's Big Brother: George Orwell's Literary Siblings* (2007).

John P. Rossi is professor emeritus of history at La Salle University in Philadelphia. He received his PhD in modern British history from the University of Pennsylvania, and while teaching for fifty years at La Salle he also taught briefly at Chestnut Hill College in Philadelphia, and at Villanova University. He is the author of seven books, most recently *Living the Promise: The 150th Anniversary History of La Salle*. Among his other books are a study of the British Liberal Party in the 1870s, a memoir of growing up in Philadelphia in the years after World War II, and three books on baseball and American history. Rossi also has written extensively on the life and times of George Orwell, including such articles as "Orwell and Chesterton" (*Thought: Fordham University Quarterly*, December 1988), "Orwell's Conception of Patriotism" (*Modern Age*, Summer 2001), and, with John Rodden, "The Mysterious (Un)meeting of George Orwell and Ernest Hemingway" (*Kenyon Review*, Fall 2009).

James Seaton is a professor in the Department of English at Michigan State University. He is the editor of *The Genteel Tradition in American Philosophy; and Character and Opinion in the United States* by George Santayana (2009), and the author of *Cultural Conservatism, Political Liberalism: From Criticism to Cultural Studies* (1996). Seaton is also the author of *A Reading of Vergil's Georgics* (1983) and coeditor with William K. Buckley of *Beyond Cheering and Bashing: New Perspectives on the Closing of the American Mind* (1992). He is a regular contributor to the "Books and Arts" section of the *Weekly Standard*. Seaton's essays and reviews have appeared in a wide variety of publications, including the *Wall Street Journal, Review of Metaphysics, American Scholar, Hudson Review, Yale Journal of Law and the Humanities, Michigan State Law Review, Society, Modern Age, University Bookman*, and many others.

William E. Cain is Mary Jewett Gaiser Professor of English at Wellesley College. His publications include a monograph on early twentieth-century American literary and cultural criticism in volume 5 of *The Cambridge History of American Literature*

(2003). He is a coeditor of the *Norton Anthology of Literary Theory and Criticism* (2nd ed., 2010), and he has coauthored with Sylvan Barnet a number of books on literature and composition. Recently he has written essays on Edith Wharton, Ralph Ellison, William Shakespeare, and Mark Rothko.

Loraine Saunders was born in Liverpool in 1967. She studied English literature at Liverpool Polytechnic and went on to become an English language teacher in Brazil, Germany, and Spain. Later, at the University of Liverpool, she completed a master's thesis on Orwell's *Nineteen Eighty-Four*, then completed her doctoral dissertation, entitled *Re-evaluating George Orwell's 1930s Fiction: An Examination of Orwell's Novelistic Style and Development*. This was turned into a book, *The Unsung Artistry of George Orwell* (2008). Saunders has lectured at the University of Manchester and Liverpool Hope University. She has contributed articles to the Blair/Orwell Forum and the Orwell Prize website. Her most recent work has been teaching English to undergraduates at King Saud University in Riyadh, Saudi Arabia.

Eugene Goodheart is the Edytha Macy Gross Professor of Humanities at Brandeis University. He has also taught at Bard College, the University of Chicago, Mount Holyoke College, Massachusetts Institute of Technology, and Boston University. Awards include fellowships from the Guggenheim Foundation, the American Council of Learned Societies, and the National Endowment for the Humanities. He is the author of eleven books of literary and cultural criticism, including *The Skeptic Disposition: Deconstruction, Ideology, and Other Matters* (1984), *The Reign of Ideology* (1997), *Does Literary Studies Have a Future?* (1999), *Darwinian Misadventures in the Humanities* (2007), as well as a memoir, *Confessions of a Secular Jew* (2001). The Christian Gauss lectures he delivered at Princeton University formed part of his 1973 book *Culture and the Radical Conscience*. His many articles and reviews have appeared in, among other journals, the *Partisan Review, Sewanee Review, New Literary History, Critical Inquiry*, and *Daedalus*.

Peter Davison has published extensively on drama and George Orwell. His twenty-volume edition of Orwell's writings—almost nine thousand pages in length—appeared in 1998 and has been followed by a further nine books devoted to Orwell's work. He has written many articles on Orwell, a half dozen of which have appeared on websites such as OrwellSociety.com, where they have attracted an international readership. He has been awarded an honorary doctorate, the gold medal of the Bibliographical Society, and been appointed Officer of the British Empire for his services to English literature.

Gorman Beauchamp is professor emeritus of humanities at the University of Michigan. He has authored a book on Jack London and over seventy articles on subjects ranging from Shakespeare to science fiction, including a number on Orwell. He anticipates being appointed Flem and Eula V. Snopes Professor of Critical Theory at Yoknapatawpha Community College sometime soon.

Peter Stansky is the Frances and Charles Field Professor of History, emeritus, at Stanford University. He has written extensively on modern Britain. He is the coauthor, with William Abrahams, of *The Unknown Orwell* (1972) and *Orwell: The Transformation* (1979). In essays and reviews, some collected in *From William Morris to Sergeant Pepper* (1999), he has written on various aspects of George Orwell, with particular attention to the enduring popularity of Orwell's best known work, *Nineteen Eighty-Four.*

Henk Vynckier chairs the Department of Foreign Languages and Literatures at Tunghai University in Taichung, Taiwan. He has written about travel literature, literary images of barbarians, life writing of Westerners in China, and George Orwell. His recent publications include the essays "Museifying Formosa: George Mackay's *From Far Formosa*" in *Sinographies: Writing China* (2008) and "Behold the Franks: Aamin Maalouf's *The Crusades Through Arab Eyes* Revisited" in the *Wenshan Review of Literature and Culture* (December 2011). He is currently coediting the book *Orienting Orwell: Orwell in/and Asia* with John Rodden and is a member of a research team studying the nineteenth-century British consular official Robert Hart and the Chinese Maritime Customs Service.

Dione Venables is the late-arriving daughter of a late-arriving father. As a result, she was twenty to thirty years younger than all her cousins, including Jacintha Buddicom, author of *Eric & Us.* This explains why she carries a broad spectrum of referred memory, stretching back into Jacintha's Edwardian childhood. Dione has had seven novels published, and she ran a literary website for five years, but now concentrates on her involvement with the Orwell Society, which has Richard Blair, Orwell's son, as its patron and already includes most of the Orwell fraternity in its membership list.

Index